Mass Communication in Africa

GRAHAM MYTTON

JOHNSON
UNIVERSITY
FLORIDA
LIBRARY

Edward A

D1367280

© Graham Mytton 1983

First published in Great Britain 1983
by Edward Arnold (Publishers) Ltd
41 Bedford Square
London WC1 3DQ

British Library Cataloguing in Publication Data

Mytton, Graham
Mass communication in Africa
1. Mass communication—Africa
I. Title
302.2'3'96   P92.A/

ISBN 0-7131-8040-0

All rights reserved. No part of this publication may be reproduced, stored in
a retrieval system, or transmitted in any form or by any means, electronic,
photocopying, recording, or otherwise, without the prior permission of
Edward Arnold (Publishers) Ltd.

This book is dedicated to the memory
of two great pioneers of broadcasting
in Africa – Alick Nkhata and
Edward 'Mfumfumfu' Kateka

Text set in Palatino
by TNR Productions, London
Printed in Great Britain at The Pitman Press, Bath

Contents

Black and white plates appear between pages 80 and 81.

Preface

I became interested in the mass media as a subject for study back in 1966, after I had been working in London as a radio studio manager. I had returned to full-time study at Manchester University as a postgraduate political science student. The idea of looking at the mass media in some of the new states came from Ken Post, who pointed out that only a minimal amount of practical research had been done in this field in Africa. There had been some very useful historical work on Africa's press, but the subject of radio had been comparatively neglected. It was clear to me that it was the latter that was rapidly becoming far more important. And yet, even in works of a general nature on the new political systems of Africa, little or nothing had been written about the main means of national communication in many of the new states – which was radio.

I am grateful to the Social Science Research Council for making funds available so that I could undertake a year's field research in Tanzania during my postgraduate studentship at Manchester. I was admitted to University College, Dar es Salaam for one year from August 1967 as a research associate in the Department of Political Science. Quite apart from the opportunities it allowed for research in the country, I found it an intellectually stimulating experience to be there at that time, for which I am grateful both to the university authorities at Dar es Salaam and to my former colleagues in Political Science and other departments. Those who gave valuable advice are too numerous to mention, but I would particularly like to thank John Condon and Belle Harris, both formerly at Kivukoni College, and Lionel Cliffe and Carl Rosberg, formerly at the University.

I was very fortunate to obtain the services of two experienced research assistants, George Shilaka and Ezekiel Ngonyani, who carried out survey research by questionnaire in different parts of the country. It is impossible to exaggerate the importance of reliable research assistants in a country like Tanzania, where a thorough knowledge of Swahili, though useful, proved to be nowhere near enough; an outsider is always hindered by cultural and other barriers from gaining anything more than a superficial understanding of the substance of Tanzanian daily life. George Shilaka, together with Clement Maganga, also translated passages from parliamentary debates, items from the press and radio broadcasts.

Many journalists and broadcasters in Tanzania took a helpful interest in my work. Though it is impossible to name them all, I would particularly like to thank Ben Mkapa, Martin Kiama, Stephen Mlatie and Abdulla Riyami.

The Tanzanian research which first aroused my interest in Africa's media could not have got off the ground without the encouragement of the late Professor Brian Chapman, through whose persistence and organizational energy I was helped on my way to Dar es Salaam. Without him I would never have started; without Professor Bill Tordoff of Manchester University and John Wilkinson of the BBC I do not think I would have been able to finish. Both men encouraged me in their different ways to continue what I had begun.

For three years after completing my studies at Manchester I was at the University of Zambia conducting similar research into Zambia's mass media, as the Zambia Broadcasting Services Research Fellow at the Institute for African Studies, University of Zambia. I would like to acknowledge the help and encouragement given me there by Jaap Van Velsen, Cherry Gertzel and Mubanga Kashoki.

In Zambia I was similarly dependent on research assistants, most notably Joseph Mwanza and Stephen Kapoyo. I owe them both a great debt of gratitude for hard work, dedication and friendship over many years.

My research project in Zambia was sponsored by the ZBS. Former deputy directors, including the late Alick Nkhata and his successor Asaf Mvula, as well as other senior officers, were always co-operative and enthusiastic about my study. They allowed me to visit the ZBS regularly, to attend staff meetings when this was useful, and kept me informed of events and changes within the ZBS. The staff of ZBS, too numerous to mention, also showed a lively interest in the project and helped in many ways, as did the former editor of the *Times of Zambia*, Vernon Mwaanga.

I am indebted to Peter Clarke for encouraging me to include a large quantity of separate material. Thanks go also to James Roberts for many detailed comments. Hilary Laurie and Kathryn Coutu also read the manuscript and made improvements.

The work involved a good deal of searching for obscure material on broadcasting and the press. (For some reason, source material on the mass media is kept by few libraries.) I am indebted to the library staff at the Universities of Zambia, Dar es Salaam and Manchester, the Institute of Commonwealth Studies in London, the Institute of Development Studies at the University of Sussex and the BBC.

My wife Janet has lived with this work for as long as I have – indeed, we met for the first time only weeks before I embarked on the project. I thank her now for her patience, which must at times have been strained by the feeling that I would never finish. She has been a forthright critic of my writing. Whatever this work's merits, it would be considerably worse without her corrections and alterations, particularly in the latter stages.

What I write here is, of course, entirely my responsibility and no one else's. I hope it will prove useful and interesting to students of Africa and the mass media, and also to African students in the future who will, I hope, take a continuing interest in their continent's communications media.

Graham Mytton   February 1983

Any views or opinions expressed in this book are my own and do not necessarily reflect those of the British Broadcasting Corporation where I now work, nor do they necessarily reflect those of the academic and broadcasting institutions in Africa with which I have been associated.   GM

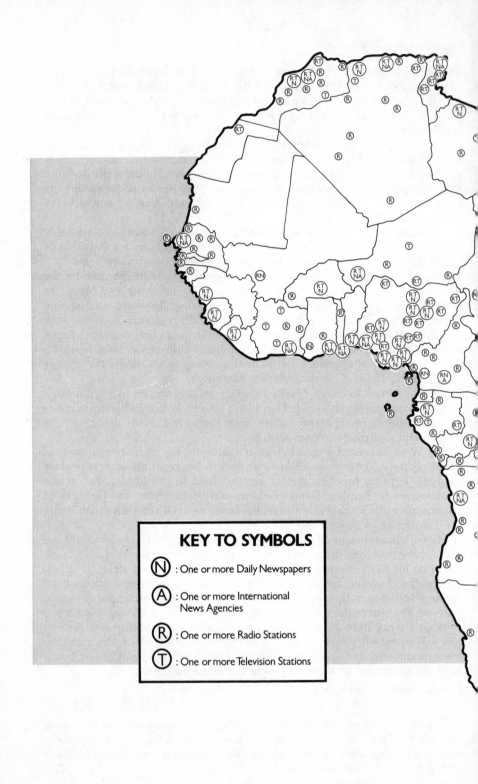

KEY TO SYMBOLS

(N) : One or more Daily Newspapers

(A) : One or more International News Agencies

(R) : One or more Radio Stations

(T) : One or more Television Stations

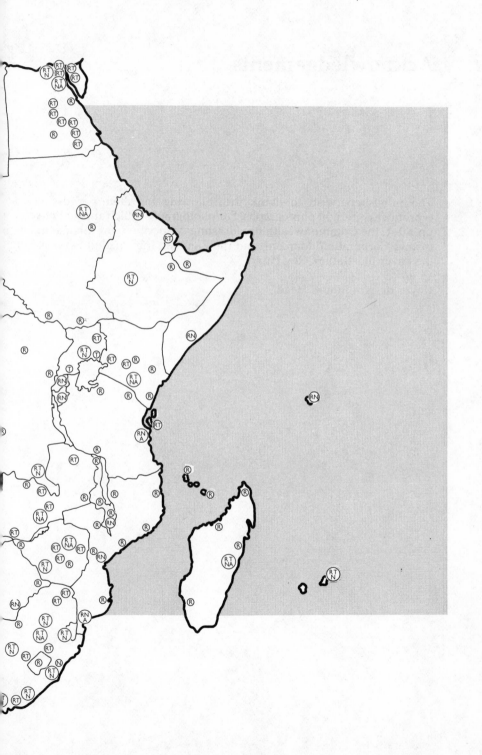

Acknowledgements

The publishers wish to thank the following for their permission to reproduce copyright photographs. For photographs which appear between pp. 80–1: the Commonwealth Broadcasting Association; the Ghana Broadcasting Corporation; Marconi; and the Zambian Information Service. For the cover illustration: Rex Parry.

Cover design: Simon Head.

1
Why Mass Communication?

Many books have been written about communications in recent years, of which a large number have focused on radio, television and the press. Others have taken a broader view and concerned themselves with human communication in a broader sense. Most describe the situation in the developed, wealthy countries as if what happens there were somehow typical of human communication in general; if they mention the so-called Third World or less developed countries at all, they do so almost as an afterthought. Yet it is a fact that the majority of the population of our small planet live in these less developed countries.

In this book, the situation that prevails in the greater part of the world is regarded as the norm. I have deliberately chosen to focus on Africa since it was there that I studied modern communications; besides, that continent possesses a number of characteristics which make it fertile ground for study. All the modes and varieties of human communication are to be found there, both the traditional historic and the new technological forms being available for the student to observe, examine and understand. Satellites carry colour TV pictures, telex messages, computer programmes and telephone calls to and from Africa, yet methods of communication that have been part of its social life for thousands of years – traditional music, dance, art, oral history and literature – still survive, and communication by word of mouth continues to be conducted in hundreds of different languages and dialects.

The social science student in the West suffers from a considerable handicap when studying modern communications: it is sometimes difficult for a person who finds it almost impossible to imagine life without the modern mass media to stand back and assess what role these play in social and political life. For the student in Africa, on the other hand, the situation is a far more interesting and rewarding one. Many students will remember television arriving in their own town or area; others may recall the coming of radio and the phenomenally rapid growth in set ownership during the 1960s. They will be able to talk to members of the older generation who saw and read the first newspapers or heard the first radio transmissions. Moreover, there are many places still without radio, and – as illiteracy is widespread – newspaper readership is as yet limited. Television remains something seen only by a minority in certain of Africa's urban areas.

The West has reached what is described as *media saturation*. Almost all homes in Britain, West Germany, France and the United States have television and radio, and most take a daily newspaper; there is ready access to other types of publication, as well as to public libraries and cinemas. In Africa the situation is a very uneven one, some countries having colour television, stereophonic VHF radio with a minimum choice of two networks plus a selection of daily newspapers, while others have no television, few radio sets and perhaps only a single daily paper. Even in countries like Nigeria, where such facilities are relatively advanced, there are many whose lives remain largely untouched by the mass media.

Why study communications at all? Communication studies may be a comparatively recent phenomenon, but the study of how man communicates is far from new. To a large extent, all those involved in the study of modern and ancient languages, literature, art, music and even history have really been studying human communications. Even the ancient philosophers of Greece, in examining difficult concepts and establishing evidence for the assertion of facts, were similarly concerned with problems of communication.

In modern times, the interest in studying communications as a subject in its own right seems to have arisen from the enormous growth in communication activity between individuals – a growth which took place not without a number of fears being expressed. People point to what they see as an increase in violence or a decline in moral standards and suggest that it is the mass media which are to blame. They also question the uses to which new communications facilities are put. The motto of the BBC, the first ever broadcasting organisation of its kind, may be 'Nation shall speak peace unto nation', but in reality things are rather different. We may be able to show an event, simultaneously in colour and with sound, to viewers in Cairo, New Delhi, Caracas and Sydney – but will they gain any deeper understanding of the world's problems as a result? Our modern, sophisticated communications systems are generally regarded as a sign of human progress, but is there a sense in which they are responsible for a deterioration in our way of life? These are real concerns, and one of the reasons we study communications is that we attach importance to resolving them, or at least to understanding the factors involved.

The development of communications is an integral part of the historical process itself. Look at a map of Africa today and you will see more than fifty independent states, nearly a third of the membership of the United Nations; thirty years ago, in 1950, there were only three states in Africa not controlled by Europeans. The years between Libyan independence in 1951 and that of Zimbabwe in 1980 marked the breakup of European empires great and small: British, French, Portuguese, Spanish, Italian and Belgian. Each of these included parts of Africa, and the map we see today is essentially one drawn by Europeans. The relevance of this point to our study of communications will be seen later. However, we should note here that this disintegration of empires coincided with a major development in mass communications. In the early 1920s radio transmissions to the public began on a large scale in Europe and America. Within only a few years radio had become a popular and widespread medium of entertainment, information and news. In 1923 just over half a million licensed radio receivers existed in Britain; by 1926 the figure was over two million and by 1946 over ten million.[1] Similar expansion took place in other industrialized coutries, but radio took much longer to arrive in Africa and develop there, for several reasons. Early radios were expensive; moreover, they used valves, which required high voltages best provided by mains supply, a facility largely confined to industrialized societies. Portable valve sets were made, but these proved cumbersome and the batteries needed to power them very expensive.

The invention in 1948 of the transistor (sometimes known as the semiconductor) was to change all this. The Americans Bardeen, Brattain and Shockley invented these small electronic devices which proved to be cheap, long-lasting and efficient. Production soon started on a massive scale, making the portable radio commonplace throughout the world. The effects of this were spectacular: radio was brought within the reach of millions, and growth in set ownership has been rapid, even in the very poorest countries, ever since. To take one example, broadcasting began in Tanganyika in 1951, by the end of which year an estimated one thousand radio receivers existed in that country; nine years later, an audience survey indicated that seventy thousand sets were in use. A further survey in 1973 showed an estimated 1.7 million radio sets in Tanzanian homes: this represented an average of more than one radio for every two households.[2]

Thus within living memory an enormous number of individuals have become radio listeners. What are the consequences of this? And what significance, if any, is there in the historical coincidence of this phenomenon with the emergence of African countries from their colonial experience? This book cannot provide a complete answer to such questions, yet it is hoped that it will stimulate further interest and research by demonstrating why mass communications are so important and pointing out the extraordinarily exciting opportunities which exist for those studying the subject.

Notes

[1]   Asa Briggs, *The History of Broadcasting in the United Kingdom, vol. I: The Birth of Broadcasting* (London, 1961), p. 18.
[2]   Tanganyika Broadcasting Corporation, *Annual Reports* (1956-1963); Market Research Company of East Africa, *TBC Audience Survey Report May 1960* (Nairobi, 1960); Associated Business Consultants, *Radio Audience Survey in Mainland Tanzania December 1973-January 1974* (Beirut, 1974).

2
Communication and Society

The West has seen a great deal of controversy about, and some rather inconclusive research into, the social and political effects of the modern mass media. What kind of power do they bestow on those who have access to, or control over, them? Do they influence political opinion? Do they help persuade people to change the way they behave? Do they remove cultural and social distinctions, or do they sustain and enhance the power of a ruling class or élite? Do they debase culture and create a mass audience by appealing to the 'lowest common denominator' of taste? Do they kill initiative and self-reliance by providing entertainment and information rather too easily? And, where they depict the less savoury side of human behaviour – namely, violence, crime and sexual perversion – do they encourage or discourage such activities? These and similar questions have been asked by students of the media in an attempt to 'fit' the mass media into their concept of society, and just as they have different concepts of the nature of society and its workings, so also have they had widely diverging views on the place of the media within society. We need not go very deeply into these controversies here. What is important for us to note is the obsession there has been with discovering *effects*, and undesirable effects at that; radio, television, cinema and the popular press seem to have been regarded as intruders in an already established social and political scene.

Mass communications research has been somewhat dominated by the United States, on account both of the media's more advanced development in that country and the higher degree of specialization in the social sciences there. Researchers looked on communications activity as a flow with a beginning and an end. In 1948 the American sociologist Harold Lasswell wrote that a convenient way to describe a communications act was to answer the questions:

Who
Says What
In Which Channel
To Whom
With What Effect?[1]

He then showed how each of these questions produced a different area of media research: control analysis, content analysis, media analysis, audience analysis and effect analysis. More recently, the English sociologist Jeremy Tunstall, while approving of Lasswell's pioneering work nevertheless bemoaned the influence of his simple classification which assumed, wrongly in his opinion, 'that the discovery of some measurable effect was the ultimate purpose of media research'.[2] Lasswell's classification suggested a flow whose ultimate goal was an audience effect. What this framework ignored was the crucial factor of feedback, of which more will be said later. Moreover, simple models such as Lasswell's can obscure the general picture by concentrating overmuch on distinct and separate communications activities.

Another drawback of Lasswell's approach was that it stressed only short-term effects, the study of which has tended to be either inconclusive or disappointing.[3] Since then, media research has shifted direction, placing less emphasis on short-term effects and more on what happens in the long term; thus far greater interest is now being shown in the place of the mass media within political and social structures. Scholars have pointed to links between the way the media are organized and the economic and class structures of their respective societies. Some see the media as part of the ideological apparatus of societies dominated by ruling classes; others, as providing for the expression of competing ideologies within a relatively free competitive or pluralist society. Most agree that the very pervasiveness of the mass media has given them an important role in the formation of political and social consciousness and attitudes.

In Africa, an ever-increasing proportion of the population has access to information previously denied it by the barriers of distance, poverty and illiteracy. New political relationships have come into being through the existence of communications media which can link government directly to the governed. The existence of a widespread radio or newspaper audience makes possible the advertising of commercial products on a large scale. The relatively small number of channels through which information and entertainment are communicated contrasts sharply with the great diversity of cultural, linguistic and social groups reached. When patterns of communication alter, corresponding changes in the social structure frequently take place. Large numbers of people who previously may have shared little other than geographical proximity begin to receive the same news, the same entertainment and the same information about their environment.

The ability of radio to span the twin barriers of distance and illiteracy makes it a medium worthy of particular interest. The coincidental arrival of large numbers of cheap portable transistor radios with the emergence of many new states in the early 1960s raised speculation about the possible contribution of the mass media in general, and radio in particular, to the solution of pressing developmental and political problems.[4]

However, poverty of resources means that few such countries possess well-developed modern communications facilities. An examination of their problems – in particular the political ones of instability and uneven development – shows these to be exacerbated by communications difficulties. A multiplicity of languages, some of which may be mutually incomprehensible, and the absence of any accepted or acceptable lingua franca are features of many recently formed African countries. Even where one language is widely spoken and understood, problems may still exist for substantial minorities, despite political pressures to adopt a majority language. Communications between the constituent parts of new countries may be difficult. Peoples may have no easy means of contact with one another because of geographical conditions and the underdevelopment of transport; governments and development agencies may themselves be able to communicate effectively with only a small proportion of a population.

It is not possible to think of politics in isolation from communication, yet much has been written about politics, both from an analytical and a historical perspective, without explicit consideration of the communications processes which pervade political life. On the one hand, political power requires the possession of information about those over whom it is exercised; on the other, the governed need to receive information from those who exercise power – no one can obey a command, observe a regulation or fulfil an obligation without knowing what these are. For the purposes of this study, *communication* is defined as an interpersonal relationship, either direct or indirect, involving the transfer of information. By *information* I mean the whole spectrum of messages conveyed through a medium of communication, ranging from the most explicit statements of fact to the most subtle influences (whether intended or otherwise) that affect the audience's picture of the world. The communications system is coextensive with the social and political system, and the high position of an individual within a communications network can bring with it social or political power.

There is a direct relationship between the structure and the organization of communications, both formal and informal, and the character of all political and social activity. A study of communications can help reveal how power and control in society are distributed. (We shall look at some examples of this later.) All social systems may be evaluated in terms of the amount, patterning, methods and content of their communications. It is the communications network of any society, of whatever size, which defines and limits its boundaries as well as governing its efficiency and capability. The relevance both of technology and of levels of economic development must not be forgotten. In what may be rather loosely described as *traditional* society, communications activity is not differentiated from other social processes: professional communicators – musicians, story-tellers and the like – are few, and information tends to flow along social, hierarchical lines consistent with relationships existing in the community. At the other extreme, in *modern* industrialized societies, communications activity is both highly organized and technically sophisticated, the existence of professional communicators allowing us to distinguish the communications process, or a large part of it, from other social processes. Interlinked with the modern, technically sophisticated system of mass communication are a multitude of face-to-face relationships where leaders of opinion who operate on an informed level play an important role.

Between these two types or extremes we can identify what may be described as a *transitional* system in which two types of communications systems operate side by side. Firstly, there is a 'modern' system based on advanced technology which centres on the urban areas and reaches the more educated, literate sections of the population. The major components of this are the modern mass media – in particular, the popular daily press and the radio. Away from the urban areas, 'traditional' systems operate. In many parts of the world these two systems are said to operate more or less autonomously, yet, increasingly, the former impinges on the latter: whenever this division exists, it is rarely a complete one.

The weakness of this rather simple analysis, put forward by the American writer Lucian Pye, is that what it says about 'traditional' systems also applies to much of the communications activity in 'modern' systems.[5] In fact, Pye's 'transitional' model is a good description of communications activity in perhaps every political system that exists, regardless of its stage of development. A more useful way of qualitatively differentiating between communications systems is according to the level of technology employed in communications activity, a level which is related both to the wealth of the societies concerned and to the proportion of total resources these allocate to modern communications activities. Technological developments may alter the patterns of communication, but change is evolutionary rather than revolutionary: traditional networks become incorporated in the new forms. There is therefore no such thing as an entirely modern system of communications (in Pye's terminology) as distinct from a transitional one. Both are marked by an interlinking of 'modern' and 'traditional' communications networks.

The technology of modern communication has allowed for greater changes in the *scale* of communications, both in terms of information content and audience reached. Early on in this century, Cooley saw the advent of railways, telegraphs, popular daily papers and telephones in the United States as bringing about fundamental changes to every aspect of American life. He identified the four areas of greatest impact as commerce, politics, education and social life. Modern techniques had widened the range of communications enormously and also introduced certain networks which were entirely new. He wrote of these developments as 'enlarging' and 'quickening' life in the country: words that have since been used to refer to radio, television and high speed travel by jet aircraft.[6] More recently, Marshall McLuhan has claimed that the electronic media, by their inherent characteristics, have introduced fundamental qualitative changes to society and made possible the increased involvement and participation of people across the boundaries of class, age group and nation.[7]

However, the new media do not necessarily bring about specific changes in society, for if the ideas and culture so communicated either remain the same or undergo little transformation the introduction of modern mass media will lead merely to the broader and more rapid spread of that content. The nature of the medium may influence the content, but there will be nothing necessarily modern in the *content* itself. Yet in most societies the introduction of the modern mass media has coincided with enormous upheavals in society and politics. This has led to the belief by some that the mass media are themselves inevitably connected with such changes.

In modern nation-states it is now impossible to conceive of politics without the existence of the mass media. It might also be said that any modern nation where rule is based on the legitimacy of majority support must develop a communications network able to cover its entire population and area – one which is capable both of transmitting and magnifying political actions so that these are felt throughout the system, and of collecting information from all parts of that system so that some sense of popular feeling and opinion can be acquired. As Pye said: 'Without a network capable of enlarging and magnifying the words and choices of individuals, there could be no politics capable of spanning the nation.'[8]

The communications process can be said to have three main functions in society: it *informs* people about their social, economic, political and cultural environment; it *links* the component parts of the society; and it *transmits* social values, norms and mores.[9] At the national level, this process performs the additional task of linking together the separate communications networks and carrying out their functions on a national scale.

How, then, is the communications network of the modern nation-state constituted? Communications networks are made up of *channels*. The most salient channels of political communication are often institutions such as parties, trade unions, pressure groups and bureaucracies; yet other organizations, not formally part of the political structure, may function as important channels of political communication. Educational or religious institutions, for example, frequently act as communicators of political as well as of social and other sorts of information. Commercial organizations and private companies can perform a similar role. Informal channels of communication must also be taken into account. Studies done in 1955 showed that informal face-to-face relationships then had greater significance in, for example, voting behaviour than did the mass media.[10] It may be assumed that informal group relationships are probably important in attitude formation in all societies.

There is definitely an awareness within totalitarian regimes of the political significance of informal social groups. Though certain individuals may be forbidden to meet others in groups, even informally, such informal relationships are, almost by definition, extremely difficult to control. The cell system is an attempt by ruling Communist regimes to formalize and institutionalize group relationships at the level of the community, the street or the workplace, and the CCM party cell system in Tanzania works in a similar way. yet less formalized relationships and groups still remain, and the kind of control sought by some absolutist regimes is difficult to achieve. It is almost impossible to institutionalize and control all the informal group relationships that may emerge at any time and in any place within dynamic social situations: a fact which imposes definite limits on the political system and on the exercise of political power.

Political communication is partly determined by the nature of the channels already available for use. In China, for example, popular art, song, dance and theatre are all used for the communication of political ideology. A similar tendency can be observed in many of the new African countries, where political élites encourage the expression of nationalist sentiments through such media.

The mass media are special channels in one very important respect: they are designed specifically for the purpose of communication. For other institutions this is merely one activity among many. Communication may – as in the case of political parties – be essential to the operation, but this is not their chief reason for existing. The mass media exist primarily to communicate.

The unique attributes of the mass media will be outlined later. It is first necessary to put them into context alongside the other channels of communication. As has been noted, the mass media are a vital part of the political power structure of any modern nation-state; the exercise of power in the modern world necessarily involves them. Their existence enables organizations such as political parties, trade unions and pressure groups to make appeals to a wider audience than they might otherwise reach. In most countries it is the mass media that represent the major source of information on parties and unions at the national level, both for members and non-members. This is the reason why so many of these try either to develop their own media (usually in the form of a newspaper) or to secure a sympathetic hearing or voice within those media not under their direct control. Of course, the situation is different in countries where political institutions separate from the government are either nonexistent or actively discouraged: here, the mass media are generally placed under the control of the ruling party, the government and its various agencies.

In countries where there is the freedom in law for the private ownership of newspapers and where the electronic mass media are obliged to be impartial, certain factors tend to work against radical or left-wing political groups and trade unions. First, starting a newspaper and keeping it going is an expensive undertaking: the freedom to publish and reach a wide audience is a one enjoyed more frequently by the rich than by the poor. Secondly, because of the need to prevent chaos on what is a limited number of airwaves, and out of fear of the consequences of a free-for-all, radio and television in Africa tend to be under governmental control, if not directly then indirectly, through a public corporation under government-appointed directors or governors. There are other, historical, reasons for centralized control. On the whole, radio in Africa was established by the colonial powers before independence and used from the outset for political, educational and administrative purposes – a practice which has continued. Moreover, in the majority of African countries the adoption of a *laissez-faire* system would result in there being few or no mass media at all. In the United States and Western Europe, the enormous purchasing power of the audience made commercial broadcasting an attractive proposition; in most of Africa, despite large audiences, the purchasing power is small. Although commercial advertising exists on radio and television, revenue sufficient to make broadcasting a viable proposition is rarely obtained. Few African countries have privately owned, mass circulation daily newspapers – South Africa and Nigeria alone have any significant number – and none has private commercial radio or television on a national scale.

What have communications to do with social and political change? Communication is a process in which information is transmitted, received, analysed and, finally, accepted or rejected. People make rational decisions based on learning and experience after assessing the significance of any new information they receive. The social 'unit', whether it be an individual, a group, the ruler or the ruled, adapts (or does not adapt) its behaviour on the basis both of acquired wisdom and fresh knowledge. If this is so, then the process of communication is intimately involved with that of change. Pye, Lerner, Schramm and others have argued – and their arguments have been very influential – that it is the communication from outside of new information which sets traditional and relatively isolated societies on the road to modernization and development.[11] Clearly, this may be true of all societies and social groups within societies, but in the new states the changes occurring as a result of such communication can be even farther-reaching. The process of nation-building is connected not only with the changes brought about as the result of communications from outside but also with the development of new networks within the changing society which replace or supplement existing ones. These new networks have to cope with new tasks and new demands, such as the need to bring together a population that is scattered, heterogeneous and multilingual.

Other writers take a somewhat different view. Elliott and Golding, for example, argue that the 'conception of developing countries emerging from static isolation, requiring an external stimulus to shake them into the twentieth century' is not compatible with the actual history of such countries.[12] Many civilizations have actually regressed under the impact of external rule from advanced countries, and the continued underdevelopment of less developed countries may be viewed as the direct result of the continued hegemony of the wealthy industrial states. The mass media systems of many less developed countries are viewed merely as extensions of economic imperialism serving the interests of that imperialism before all else. The writers hold the view that the main determinant of change is the impact of international economic forces. Unfortunately, they take their critical analysis of most theories of the mass media no further. It is easy to accept the proposition that the distribution of economic power in the world is a major constraint on social and political development in less developed countries.[13] It can also be argued, convincingly, that changed economic circumstances alter power relationships and may promote consequent social and political change. Yet none of this excludes the possibility of change as the result of the communication of new information. While it is true that patterns of communication generally reflect social, economic and political realities and relationships, and influence further political and social change accordingly, this does not always happen; communications activity within a social or political system is not always in support of the status quo. Elliott and Golding point out that the mass media do not operate autonomously, but this does not mean that the opposite is true and they are simply the instruments of a ruling élite: power is to some extent shared between the ruling class and the media operators so that, like other established forms of social communication, the media do not always operate as socially conservative influences. Many Third World countries are in the grip of powerful international economic forces and may be dominated by the power of multinational corporations, yet here and there cases emerge where the mass media are able to 'go against the grain'. Just as in the capitalist democracies socialist scholars and writers can be heard speaking and writing against the tide of political and economic power, so in Africa can the press and radio be found to carry messages which do not reflect the interests of the ruling élite. Ownership and control of the mass media usually reflect existing power relationships, yet the situation is more complex than this: the process of mass communication is social and cultural as well as political and economic, and the influences received from society at large are extremely significant.

A useful concept for a better understanding of communications is that of *feedback*. By this we mean the process whereby a communications network 'produces action in response to an input of information, and includes the results of its own action in the new information by which it then modifies its subsequent behaviour'.[14] A failure of feedback stops essential information getting through to where it is needed. Innumerable examples of this can be found. Let us first think of a man writing letters to a friend. He posts them each week to the same address but never gets a reply: his friend has in fact moved, and the letters have not been forwarded. The letter-writer is not getting the feedback he needs which would enable him to modify his behaviour appropriately and make his communication effective.

What is true of individual behaviour as shown in this rather mundane example is true of many other types of human activity. Most of the things we do in daily life involve modifying our behaviour according to feedback from either our environment or some object of our actions. If you say something and are not understood, you may repeat yourself, saying the same thing in another way. We know this feedback is important: its failure can lead us into making mistakes and continuing to do so because we have no way of knowing that we are in error.

On a larger scale, effective feedback may be crucial to political stability. In a number of cases where feedback in a political system has either broken down or been blocked, serious consequences have arisen for the system as a whole. The irony is that it is often governments themselves which are the blockers; as a rule it is they who stop the free flow of information. Political élites may actually strive to perpetuate their policies by blocking all incompatible experiences both from themselves and from the community. Alternatively, policies may be perpetuated by the blocking of feedback to the policy makers. Such cases are not hard to find: many contemporary problems of government arise at least in part from poor communications between the ruled and the rulers. Those occupying central positions of power generally have access to information, of great variety and scope, about people under authority. This information may contain a great deal which shows the existing political authority in a bad light, such as evidence of the corruption of public officials, anti-government activity, the failure of policies designed to achieve specific ends, government inaction in the face of drought or famine, and so on. The government may not allow this information to reach a wider audience, restricting it to a narrow circle within the ruling élite.[15]

A government committed to a particular ideological goal or policy may block all information which might indicate failure or in any way raise doubts as to the desirability of that goal or policy. Such a blockage may occur at any level. Individual officials or politicians in power may block feedback to another key person or key group in order to prevent possible undesired consequences. Governments everywhere try both to hide information which they regard as potentially damaging and, with varying degrees of success, to block the flow of such information to the public. In the process they may also control information that is not damaging; information control is one of the components of political power. Nevertheless, feedback is necessary in a social communications network if *appropriate* modifications are to be made or action taken in response to information coming from the environment. In a political system, the 'nerves of government' need to be sensitive to feedback and even to seek it out if that system is to be legitimate and accepted.

Weak, inadequate or inappropriate communications networks in machines lead to inefficient working or actual breakdown – think of a fuel gauge, an oil pressure meter or a water thermometer in a motorcar. The same is true of social systems. It is therefore appropriate to look at some of the factors that work against effective communication within any society.

In many new countries a communications gap exists between town and country. There are often two types of communications network operating more or less autonomously: the urban communications network may not be at all responsive to what takes place in the various village systems, and at the village level, communications from the urban areas may be seen to contain little of local relevance. In addition, gaps are to be found both within the towns themselves and between the various rural localities. The latter can have serious political consequences. Villages and other small-scale societies are frequently quite separate, autonomous communications entities; they may, in fact, have little communication with each other beyond quite a short distance. This situation can prevent the inhabitants of rural areas from pursuing common interests. If peasants act politically at the national level at all, they tend to do so independently and without cohesion. They are thus rarely able to challenge urban leadership.

None of this should suggest that a duality or a diversity of communications networks within a national system necessarily implies lack of cohesiveness. Nevertheless, it is the quality, quantity and range of linkages between communications networks which are the measure of the cohesiveness of the system as a whole. The cohesiveness of all types of organization depends partly on the integration effected by the communications network. Improvements in the range, content and efficiency of political or national communication tend to bring about corresponding improvements in the more general capabilities of the society or nation: if channels of communication are not developed, neither does the system as a whole.

A number of other barriers to communication are found in rural areas. There are, of course, the natural ones: the effect of weather on transport, the influence of solar activity on radio transmission, and obstacles such as mountain ranges, rivers or marshes. Many new states cover vast areas, whose populations are separated by long distances. Poverty prevents the expansion of transport and trade, both major factors in the promotion of communication. The social obstacles which frequently exist are the most difficult to overcome, and these fall into two types. Firstly, there is frequently a great diversity of languages; the mutually incomprehensible languages spoken in many new states reflect the continuing existence of traditional communications barriers. National leaders in government may have to use a language not understood by the majority of the inhabitants. Translation from one language to another requires skills and manpower, and even then the problem remains of the equivalence of concepts between languages. This language barrier may be the most stubborn. As one writer has put it, it might be easier to blast through a mountain to bring two divided communities together than to get them to speak each other's language.[16]

The social structure itself is a vital influence on communications. It regulates the relationships between the communicator and the audience by assigning roles to each. Certain relationships of kin, marriage and social affiliation or class are strongly governed, and face-to-face communication and association greatly affected, by the nature of that structure. Habits or patterns of behaviour anchored in the culture of society structure communications networks which in turn reinforce these habits and patterns. It is here that one finds the second type of social obstacle.

In certain societies, according to one writer, the process of communication has a social function over and above its information content or 'truth value': a statement is valid only if it comes from the right source. This is a feature of many small-scale traditional societies, but in western societies too, the act of communication is often more important than the information communicated.[17] It is false to suppose that the person who refuses to answer certain questions on the conviction that whatever he or she had to say would have no value is found only in traditional society. Lerner noted during his research in the Middle East, which involved the extensive use of questionnaires, that peasants refused to answer questions requiring the subject to put himself or herself in another person's shoes. He seemed to make the curious assumption that this was an attribute only of the kind of society he was studying.[18]

An important point needs to be made here: the existing social structures of traditional society, and therefore also the existing communications networks, are constantly being challenged from outside. This challenge can be resisted as new ideas and messages are filtered through existing communications structures. Such a process is characteristic of all societies. New ideas, new messages and new information of various kinds rarely have direct effects but instead operate through a nexus of existing beliefs and attitudes which help determine the ways in which they are received and interpreted.[19] Of particular importance in this process is the influence of opinion leaders.

Communications facilities and technology are closely related to economic resources. Lack of money is often the most serious obstacle to their development. Underdeveloped transport means not only that trade and travel are hindered but also that the communication of information is affected. In Africa, the roads and railways were built by the colonial powers mainly for their own purposes – exploitative or extractive trade, defence and administration – which is why transport and communication, both between states and within many of the states themselves, are still difficult.

Indices of economic development and of the level of development of communications facilities are closely related. The modern mass media impose a burden on limited economic resources, and other claims on resources are usually felt to have priority. The invention of the transistor has brought radio receivers within the reach of many, but both the cost and upkeep of the broadcast and transmission equipment needed to serve a large country and the manpower required to broadcast effectively to a heterogeneous and multilingual nation, present further barriers to the development of this medium. The press is similarly hampered. A daily press cannot flourish without a substantial urban wage-earning readership, and newspapers are expensive to launch and to produce. Daily newspaper sales throughout most of Africa south of the Sahara and north of the Limpopo are extremely low.

What makes the mass media different from other forms of communication? Janowitz has provided a famous definition, seeing mass communications as comprising 'the institutions and techniques by which specialized groups employ technological devices (press, radio, films, etc.) to disseminate symbolic content to a large, heterogeneous and widely dispersed audience'.[20] The term 'mass media' is used to refer to the devices or means of communication, which include the mass circulation press, television, radio and films as well as posters, advertising in general, gramophone records and best-selling literature. The mass media are directed towards audiences which are *large* and *heterogeneous*; their size and heterogeneity will vary between media. In less developed countries, for example, the radio audience is generally more heterogeneous than the newspaper-reading public. The latter is confined to the literate and, for the most part, to the urban areas.

Mass media content is public: it is open to all, except when legal prohibitions intrude and except for the barriers of language, literacy and economics. These barriers vary considerably among societies. In some, legal restrictions on media production and distribution are few; in others, the law may both prevent the dissemination of various forms of information which originate outside and limit the ownership of and access to the media within. Language does not present a barrier to the same degree everywhere, it is true; nevertheless, in multilingual countries the mass media cannot be open to everyone unless they employ languages which are universally understood. In the majority of African states, and to a varying degree, groups exist which are excluded from the mass media audience because they are unable to understand any of the languages used.

Illiteracy represents a considerable barrier in much of the world and one which is being sidestepped by radio and, to a lesser extent, by television and film. But, as Everett Rogers has pointed out, the impact of illiteracy is not confined to reading ability alone: a literate person is also better able than an illiterate to understand the content of electronic media such as television and radio. Literacy tends to lead to 'different mental abilities, such as a capacity to deal with abstract symbols, to an interest in cosmopolitan events outside the peasants' village, and to a general motivation to modernise, all of which are evidently partially independent of mass media *per se*.'[21]

If mass media content is, broadly speaking, public, access to the source is far from being so: formal organization and the mastery of special techniques and skills are required. Due to the complexity of these and the expense involved, the mass media are, almost everywhere, owned or controlled by governments, large public or private corporations or wealthy individuals.

These media achieve simultaneous, or near-simultaneous, contact with their audience, and that audience is in turn characterized by remoteness, to a greater or lesser degree, from the source. Radio and television achieve complete simultaneity, whereas the press and the cinema do not. This simultaneity of the broadcast media is one of their most important and distinctive characteristics. The fact that information can be passed rapidly to a large number of people at once has vital implications – particularly, for example, in times of war or of crisis, when public attention is focused on national events. The ability of radio and television to reach directly and simultaneously into the homes of individuals and families has become a major power resource of political leaders in both authoritarian and liberal regimes.

The relationship between the mass media and its audience is both anonymous and impersonal. The audience is a collectivity unique to contemporary society: an aggregate of individuals engaged in virtually identical forms of behaviour, unknown and unknowable to each other. The mass media are unique in another respect, in that they are predominantly one-way channels of communication. The audience has no immediate way of communicating with the source. Individual listeners, viewers or readers are able to communicate with radio and television stations and newspapers, but such communication is generally delayed and is in any event neither a necessary nor an integral part of mass communications activity. Little immediate feedback occurs, except in a negative sense.[22] If a newspaper is disliked or found not to be useful, it will not be bought; if a radio station broadcasts boring programmes, it will lose listeners. While it is true that many media institutions deliberately seek out the views of their audience through some form of market or audience research, this provides at best only a very limited kind of feedback of information.

With mass ownership of transistor radios, political élites were provided with a greatly improved means of downward communication. Consequently, mass media content in less developed countries tends to be heavily dominated by information – including a great deal of propaganda, direction and exhortation – from the political centre. The low level of development of mass media facilities, with little reporting from the rural areas, means that the media of poor countries tend to be far more restricted as channels of national communication in the real sense than is often the case in wealthier states. In developed systems, radio, television and the press are able to provide both an important degree of horizontal communication and a kind of upward communication that are generally lacking in the new states, with their relatively limited mass media facilities. For example, the press and broadcasting in Europe and the United States can act as useful channels of information for decision makers. They also inform sections or groups in society about other sections or groups. This is less often the case in the new states of Africa.

Another significant characteristic of the mass media (and one already mentioned) is their ability to bypass existing social relationships in the fields of politics, religion, kinship, caste or class. They can make inroads into the authority of existing institutions. This is, of course, one of the reasons why in many states the media are placed under strict political control. Conversely, even when not formally controlled, and even when the existing institutions are capable of accommodating themselves to any threat, the mass media are themselves influenced by social and cultural norms. Like their audience, the communicators are members of groups within society as a whole, and their behaviour in mass media activity is affected by the relationships and attitudes existing within such groups. Because of the media's ability to cut across existing social relationships new mechanisms, both formal and informal, are developed in order to control them.

> The result is to ensure that the selection and editing of content is guided by the prevailing laws and social norms, and generally to turn the mass media themselves into agencies of control which reinforce dominant cultural and institutional patterns.[23]

This point is a vital one and has a considerable effect on the role of the mass media in nation-building and modernization.

The growth of the mass media has coincided with the emergence of a large number of new nations in Africa and Asia. Communication is crucial to the process of change, and the media offer numerous advantages to under-developed areas for the rapid development of education and the communication of information – a notable example being the way radio can overcome the problem of illiteracy. Certain writers and institutions have been highly optimistic about the possible role of the media, particularly radio, in speeding development and nation-building.[24] Similar optimism had been felt earlier in the West with the arrival of the popular press. Cooley saw the technical progress that facilitated the growth of the mass circulation press in the United States as making it possible 'for society to be organised more and more on the higher faculties of man, on intelligence and sympathy, rather than on authority, caste and routine'.[25] More recently scholars have been less sanguine. Yet the basic point they make is the same: the mass media can bring about a breakthrough in 'traditional society' by offering alternatives to people, opening up to them new prospects and opportunities and showing, or helping to show, the way to education, health and prosperity. The mass media are credited with assisting in the breaking down of barriers of language, caste and culture between individuals. In the same way, it was once hoped that greater communication between peoples would bring about greater understanding within nations and, eventually, between nations.[26] This optimism has proved ill-founded, but the impact of the mass media in the newly independent, technologically less advanced countries is nonetheless important: these media provide a communications network necessary for spreading information to a widely dispersed and partially literate public. Other writers state the opposing view that the mass media are not so much catalysts for social change as cultural mechanisms for maintaining the social order.[27] This may well be the case in established political systems (although their role in maintaining order may at times be questioned), but in the less developed, so-called emergent nations the mass media are almost inevitably bound up with social change – and not always along the lines envisaged for them.

The governments or ruling élites of many developing countries are actively engaged in promoting economic and social change. It is true that in so doing they may be maintaining or increasing their own political and economic power; yet at the same time they do involve the media in the promotion of social change. In other words, the kind of social change which involves advances in the economy, education, behaviour, life patterns, public health and nutrition of the country may be promoted by the mass media at the behest of the political élite as part of its mechanism for maintaining and enhancing the social order. While the media may indeed be used as agencies of control, this does not mean that they are unable to promote social or political change.

Notes

[1] Harold Lasswell, 'The Structure and Function of Communication in Society' in *The Communication of Ideas*, ed. Lyman Bryson (New York, 1948), p. 37.

[2] Jeremy Tunstall, *Media Sociology* (London, 1970), p. 5.

[3] J.T. Klapper, *The Effects of Mass Communication* (New York, 1960). An attempt to look back and discover what American research had achieved in the preceding twenty or so years.

[4] See, for example, Wilbur Schramm, *Mass Media and National Development* (Paris, 1964).

[5] Lucian W. Pye, 'Models of Traditional, Transitional and Modern Communications Systems' in *Communications and Political Development* (Princeton, 1963) pp. 24-29.

[6] Charles Cooley, *The Significance of Communication* (1909), reprinted in Berelson and Janowitz, *Reader in Public Opinion and Communication* (New York, 1966), p. 151.

[7] Marshall McLuhan, *Understanding Media* (London, 1964), pp. 317-360.

[8] Pye, *Communications and Political Development*, p. 6.

[9] Harold Lasswell, 'The Structure and Function' in Bryson, *Communication of Ideas*, p. 37.

[10] Elihu Katz and Paul F. Lazarsfeld, *Personal Influence* (New York, 1955); Bernard Berelson, Paul Lazarsfeld and W. William McPhee, *Voting: A Study of Opinion Formation in a Presidential Campaign* (Chicago, 1954); Paul F. Lazarsfeld, Bernard Berelson and Hazel Gaudet, *The Peoples' Choice* (New York, 1948); and Elihu Katz, 'The Two-Step Flow of Communications: An Up-To-Date Report on an Hypothesis', *Public Opinion Quarterly*, XXI, no. 1 (Spring 1957), pp. 61-78.

[11] Pye, *Communications and Political Development*; Schramm, *Mass Media and National Development*; Daniel Lerner, *The Passing of Traditional Society* (New York, 1958).

12   Philip Elliott and Peter Golding, 'Mass Communication and Social Change: The Imagery of Development and the Development of Imagery' in *Sociology and Development*, ed. Emmanuel de Kadt and Gavin Williams (London, 1974), p. 274.

13   Robin Jenkins, *Exploitation* (London, 1970).

14   Karl Deutsch, *Nerves of Government* (New York, 1966), p. 88.

15   Ethiopia during the last years of Emperor Haile Selassie's rule is a case in point. The disastrous drought and famine killed thousands of people. There is little doubt that the Emperor knew, but no mention of the situation was permitted in public either via the press or radio. The result was that the true nature of the disaster was either glossed over or not realized by many people not actually near the scenes of greatest hunger. For a good account of the period see Patrick Gilkes, *The Dying Lion* (London, 1975).

16   Leonard Doob, *Communication in Africa* (New Haven, 1961), p. 165.

17   Ithiel de Sola Pool, 'The Mass Media and Politics in the Modernisation Process' in Pye, *Communications and Political Development*, p. 243.

18   Lerner, *The Passing of Traditional Society* (New York, 1958).

19   Joseph Klapper, 'What We Know About the Effects of Mass Communication: The Brink of Hope', *Public Opinion Quarterly*, XXI (Winter 1957-58); Katz and Lazarsfeld, *Personal Influence*.

20   M. Janowitz, 'The Study of Mass Communication' in *International Encyclopaedia of the Social Sciences* (New York, 1963), vol. 3, p. 42.

21   Everett M. Rogers, *Modernisation Among Peasants: The Impact of Communication* (New York, 1969), p. 115. Rogers claims that the acquisition of literacy introduces a qualitative change. I am not convinced that he is right in every respect: I have met many illiterates who show considerable interest in events outside their village, with considerable motivation to modernize, and with remarkable ability to understand and use abstract symbols. It is, however, true that literacy tends to increase these capacities. The difference therefore may be quantitative rather than qualitative.

22   A limited kind of direct feedback has been introduced on radio (mainly in the developed countries) with 'phone-in' programmes, and a somewhat different and also limited kind of feedback is integral to some of the cable systems of television now being used in the United States. Here and elsewhere I am discussing more orthodox forms of broadcasting.

23   Dennis McQuail, *Towards a Sociology of Mass Communications* (London, 1969), p. 18.

24   See Schramm, *Mass Media and National Development*; and UNESCO, *Mass Media in the Developing Countries*, Reports and Papers on Mass Communication, no. 33 (Paris, 1961).

25   Cooley, *The Significance of Communication*, p. 160.

26   *Ibid.*

27   Elliott and Golding, 'Mass Communication and Social Change', in de Kadt and Williams, *Sociology and Development*, p. 230.

3
The Changing Networks

It would be absurd to make too many broad generalizations about communication in Africa, or in any other large area of the world for that matter. Nevertheless, different regions have certain features in common. The first and most significant is the presence of the new technology – radio, television and modern printing techniques have arrived in most parts of the continent – but the spread of that technology is very uneven, both between and within individual countries.

The mass media in Africa are underdeveloped in comparison with most of those in the rest of the world. The number of newspapers is limited, some countries being without a single daily paper. Few dailies have large circulations, and few reach readerships of any size beyond the major towns. Although radio stations have been set up in every African state, their transmitting power is often weak and the number of networks within most countries small. Television is certainly underdeveloped: in some countries it does not even exist. Where it has been introduced, it is chiefly confined to a small number of viewers in those towns where mains electricity is available.

In the majority of cases the electronic mass media belong to, and are controlled by, governments. In 1982 there were only three privately owned commercial radio stations on the entire continent, plus three stations run by churches and missions and four relay stations used by the external services of the United States, West Germany and Holland.[1] The power of the press is likewise concentrated in the hands of the few, most daily newspapers belonging either to governments or ruling political parties. The only countries with significant levels of private ownership and competition are South Africa, Nigeria and – to a lesser extent – Kenya. In the days when many African countries did have privately owned newspapers, these were generally dominated by companies based in the former colonial territories: for example, the British-based group Lonrho once owned papers in Tanzania, Uganda, Zambia and Kenya. The Mirror and Thomson newspaper companies, also based in Britain, had interests in English-speaking West Africa, while French press interests dominated Francophone West Africa. In the early 1960s, when all French West and Equatorial African colonies gained independence, the region had only three daily papers, all of them belonging to Charles de Breteuil, a French businessman.[2] On the whole, such outside private interests have now been taken over – generally by the governments of the countries concerned.

Moreover, remarkably few media outlets or channels exist within each country. Accurate information on this is notoriously difficult to come by, but the following can be regarded as a close approximation to the number of media facilities in African countries. Comparable figures are given for Europe and North America.

Number and circulation of daily newspapers, 1977

	Number of dailies	Estimated circulation (millions)	No. of copies per 1,000 inhabitants
All Africa	180	9	21
Africa excluding Arab states	150	5	15
Europe	1,740	127	264
North America	1,950	67	281

Source: UNESCO, *Statistical Yearbook* 1978-79, p. 867.

Radio facilities

Radio transmitters	1965	1970	1975	1977
All of Africa	500	680	730	790
Africa excluding Arab states	400	560	580	630
Europe	4,170	5,240	5,980	6,190
North America	6,170	6,770	8,530	9,190
Radio receivers				
(a) Number (millions) in Africa	10	16	28	31
Africa excluding Arab states	6	8	17	20
Europe	110	138	155	188
North America	251	306	424	466
(b) *Receivers per 1,000 people*				
Africa	33	45	70	73
Africa excluding Arab states	24	31	55	62
Europe	249	299	327	381
North America	1,173	1,353	1,793	1,942

Source: UNESCO, *Statistical Yearbook* 1978-9, pp. 871-872.

Television facilities

Television transmitters	1965	1970	1975	1977
Africa	100	140	230	250
Africa excluding Arab states	55	70	120	130
Europe	3,550	7,900	14,900	16,300
North America	2,820	3,850	4,360	4,420
TV receivers				
(a) *Number (millions)*				
Africa	0.6	1.2	2.5	4.7
Africa excluding Arab states	0.1	0.3	0.6	2.1
Europe	·59	90	114	126
North America	76	92	133	145
(b) *TV receivers per 1,000 people*				
Africa	1.9	3.4	6.2	11
Africa excluding Arab states	0.4	1.1	2.0	6.5
Europe	132	196	241	264
North America	355	407	562	604

Source: UNESCO, *Statistical Yearbook* 1978–79, pp.873–874.

Growth in circulation of daily newspapers in selected African countries, 1959 and 1980

Country	1959	1980
Cameroon	7,000	30,000
Ethiopia	45,000	43,000
Ghana	200,000	425,000
Guinea	600	10,000
Ivory Coast	9,400	150,000
Kenya	32,000	178,000
Liberia	1,000	10,000
Nigeria	260,000	1,300,000
Senegal	20,000	31,000
Somalia	2,000	12,000
Sudan	30,000	26,000
Tanzania (mainland)	23,300	90,000
Togo	1,650	10,000
Uganda	65,500	35,000
Zambia	18,000	120,000

Source: Arno Huth, *Communications Media in Tropical Africa* (Washington, 1960), p. 168; George Thomas Kurian, *World Press Encyclopaedia*, 2 vols. (London, 1982), *passim*; *The African Book World and Press: A Directory* (Oxford, 1980), *passim*.

Africa possesses fewer media facilities per head of population than any other continent. The figures on which the charts below are based come mostly from UNESCO and are not completely reliable; they are, however, useful for purposes of comparison.

It is difficult to assess the precise significance of Africa's backwardness concerning the media: numbers of radio receivers tell us little, and we should be very careful in making assumptions based on such evidence. Note that there are very nearly two radio sets for every inhabitant of continental North America, and that in the United States itself, the proportion is very much higher. Nevertheless, this should not be taken to mean that the average American listens to the radio more often than anyone elsewhere. Media saturation in rich countries is directly attributable to personal wealth; the spread of media facilities in the less developed countries reflects the uneven distribution of limited wealth without necessarily reflecting a proportionately less significant role for the mass media.

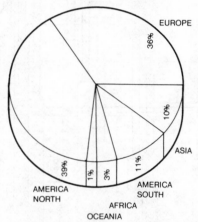

1 World distribution of radio broadcasting transmitters 1974.

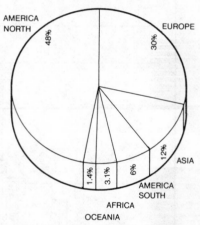

2 World distribution of radio receivers 1976.

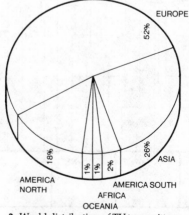

3 World distribution of TV transmitters 1974.

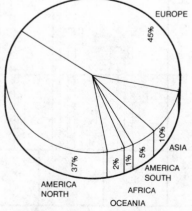

4 World distribution of TV receivers 1976.

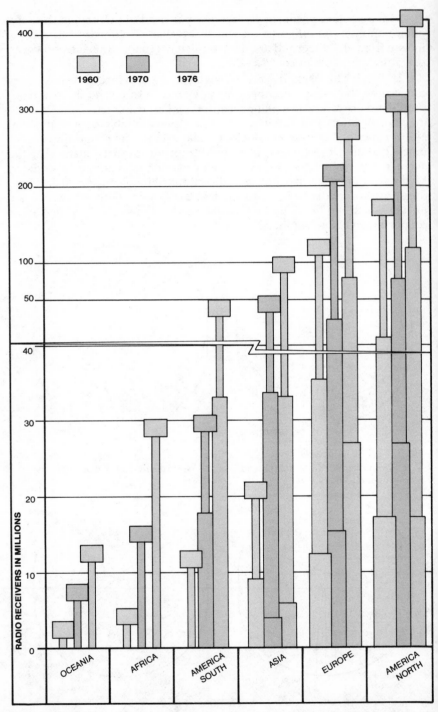

5 Total number of radio receivers by continents: 1960, 1970 and 1976 (in millions).

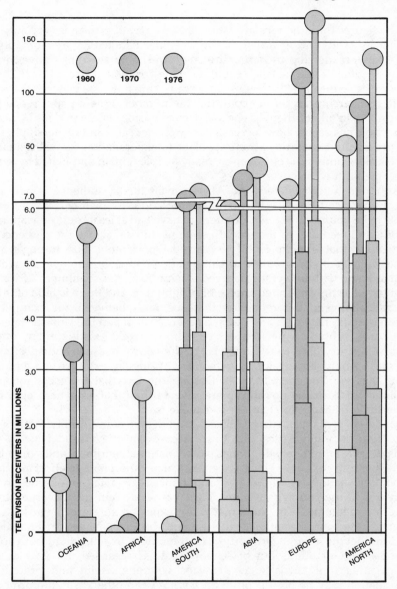

6 Total number of television receivers by continents: 1960, 1970 and 1976 (in millions).

Notes

Charts 1 to 4 show how the world's transmitters and receivers are proportionately distributed. For comparison, note that Africa has about 11% of the world's population and about 20% of its land area. Charts 5 and 6 show the enormous growth of set ownership in Africa. The continent nevertheless has a very long way to go before reaching the saturation levels of Europe and North America. Note that in North America there are considerably more radio receivers than people! Source: UNESCO, *Statistical Yearbook* 1978-79 (Paris 1980), pp. 859-864.

The figures for radio receivers show that the rate of growth is very much higher in Africa and Asia than in the wealthier nations. Figures for daily newspaper readership are harder to analyse and complete comparative data for individual years unavailable, but it is noteworthy that, according to the data we have, the growth of newspaper readership nowhere matches that of radio listenership. In certain countries the number of newspaper readers has grown; in others, there has been a decline during certain periods. Africa as a whole has seen a slow increase in newspaper sales and readership, yet the press still reaches only a minority of the total population. Radio listeners are far more numerous but, even so, many people remain untouched by any mass medium whatsoever.

Although heterogeneous, the African mass media audience is not an evenly balanced cross-section of the population. Its members are more likely to be young, to be town dwellers, to have had at least some education, to be employed and to be male. In spite of this imbalance the audience, particularly that for radio, is still very mixed. For example, those tuning in to a particular radio programme might include people with no education as well as some with university degrees. The radio audience in most African countries has only a limited choice of programme, and there is little of the specialization and differentiation that one finds between, for example, different radio networks and newspapers in Britain and the United States. One, or possibly two, newspapers or radio networks existing in any one African country have to try to appeal to the widest possible audience: no easy task when you consider the diversity of language, culture and ethnic groupings which generally exist. Despite the fact that the mass media audience in Africa is possibly more diverse than that anywhere else, it nevertheless has fewer channels to choose from.

Media content is also marked by a certain degree of uniformity. With the exception of South Africa and, to a lesser extent, Egypt and Nigeria, a considerable amount of attention is paid to national sentiment and symbols in the handling of news. There is a great deal of exhortation to effort for the good of the nation as a whole, and prominence is given to the speeches and activities of the country's leaders. This is true of countries governed by differing ideologies. The mass media are expected, to a greater or lesser degree, to support the national government. Moreover, many African radio stations devote a large proportion of their time to education, both for schools and for adults out of school. Radio is regarded not only as a propaganda tool but also as a means whereby useful and practical information may be passed on to an illiterate and otherwise uninformed public.

However, it should not be assumed that because the mass media are modern phenomena their cultural content necessarily reflects modernity. Must they always convey a message of nation-building, development and progress? Can they not also extend and strengthen the existing culture and values in the face of change and uncertainty? Broadcasting stations in much of Africa draw heavily on existing traditional culture ('traditional' generally being used here to refer to a large number of separate, or only loosely related, cultures).

Technology has made it possible to send out messages to more people than ever before: only the messages themselves need not be new. Often they are very familiar ones. Radio stations are not forever broadcasting improving talks on health, agriculture, government plans for development, and the rest; for a good part of the time they also broadcast material which is familiar to the listeners: traditional music, stories, words of wisdom from respected elders, and so on. Instead of reaching a handful of people in a host of separate small towns or villages, these messages can now reach thousands or millions. Someone once called the mass media the 'magic multipliers', but it is what they multiply that matters, and too little attention has been paid in studies of African radio to what radio – and, by extension, television stations and newspapers – actually say and do.

When radio started in Northern Rhodesia and began to spread among the African population there, it was taken up enthusiastically by those able to afford the early portable sets. These were relatively inexpensive: within the reach of the average urban worker and of many prosperous rural dwellers as well. The new invention was hailed in one white settler newspaper over the border in Southern Rhodesia in the following terms:

> In every hut in every village there may yet be a shiny instrument a source of entertainment and a new kind of 'fifth column' in the battle against ignorance and apathy.[3]

Letters from the first listeners to the new radio station in Lusaka speak of the many different pleasures that possession of this new invention brought. To a large number, it was simply a precious and remarkable novelty; to others, it provided evening entertainment to be shared with their families. To some, it brought interesting information they otherwise would not have had. Here are just a few examples of what they wrote:

> We have since been enjoying our sets very much inasmuch as we can get news from all over the world. We can listen to the music from Lusaka, Lourenço Marques, BBC, etc. The Malipenga Dance from Lusaka, the Rumbas, Tangos and Khongas from Lourenço Marques are much enjoyed too.

> More and above this, I thank the Government by letting Africans to possess the wireless. I hope the Government will still (go) on favouring we Africans to get precious things.

> I am now one of the proud wireless owners. Surely it gives very loud and interesting music.

> I am very pleased to have bought a radio set at a very low price. My fellow Africans let us praise the God for His kindness He has done to us. Long ago Africans were not suspected to buy such a big thing, but by now we are lucky in possessing these 'sets' and talk to each other as of the same village.

> I did not know that from Lusaka there can come words as if the one speaking is just with me in my house and when they are singing as if they were with me in my house. My wife and I are praising the Governor for having sent the District Commissioner walking for eight miles to come and bring me a wireless set.

To me every evening is a jolly evening and makes home a happy home. I like the set more than important things that I have bought with much money in my life.

I have pleasure in telling you that ever since in my life I never had anything which could please my life (better) than the wireless I have got.

I am thanking you for the great work that you are doing in enabling us to have such happy evenings.

I was the second African to buy a set in Serenje, the first being my father-in-law, Mr. B. Ngoma, and many others have bought them seeing that they are very educative indeed and at the same time they bring joy at the house.

At 444 miles away on the Great North Road always people come around to listen in and are very pleased. Number of them is about 25 to 40 people. So, Sir, we are all very happy indeed.

A few words from very far away where I stay. I was always going to listen to some wireless news and today I bought one wireless but people are coming wonderful to listen.

I bought a wireless set on 5.12.49 and now I am able to hear news from far and near, Lusaka is no longer a distance to me.

To those of you who possess these good things, I pray you not to be hard on the people when they want to listen to your sets. Let everyone listen, because it is by his listening that he will encourage his daughter and himself to follow the way to progress.

The news which we listen through our wireless sets have taught us many things and some of these are:
(1) Agriculture, (2) Building villages at a suitable place, (3) Digging and building wells and dams, (4) Latrines in villages, (5) Care of children, (6) Education of Girls, (7) How to improve Livestock and (8) many other things. The Broadcasting Officer should know that we bought wireless sets in order to use them and we are doing so . . .

My receiver came a few days ago, and it has been into operation for only a week and during this first week, I have learned quite a lot of things which most of the people, I mean those who have none, do not know. I hear news from all over the districts in Northern Rhodesia, Southern Rhodesia, South Africa and Nyasaland. I hear also some of the important events happening in Europe and so many other European countries through the Central Broadcasting Station Lusaka. What a great favour![4]

This is necessarily selective, but there can be little doubt that radio soon became a very important medium throughout Northern Rhodesia. It would not be too fanciful to suppose that its presence helped bring about a sense of unity and nationhood in that large territory of some seventy tribes in eight or nine groups speaking mutually incomprehensible languages.

Reading through these letters and many others which have reached the Zambia Broadcasting Services in recent years, one is struck first of all by the tremendous pleasure people get from listening to the radio – a pleasure which was, of course, especially intense when the wireless was new. The excitement and happiness it provided was evident in almost all the letters. But soon, as some of them indicate, it took on an added significance:

> I feel proud when I switch on my Saucepan Special and have the whole world in my hut.[5]

Into an increasing number of huts came not only music both familiar and unfamiliar, but also news from the capital city, from other parts of the country and from abroad: different views, different cultures, different voices. Whatever the radio transmits reaches a national audience. This means a significant change in patterns of communication. The extent of that change will of course depend on the diversity within the society, but radio on a national scale can contribute to a cross-fertilization of ideas throughout the entire community.

Radio broadcasts are often very varied, and the individual listener is able to be selective, paying attention only when he or she wants to. Thus radio may play both a change-orientated and a conservative role. It can provide information about the possibilities for improvement, explaining the changes that may be taking place. It can announce and promote, among other things, political campaigns aimed at reducing poverty, ignorance and disease. It can tell people that a better way of life is possible or attainable and describe the constraints on development. It can help raise the general level of political consciousness, providing its audience with a view of their wider national community. Yet it can, at the same time, act as a conservative force and a stabilizing influence by giving the impression of continuity and stability amidst uncertainty and apparent upheaval.

Another role exists for the mass media. In certain countries they operate more as an extension of the media of the developed world, and consequently portray the ideas, values and culture of rich societies. This seems to be especially true of the cinema and television. Few African cinemas ever show feature films made locally, and only a tiny proportion of the films screened by commercial cinemas or at rural open air film shows are the work of that continent's film makers. Where television is concerned, the situation is scarcely different: some African TV stations purchase as much as 80% of their material from European and US sources. Governments that have tried to end this dependence have sometimes encountered stiff resistance from the mostly urban and relatively privileged audience.

Similarly, many African newspapers carry a high proportion of foreign material, ranging from strip cartoons to feature articles. A great deal of this comes from agencies and press companies in Western countries, but African papers increasingly also carry feature articles either supplied free of charge or even paid for by the countries concerned. Radio is, as a rule, far less dependent on foreign material, though there is great variation in this and the majority of African radio stations play at least some western popular music; however, the trend seems to be towards greater indigenization.

The most powerful outside influence on the content of all the mass media in any African country is the news. For the bulk of world news, including that of other countries in Africa, African media depend on one or more of the five main international news agencies: Reuters (UK), AFP (France), AP and UPI (USA), and Tass (USSR). Even in those countries whose mass media have steadily reduced their dependence on foreign sources for other types of material, the reliance on one or any combination of the five agencies for world news is almost complete. Without these there would be virtually no foreign news, for few of the African media have their own sources of such information. Even when agency material has been substantially rewritten, the view of the world it gives to African audiences is one that is largely determined outside the continent and in a different cultural, political and economic environment. Attempts have been made to change this situation, notably in the so-called Non-Aligned News Agencies Pool launched in 1976, but for news of international diplomacy, wars, emergencies of various kinds, political and other news of other countries, the African media as a whole continue to depend on the news agencies, and on the four western ones in particular.[6]

Reuters and AFP are the most significant, both in their coverage of Africa and in the number of African customers using their services. Each has regionalized news services for Africa which try to take local demands into account. Such regionalization is expensive for the agencies, which do not, in any case, make much of their money in Africa. They need to be able to report from as many places as possible: access to certain countries may depend on their provision of services which show regard for local news requirements. Nevertheless, denial of access is not uncommon. Despite its importance as Africa's largest nation and a major oil producer, Nigeria received little news attention in the years 1976 to 1980, mainly because access was refused during that period to three of the four western agencies as well as to most visiting journalists. As a result, the Nigerian elections of 1979 – which were, by any standards, newsworthy and of great significance internationally – were given a very meagre coverage by the world's media. It is worth noting that this lack of coverage applied also to the African media outside Nigeria. If the major agencies ignore or barely report a story, the world's media, including those of Africa, will give it the same treatment: the agencies thus have an important 'agenda-setting' role. Some media, of course, try to escape from their reliance on the agencies – but what criteria do they use for news values? The irony is that those few newspapers or radio stations in Africa which can afford their own foreign coverage in the form of correspondents and reporters tend to send them to places that are already well covered by the agencies – the United Nations, Paris, London or Washington – instead of supplementing the activities of the agencies where these are desperately weak. An obvious case in point is Nigeria, where, except for the Ghana News Agency, no other African country's news medium maintains a correspondent. For similar reasons the conflicts in Chad, Ethiopia and the Western Sahara have gone largely unreported except when the international agencies have been able to give coverage.

Poverty and lack of resources are to blame for the dependence of Africa's mass media on foreign sources for material as well as for technology. It should nevertheless be recalled that most of the research into the media has been carried out in the United States, and one should question the applicability of such findings to the situation in Africa. As one writer has warned, the frames of reference and terminology are the products of mass society in an electronic age.[7] The mass media in Africa operate in a very different environment. There are few channels, and only in certain towns do the mass media gain anything like the saturation coverage reached in western countries. The audience is for the most part illiterate, uneducated and rural; television, cinema and the press are largely confined to the urban areas. Moreover, in the majority of African countries, severe language problems have to be overcome. If, then, the mass media of Africa are seen to be different in most other respects, it would indeed be surprising to discover that they produced effects similar to those produced by the media in richer nations. Yet this is the mistake commonly made by those who draw for guidance on research carried out in the United States. Real opportunities exist for fruitful study of the media's role in less developed countries. Even in African countries at similar levels of economic development the media differ in their role, in the social and political control exercised over them, and in other ways. They must therefore be expected to produce different results.

When considering possible effects it is essential to formulate questions that are both relevant and answerable. Too often in studying writings on the mass media one is struck by questions which seem to imply that it is possible or meaningful to talk of modern society without the mass media, when the two are in reality inseparable. Consider these two examples of questions on the effects of the media:

How are people's relations with each other affected by the use of the mass media as a means of social communication?

What are the social consequences for the organisation of society and its institutions of the use of mass communications with its capacity to bypass existing channels of influence and set up competing forces of authority?[8]

These and similar questions appear to treat the mass media as if they were intruders playing an unwelcome and inappropriate role. It is quite wrong to regard the modern mass media in this way. They are now – or are in the process of becoming – absorbed into a total order of things wherein they, together with other institutions, play a part in influencing behaviour, contributing to knowledge and helping either to prevent or bring about change.

What role, then, do the mass media play in the lives of their audience? What do people go to the media for, and what use do they make of them? In order to answer these questions one needs to look not only at the potential of the mass media in terms of their content, spread and control but also at the disposition of the audience. What happens to the individual at the end of the mass communications chain is determined by his background and needs. One is unlikely to be affected by media content which one either has no use for or rejects as being irrelevant to one's perceived needs. Multiply the role of the mass media played in the life of each individual, and you may be able to see the role they play in society as a whole. Yet sociologists do not seem very clear about the position of the mass media within an overall view of society. They leave unanswered the main question, that of the real and specific functions of the mass media.[9]

If the communications process has three main social functions – to inform people about their environment, to link component parts of the society, and to transmit social values and norms – it will be seen that these are performed by the mass media in rather special ways, ways which are essential to the process of nation-building. In less developed countries with poor transport facilities and long distances to be covered, radio can play a major role in carrying information to a national audience; in many new nations there is little else in the way of *national* political communication. If governments want to keep their people informed they must have access, whether direct or indirect, to some kind of mass media system. The exercise of political power requires the communication of information from rulers to ruled, and it is the mass media which can convey this information. Not surprisingly, research has shown a high correlation between mass media exposure and knowledge of political matters. Well-informed people are mostly those who either listen to the radio or read a daily newspaper, on a regular basis.[10]

Even when there are many people not routinely exposed to the mass media, news can nonetheless reach a wide audience. For instance, I noticed in June 1966 how rapidly the news of Robert Kennedy's assassination travelled through villages in Kilimanjaro District, Tanzania. I have been told that the same thing happened when Martin Luther King was killed in April 1968. Similarly, in Zambia in 1970 news of a disaster at a copper mine in Mufulira spread rapidly by word of mouth from those who had radios to those who did not. In this way the radio can speed the dissemination of certain kinds of news to people who are not ordinarily radio listeners.

The mass media play a major role in the spread of information within any political system which places some importance on informed decision-making at all levels, whether in democratic elections, through local government or at the various levels of a state bureaucracy. They can broaden the policy dialogue. This has an important consequence for nation-building when

> the media cover the national news, the national problems and the statements and arguments of leaders as to what policies should be adopted. Thus the theater of policy discussion is widened until it begins to be as wide as the nation. As this happens, during development, the conditions of national participation are set up, national empathy is encouraged, and all the requirements for developing as a nation are brought within reach.[11]

The mass media can focus attention on issues and influence both debates and decisions, but in so doing they can also *impose* a way of looking at events which influences those debates and decisions. By concentrating on certain issues and ignoring others they give an image of events that reflects the bias, conscious or unconscious, of those who control them. The prejudices of the communicators, which perhaps reflect the prejudices of at least some groups in society, become magnified by the process of mass communication. In this way the media, whether politically controlled or not, are able to influence the way we ourselves interpret events. Many examples could be cited in support of this. In 1978 a local rebellion took place in the mining town of Kolwezi in Shaba Province, Zaire. A large number of local people, as well as some foreign-born *black* people in the town, were killed in the fighting between the rebels and the Zairean army. The story was reported by the world news media almost entirely in terms of the fate of a small number of the town's European residents. After the event, most people, as I recall, remembered the Shaba disturbances story as being about the threat to the lives of white people living in an African country; in fact, this had almost nothing to do with what happened. Any student of the media will doubtless be able to draw upon some event or series of events from his or her own experience which may illustrate a similar, if less spectacular, example of media influence on the way reality can be defined for us.

The siting or physical position of the mass media, in particular that of the radio, make them important in another respect. They appear to be 'at the centre of things', and have the ability to confer status on individuals and groups. It is significant that at the time of a coup one of the first targets for the insurgents is the national radio station. Yet this power to bestow authority is not confined to those already occupying positions of power:

> Recognition by the press or radio or magazines or newsreels testifies that one has arrived, that one is important enough to have been singled out from the large anonymous masses, that one's behaviour and opinions are significant enough to require public notice.[12]

Note how, when a well-known person is ignored by the media for a time, people ask: 'Whatever happened to X?' He or she may in fact be as active as ever!

A major component of the process of nation-building is the so-called widening of horizons brought about by the mass media. In developing countries, this is generally caused by the arrival of radio. Schramm quotes an African listener describing the impact of radio on his life:

> The radio can take a man up to a hill higher than any we can see on the horizon and let him look beyond.[13]

The letters quoted earlier, sent to the radio station in Lusaka, Northern Rhodesia, imply a connection between knowledge and progress or modernization. Whatever its actual effect may be on listeners' behaviour, the radio can impart knowledge or information about alternative ways of life or of doing things. Not infrequently, it is from the mass media that a person first hears of new ideas. However, this can lead to a difficulty which has been referred to as the 'revolution of rising expectations'. The audience may be encouraged to want something without being shown how to achieve it. Mass media can encourage desires for things which may not be readily available; aspirations may be more easily raised than satisfied. The presence in society of gross inequalities between an urbanized, educated minority and a rural peasantry, combined with the wide dissemination of mass media content, might therefore be expected to result in political instability. Once again, it is the content of the mass media which is a vital consideration.

If the mass media are able to raise aspirations, are they not also able to stimulate economic progress? It may be true that by providing information about change and the possibilities for development they can create a 'climate' in which 'development is stimulated' – but what evidence do we have that people are in fact stimulated to 'take another look at their own current practices and perspectives'?[14] One of the very few pieces of research in this field carried out in an underdeveloped country – among uneducated peasants of an Andean village in South America – showed a positive correlation between high mass media exposure (mostly to radio) and the adoption of new farming practices by villagers, together with higher aspirations for their children.[15] Yet it was not shown that the one *caused* the other. It is possible that these villages bought radio sets and listened to them because they already possessed these attributes. In other words, there was no evidence that by becoming radio listeners peasants then became achievers or modernizers.

Social barriers to the communication of new ideas frequently play a large part in resistance to change. New ideas are filtered through a psychological screen made up of the person's previous experiences, beliefs, present practices and attitudes. People may see new ideas as a threat. Messages are accepted if they fit or can be made to fit; otherwise, they may be rejected or distorted.[16] Karl Deutsch has made an interesting proposition regarding communication within a political system:

> The extent of the effect of the introduction of new information into a political or economic system might well be related among other things to the extent of the instabilities that already exist there.[17]

This is central to the consideration of the role of the mass media in developing countries. In the narrower sense of building a national consciousness, the mass media can play an active role without challenging a large number of existing attitudes. This they can do either by diverting attention away from parochial affairs and towards national interests or helping to arouse nationalistic sentiments, thereby drawing people closer together despite their differences. They may well be able to achieve little else. If, however, society is in a state of change and the mass media operate in the service of that change, it is likely that their impact will be both considerable and wider-ranging.

Assuming that the mass media are new in content as well as form, can we then make assumptions about their effects? The answer, unfortunately, is no, because we cannot measure effects without taking account of audience attitude. Are individual members of the audience interested, and are they motivated to learn new ideas? Radio in its early days obviously had great novelty value, as the reports from Northern Rhodesia indicate, and its impact then was no doubt considerable. In recent years the media may have become a mere palliative – something that makes an unpleasant or difficult life more bearable.

It should not be forgotten that there is often a difference between what is intended and what is perceived. Even specifically designed mass media campaigns can fail when the selective perception of the audience plays a negative role. There was a famous campaign in the United States which attempted to ridicule those who were racially prejudiced, but which in fact gave the target audience the wrong message: it was thought that the cartoons of 'Mr Bigott' actually supported racial prejudice.[18] If people come into contact with messages that conflict with deeply-held beliefs and practices they frequently misinterpret, distort or reject them.

Numerous scholars have noted the importance of small groups in social communication and decision making. Rogers, among others, has suggested that while the mass media may be effective in creating knowledge about new ideas, interpersonal channels of communication may be more effective in helping to form and change attitudes towards such ideas. Perhaps when the objective is persuasion, 'we should largely depend on word of mouth channels rather than the mass media'.[19] This is why in a number of countries encouragement has been given to mass media campaigns combined with small, organized groups under carefully selected leadership. In China, for example, people were organized into media forums, where cadres attempted to control the mediating influences. The audience received and discussed media content in controlled conditions.[20] In groups, individuals are thus able to discuss problems related to culture, religion, tradition or social structure that might otherwise work against desired change. Neurath shows how in India the mass media can play a role in encouraging agricultural innovation when utilized in combination with organized interpersonal discussion.[21] Studies in Ghana and elsewhere show much the same thing.[22]

The political and economic system within which the mass media operate partially determines their role. Radical thinkers like Raymond Williams have said that the media of western countries produce routine 'mass culture' which, together with routine thinking, can 'insulate us from reality'. It is characteristic of the mass media that they appear to simplify news, make stereotypes of people and events, and tend to take note only of information that is immediate and therefore also ephemeral. In the West, a large proportion of media content appears 'designed to relax, encourage personal consumption, provide vicarious thrills or escape in one form or another.[23] In certain less developed countries the mass media are developing along similar lines, whereas in others this tendency has been arrested. In most new countries of Africa, the mass media are under government control, and it is these governments which will determine their direction.

Notes

1   *World Radio-TV Handbook 1982* (Hvidovre, Denmark, 1982).
2   Rosalynde Ainslie, *The Press in Africa* (London, 1966), p. 135.
3   *Bulawayo Chronicle*, October 15th 1948. Eight months later, an editorial in the paper warned of the 'dangers' of Africans listening to radio broadcasts other than those over which the settlers had control. It was also worried that

uneducated Africans would misunderstand what they heard from the colonial stations and that there could be tragic results. *Ibid.*, June 10th 1949.

4   Harry Franklin, *Report on 'The Saucepan Special'* (Lusaka, 1950). The so-called 'Saucepan Special' was an inexpensive, portable, valve radio set housed in a metal case like a small saucepan. It required a heavy and cumbersome battery to power its valve amplifier, and the battery cost as much as a fifth of the total price of the set. But it was the first widely available and cheap set on sale anywhere in Africa that did not require mains electricity and was both reliable and sturdy. Within ten years it was superseded by transistor portable radio sets.

5   Peter Fraenkel, *Wayaleshi* (London, 1959), p. 20. Fraenkel's personal and entertaining account of broadcasting in the early days in Lusaka is a worthwhile read.

6   For the best analysis of the agencies and their influence over flow of news around the world see Oliver Boyd-Barrett, *The International News Agencies* (London, 1980).

7   Simon Othenburg, 'Commentary: Rural Sociology and Communications', *Canadian Journal of African Studies*, 3, no. 1 (Winter 1969), pp. 232-9.

8   Dennis McQuail, *Towards a Sociology of Mass Communication*, p.79.

9   See, for example, J.W. Riley and M.W. Riley, 'Mass Communication and the Social System' in *Sociology Today*, (eds.) R. Merton, L. Brown and L. Cottrell (New York, 1959), p. 577.

10   See pp. 90-92.

11   Schramm, *Mass Media and National Development*, p. 137.

12   Paul F. Lazarsfeld and Robert K. Merton, 'Mass Communication, Popular Taste and Organised Social Action' in *Mass Communications*, (ed.) Wilbur Schramm (Urbana, Illinois, 1969), p. 408.

13   Schramm, *Mass Media and National Development*, p. 127.

14   *Ibid.*, pp. 131-132.

15   Paul J. Deutschmann, 'The Mass Media in an Underdeveloped Village', *Journalism Quarterly*, 40 (1963), pp. 27-35.

16   Klapper, *The Effects of Mass Communication*, p. 50.

17   Deutsch, *Nerves of Government*, p. 147.

18   Eunice Cooper and Marie Jahoda, 'The Evasion of Propaganda; How Prejudiced People Respond to Anti-Prejudice Propaganda', *Journal of Psychology*, 23 (1947), pp. 15-25.

19   Everett M. Rogers, 'Communications Research and Rural Development', *The Canadian Journal of African Studies* (Winter, 1960), p. 216.

20   Frederick T.C. Yu, 'Campaigns, Communications and Development in Communist China' in *Communication and Change in the Developing Countries*, (eds.) Daniel Lerner and Wilbur Schramm (Honolulu, 1967).

21   Paul Neurath, 'Radio Farm Forum as a Tool of Change in Indian Villages', *Economic Development and Cultural Change*, 10 (1962), pp. 275-283.

22   UNESCO, *An African Experiment in Radio Forums for Development: Ghana 1964/1965*, Reports and Papers on Mass Communication, no. 51 (Paris, 1968).

23   Raymond Williams, *Communications* (Harmondsworth, Middlesex, 1968), p. 100.

4
Communications and Political Power

Africa's media in action before independence

To write adequately about Africa's press, radio and television would require a succession of books. What follows is therefore only a brief outline, with a closer examination of certain areas. There are more than fifty countries in Africa, of which each has radio, most have a daily press and many have television. Their present media facilities owe much to their history. Though a certain amount of work has been done on the history of Africa's media, there is room for research on a far larger scale.

Africa's modern print and electronic media developed as the direct or indirect result of contact with Europe. Few African societies had a written language, and in those that did, printing was either unknown or undeveloped. Arab traders brought literacy to West and East Africa, but the technology of printing came from Europe and the United States. European colonialism south of the Sahara meant that most literacy, and therefore most printing, was in a European language. This has important implications which are worth considering more closely. Traditional oral forms of communication, which played a central role in the maintenance of social and political order – ensuring continuity and reinforcing values and norms of behaviour – was gradually confronted by a quite different form based on the new technology of print and, generally, on a foreign language. If an African language was used, it was a lingua franca, one not necessarily employed in traditional oral communication. Thus the introduction of the new print media marked the beginning of a break with the past. It must be stressed that the literacy barrier is a double one. Of the many Africans who learn to read and write, a large number, perhaps the majority, rarely see their own mother tongue in print. Certain languages have still not been written down; others exist in written form only as the Bible or sections of it. Literacy and education tend therefore to reduce linguistic diversity and to enhance major languages at the expense of minor ones. Radio has therefore proved less restrictive, being able to reach many more individuals through a greater number of languages. Head listed over 175 indigenous African languages used in radio broadcasting in 1973.[1] His list was incomplete, and the true total today certainly exceeds 200. Yet this still means that over a thousand African languages are not heard on the radio.

The legacy of the press

The press is far older in Africa than is generally supposed, the first newspapers probably being those that appeared during the Napoleonic occupation of Egypt in 1797. In South Africa, the *Cape Town Gazette* first appeared in 1800, and a year later, the *Royal Gazette* appeared in Freetown, Sierra Leone. The first truly indigenous press was almost certainly that of Egypt, which began to appear during the nineteenth century; but it predated black Africa's press by only a few years. Slaves returning from the Americas to the West African coast soon established local papers. Of these, the earliest was probably founded in Liberia, where in 1826 Charles Force started the monthly *Liberia Herald*, whose motto was 'Freedom is the Brilliant Gift of Heaven.'[2]

In 1858 Charles Bannerman, the first African editor in the British colony of the Gold Coast (now Ghana), started the *Accra Herald*. At first he had no press but, undaunted, wrote the paper by hand! In 1859 missionaries published Nigeria's first paper, which was also the first African paper in an African language. It was called *Iwe Irobin fun awon ara Egba Yorubas* ('the newspaper for Egba and Yoruba people') and was priced at 30 cowries! Four years later, Nigeria's first English language paper appeared – the *Anglo-African*, published by a West Indian, Robert Campbell. In Sierra Leone, the short-lived *Royal Gazette* was followed by others, including the *African Interpreter and Advocate*. The economic base of these early newspapers was fragile, and few lasted long, but they were significant in their expression of early educated and urbanized African opinion.

Political protest and the expression of informed African opinion soon became the dominant theme of the West African English language press. In the Gold Coast, J.H. Brew, Timothy Laing, Casely Hayford, Attoh Ahuma and James Mensah Sarbah founded a strong tradition of political satire that was to last well into the nationalist period. These papers played an important role in trying to raise an early consciousness of nationalism and pride in the face of colonial dominance and alien values. Thus Attoh Ahuma (who was also known as a clergyman, the Revd S.R.B. Solomon) joined with another local churchman, the Revd Eggijir Assam, to launch the *Gold Coast Aborigine*, in which they promised to redress what they saw as the colonial imbalance in the education of local Africans:

> Most of our youth are acquainted with the history of England with such precision and to such a degree that it astounds the Briton, and yet these cannot tell a B from a bull's foot in the history of this country.

The two men therefore began to produce a series of articles on local African history in order to show that Africa also had a past worth recalling.

By the end of the nineteenth century thirty-four newspapers had appeared in Sierra Leone, nineteen in the Gold Coast, nine in Nigeria and one in the Gambia. During the 1890s four major papers were operating in the Gold Coast, two being published in Accra and two at Cape Coast, two hundred miles away. They carried an amazing amount of news, considering the difficulty of surface transport and the absence of telephone and telegraph. Kwame Nkrumah later referred proudly to the enterprise of these pioneer pressmen:

> The astonishing thing about these editors and their small band of journalistic collaborators was how they managed to build up a secret intelligence and newsgathering service along the coast, which involved, beside the normal hazards of anti-colonialist activity, the danger of some of them finding a premature watery grave. In those days there was no proper road between Cape Coast and Accra . . . so these editors and their co-workers worked their clandestine way by canoe along the coast to the capital, Accra. There they ferreted out all the latest material that could be used against the colonialist government, and then they paddled their dangerous way back to Cape Coast. All these activities were done at night. It was always a puzzle to the British administration in Accra as to how these newspapers were able to appear in Cape Coast with such 'hot' news so quickly. Nevertheless these and other journalists did much to spread the doctrine of equal rights for Africans, especially as schooling began to widen out gradually and we were becoming conscious of ourselves as political beings.[3]

Despite their attempts to express opposition many of these early papers still looked to the press of Europe as models. In 1883 Owen Macaulay's *Eagle and Lagos Critic* was founded, having as its aim the infusion into 'the minds of the community the fondness for reading for its own sake'. It carried accounts of the debates in the British Parliament as well as reports on local cricket matches, and leavened its rather serious tone with Victorian English jokes. The reliance of some of Africa's English language press for some of its lighter material on foreign sources continues today, as can be seen from the number of papers which take English and American comic strips such as *Modesty Blaise, Andy Capp, The Gambols, Garth, Peanuts* and *The Perishers*.

The West African English language press rapidly took on a more militant and nationalist tone, particularly in Lagos, Nigeria, thanks to John Payne Jackson. Born in Liberia, Jackson had learned printing at a mission school. He became a trader in Nigeria and when this career failed, worked for a time as a clerk to Richard Beale Blaize, publisher of the short-lived *Lagos Times*. Though the two men fell out, Blaize is thought later to have financed Jackson when he started the *Lagos Weekly Times* in 1890. They quarrelled again, but this time Jackson had established his reputation as a journalist, and kept control of the paper. From January 1891 it appeared as the *Lagos Weekly Record*, and was for forty-nine years an outspoken critic of colonialism. In 1913, Jackson produced a vigorous attack on the new governor, Sir Frederick (later Lord) Lugard. He also campaigned actively on behalf of the people of neighbouring Dahomey in their struggle against the French. Jackson died in 1915, the editorship being taken over by his son, Horatio.

In 1925, Herbert Macaulay produced West Africa's first successful daily newspaper, the *Lagos Daily News*, which was a mouthpiece for his National Democratic Party. From 1933 a rival party, the Nigerian Youth Movement, also had its own paper, the *Daily Service*. More important than either of these were Nnamdi Azikiwe's *West African Pilot*, started in 1937, and a series of other papers he launched in the succeeding years. By 1940 the *Pilot* had outstripped all other West African papers in circulation, achieving daily sales of 12,000. An outstanding West African nationalist and journalist, Azikiwe at one time owned six papers. He also subscribed to Reuters (received in morse by radio) and was for a while a Reuters correspondent in the region.

The press of the Gold Coast also reflected and stimulated the activities of nationalists and of the burgeoning political parties. In 1948 Kwame Nkrumah founded the *Evening News*, which became the paper of his Convention Peoples Party.

The CPP warned its readers to read the *Evening News* daily to enable the national headquarters to guide the country to victory.[4]

When independence became assured, further party newspapers appeared as it became clear that owning a newspaper was a necessary part of a successful political campaign: for example, in Nigeria, Azikiwe and his NCNC party controlled ten newspapers in 1959, while their rivals, Obafemi Awolowo and the Action Group, controlled fourteen. The parties of Sierra Leone and Gold Coast similarly had one or more newspapers each.

In addition to this flourishing political press there existed other influential papers. The British Mirror Group under Cecil King established a significant foothold in the English language press of West Africa. It purchased the *Nigerian Daily Times* in 1947 and brought great technical improvements to the paper. Prior to this, local papers had rarely carried pictures; those that were used had first to be made into printing blocks in London – a process which could take six weeks. When the veteran Nigerian journalist Abiodun Aloba began his career in 1944, no paper was able to process pictures locally, none had teleprinters and few even had telephones. Stories of even the most important events often depended on the post.[5] Cecil King's entry into the field of newspaper publishing changed all this. His Mirror Group papers were non-partisan, but they were, equally, not identified with colonial rule. They recruited and trained some of West Africa's best journalists, building on the already established foundations of newspaper readership and reporting. Most significantly, Mirror papers introduced modern printing techniques, processed photos locally for immediate use and speeded up the presses. After the first rotary press was established at the *Daily Times*, that paper's circulation soared from 25,000 in 1951 to 55,000 in 1955; ten years later, it reached 120,000 copies daily. In 1950, the group established the *Daily Graphic* in the Gold Coast, and in 1952 it bought the *Daily Mail* of Sierra Leone. These well-produced papers were a major challenge to the indigenous political press, some of whose publications failed to survive as a result. The Mirror Group eventually sold all its papers in West Africa to local interests. In the case of Ghana, the *Daily Graphic* was sold to the Nkrumah Government in 1965.

In the vast area of West and Equatorial Africa, formerly ruled by the French, the press was far slower to develop. The somewhat different style of French colonial rule and the region's more scattered population were two major reasons. The policy of the French was to form a small native élite, known as *évolués*, who learned their language and culture. It was also French colonial policy for there to be larger concentrations of Europeans in their territories. This led to the establishment of French language newspapers, edited by Frenchmen, which catered for a combined European and *évolué* readership. The latter identified far more closely with French culture than their counterparts in Nigeria or the Gold Coast ever identified with the British. A measure of the extent to which *évolués* were drawn into French life was the fact that President Houphouet-Boigny of the Ivory Coast was previously a member of five successive French cabinets during the 1950s.

The French discouraged the establishment of indigenous African publishing. All the early newspapers – such as *Le Réveil du Sénégalais*, launched in 1886 and *L'Union Africaine*, in 1896 – were published by Frenchmen. The first paper in Abidjan, Ivory Coast, to be owned and edited by an African appeared in 1935.[6] The *Eclaireur de la Côte D'Ivoire* became a popular anti-colonial paper voicing grievances against the police and some of the chiefs, and campaigning for the unemployed and farmers hit by the world recession. Between 1928 and independence the Ivory Coast had some fifty newspapers, but few of them lasted long. The Frenchman Charles de Breteuil launched a chain of newspapers in French West Africa which included *Paris-Dakar*, started in Senegal in 1933, and *France-Afrique* (later renamed *Abidjan-Matin*) established in the Ivory Coast in 1938. After the war, *La Presse de Guinée* was launched in Conakry and *La Presse du Cameroun* in Yaoundé. All of these were originally produced by Frenchmen for Frenchmen.[7]

The educational and cultural gap between the élite *évolués* and the rest of the African population was noted by Almond and Coleman as a 'marked discontinuity in communication' between the two; at the same time, between this African élite and European Frenchmen, 'one could argue that a unified communications process tended to develop'.[8] Both these processes were more evident in the French than in the British territories, say the authors, who nevertheless caution against making too much of this. For, while Léopold Senghor and Houphouet-Boigny were able to communicate with their political colleagues in Paris, they had nevertheless not forgotten how to communicate with their own people.

French restrictions on an African press were lifted after the Second World War, and between 1945 and independence in 1960 thirty-six newspapers emerged and disappeared in Abidjan alone. These mostly reflected the emergence and subsequent disappearance of various political groupings and parties. By the time self-government had been achieved in 1960, Felix Houphouet-Boigny's *Parti Démocratique de la Côte d'Ivoire* (PDCI) had defeated all other parties, whose papers disappeared with them.

In writing about the press of French-speaking West Africa before 1960, one is referring mainly to Abidjan and Dakar, where the *évolués* were concentrated. West and Equatorial French Africa then broke up into fourteen separate, independent countries. Outside Senegal and the Ivory Coast there was very little press to speak of in the pre-independence period: illiteracy was even higher than in the British territories, and the small, educated élite could not easily sustain newspapers. There were exceptions, notably in two Francophone countries which were originally colonized not by France but by Germany. *Elolombe ya Kamerun* ('The Cameroon Sun') was an early mission paper of that German colony, and others existed, both in German and the local languages. Togo had a Catholic monthly, *Mia Holo*, that first appeared during German rule and survived into modern times. In Dahomey, a few African papers emerged as early as the 1920s. As far as I have been able to discover, the first papers in French West Africa to be owned and controlled by Africans were *Le Cri Nègre* and *Le Phare du Dahomey*. Elsewhere, there is little to report. The political awakening that followed the Second World War and the period when French West Africans were able to elect members to the French Parliament saw the establishment of a few party papers, but few Africans could read them and their circulations were extremely low. Cameroon was something of an exception in having a number of privately owned papers: *L'Echo du Cameroun, Dialogue, Le Petit Camerounais* and *Les Nouvelles du Mungo*. French repression prior to independence, and President Ahidjo's tight control after 1960, effectively killed off this brief flowering. Rosalynde Ainslie commented in 1966 that 'many of Cameroon's finest journalists now work abroad'.[9]

This brief survey of the Francophone African scene should not ignore the rather curious case of Madagascar, which, at the time of its independence, could boast seventeen dailies with a total circulation of 20,000 copies as well as forty-four other papers and magazines.[10]

In East and Central Africa the press developed along very different lines, reflecting chiefly the contrasting nature of that region's contact with Europe. While contact between Europe and West Africa can be traced back many hundreds of years, it was only during the middle of the nineteenth century that Europeans arrived in any numbers in East and Central Africa. There are still those alive today in Zambia, Malawi and Uganda who remember the establishment of the first European *boma* in their area. An even more important feature was that many Europeans came not to administer but to settle permanently, which they did on a large scale in Kenya and Zimbabwe, smaller numbers also being found in Zambia and Tanzania. In addition, the British brought in large numbers of Indians who settled in Kenya, Tanzania and Uganda. Both immigrant groups have been important influences on the press.

The Germans, who had colonized Tanganyika in 1885, started a paper in Dar es Salaam four years later: the *Deutsch-Ostafrikanische Zeitung*. Earlier still, in 1888, the Universities Mission to Central Africa (UMCA) had had the distinction of founding German East Africa's first newspaper, *Msimulizi* ('The Reporter'), to be followed by *Habari ya Mwezi* ('News of the Month') in 1894. These papers were also the first in Swahili. *Habari ya Mwezi* was the first in East Africa to employ an African editor: Samwil Sehoza was appointed to the post in 1908.[11]

The German press disappeared after Germany's defeat in the First World War, while the missionary press, though of some historical interest, did not give rise to publications of any major importance. The English white press, on the other hand, was to play an important part in the colonial history of East Africa. Whereas the major newspapers of Nigeria and the Gold Coast were organs of protest and political agitation, those of East Africa were, from the start, 'vehicles for the culture and concepts of the rulers, with the considerable resources of white capital at their command'.[12]

In 1902 the weekly *African Standard* was launched to serve the growing number of white settlers and administrators in British East Africa. In 1910 it moved from Mombasa to Nairobi, changed its name to the *East African Standard* and became a daily. Later, after Tanganyika had become British, the company producing the *Standard* was invited by Tanganyika's governor to set up a paper in Dar es Salaam. Thus the *Tanganyika Standard* was launched in 1930.[13] These Kenyan and Tanganyikan papers took similar lines, generally representing the interests and point of view of the white settler. During the 1950s the *Tanganyika Standard* supported the United Tanganyika Party, which campaigned for racial 'partnership' and was outspoken in its opposition to TANU and African nationalism. Although it was certainly read by a growing number of Africans and Asians, it remained firmly rooted in the culture and outlook of the small, mainly British, white community. Under the trusteeship system of the United Nations, visiting missions were sent to Tanganyika regularly to report on the situation there. From the beginning, these pressed strongly for African political advancement. In 1954, for example, one of them called for a majority of Africans to be on the unofficial, i.e. representative, benches of the legislative council within three years and for self-government within twenty to twenty-five years.[14] On the day the document was published, the *Tanganyika Standard* termed the proposals 'irresponsible and mischievous', claiming 'the great majority of the African population are solidly behind the Government in its present policy'.[15]

It was, however, less strident in its opposition to African nationalism than its sister paper, the *East African Standard* of Nairobi, and when TANU won the elections in 1958, it shifted its ground, coming to terms with political change and lending its support to African nationalism as represented by what it regarded as the moderation of Nyerere. Nevertheless, it continued to be critical of what it felt to be the excesses of some of TANU's more extreme and strident members and officials. This policy was to be carried over into the post-independence period.

Whilst supporting the Government in its efforts towards development, the paper remained cautiously critical of most manifestations of militancy on the part of TANU politicians and others. It also retained something of its settler image in its news coverage, features and leisure articles until it was nationalized in 1970.[16]

There existed other newspapers aimed at the European market, such as the daily *Tanganyika Opinion* and the weekly *Tanganyika Advertiser*, but their circulations were low and they mostly disappeared long before independence. The white press of Kenya had a far larger market to attract and was altogether more viable: a considerable number of Kenyan newspapers and magazines were readily available in Tanganyika. Apart from the *East African Standard* there were the *Kenya Weekly News* and the Swahili weekly, *Baraza*. Launched in 1939, the latter remained the Standard Group's only venture into the Swahili language press and, like the *Tanganyika Standard*, began as a result of a government initiative. It was set up at the outbreak of war, when the British wanted to explain events to the African population in

East Africa, and became self-supporting within two years. Until 1946 editorial policy was a Government responsibility.[17] The Standard Group also owned the *Uganda Argus*.

Asians in East Africa had their own newspapers. In Kenya and Tanzania Asian dailies and weeklies existed in both English and Gujerati. After the Second World War they began to support African nationalism.

The African press in East Africa had a somewhat patchy beginning. In Kenya, the Kikuyu Central Association published *Mwigwithania* in 1928. It was edited by the young Jomo Kenyatta, who halted publication in 1934 when he went to England. After the war a series of anti-colonial, anti-settler, Kikuyu language newspapers existed that went mainly unchecked because the British colonial administrators knew Swahili but not Kikuyu. These papers were ruthlessly suppressed during the Mau Mau Emergency of 1952. However, the importance of the press in forging links between people had now been demonstrated. The establishment of this network proved to be a critical factor in African nationalism during this brief period in Kenyan history when the press played a role similar to that of the nationalist press in British West Africa.

The African press in Tanganyika was slow to develop. *Habari ya Mwezi*, started at an early date by the UMCA, has already been mentioned, but failed to become an important vehicle for African opinion. Other missions joined in: from 1910 onwards the German Protestant Mission produced *Pwani na Bara* ('The Coast and Hinterland'), which by the outbreak of the First World War had reached a modest monthly circulation of two thousand copies.[18] Like a number of other mission or Church papers then and since, *Pwani na Bara* leavened its religious content with a generous amount of secular news (its first edition contained articles on the Kaiser's birthday, the Nyamwezi Chief Mirambo and zeppelins) but the missionary press was nevertheless to remain very small.

These were very early days in Tanganyika's modern development, and still only a tiny handful of Africans could read. Advances were made in education, and the number of literates grew in the period 1910 to 1945, but it is important not to overestimate this growth. Even at independence in 1961, probably not more than ten per cent of the country's African population could read and write.[19] However, in the period leading up to the birth of nationalism, this small number of literates formed a politically important minority.

The colonial government entered the field of the press soon after the German defeat when in 1923 it introduced *Mambo Leo* ('Affairs of Today'). Edited by the Department of Education, its stated purpose was to educate Africans. It was 'non-political' and 'non-controversial' during the interwar years. In addition to world news (carefully interpreted by the staff of the Department), and articles on current affairs and subjects of local interest, the paper carried explanatory and instructive articles on agriculture, health and sanitation. In the beginning it had a circulation of two thousand; by 1930 it was selling nine thousand copies per month at ten cents. Sales continued to rise, its price being held down so that by 1953, fifty thousand copies were sold each month.[20] After the Second World War the paper came under the

Information Office (later renamed the Public Relations Office) whose policy was to explain and promote the achievements and aims of the territory's government. Through *Mambo Leo* and its other newspapers, this government also aimed to present British news and the British way of life to the people of the country, in particular to those without access either to the British press or the BBC. *Mambo Leo* took on a new importance in the 1950s, when the Government hoped it would help stave off the march of nationalism. It placed great emphasis on the Government's efforts in education, perhaps believing that this approach would evoke a sympathetic response from its recently educated African readership. Most editions carried stories stressing the amount of money being spent on improving conditions for Africans in the country, and special attention was given to items concerning stories about the funds provided for health and education by the Colonial Development and Welfare Fund and other British official sources. However, as Omari has pointed out, the paper also printed letters from readers who took a nationalist point of view, and tried to provide answers to them.[21] Moreover, it reported some of the speeches and activities of Nyerere, who led the nationalist party (TANU) from its formation in 1954. When the UN Visiting Mission made its various reports, *Mambo Leo* was at pains to explain British policy on political advance for Africans.[22] Its success in reaching what were, by East African standards, very healthy circulation figures encouraged the Public Relations Department to launch a second paper in 1951. This, *Mwangaza* ('Light'), was later to become the first Swahili daily, but although it cost only three cents it never achieved sales higher than about 1,400.[23] At first *Mwangaza* was sold only in Dar es Salaam, but sales were eventually extended to Tanga, the country's second town. It relied on government subsidy and was closed at the end of 1958. *Mwangaza* seemed dedicated, even more so than *Mambo Leo*, to opposing the nationalists. Omari describes how the paper printed many letters from readers in support of the Government, but it also published others strongly in favour of nationalism and independence. The latter were sometimes answered by editorial comments to the effect that the country was not ready for African self-government. Omari gives a translation of an interesting example in reply to a reader who had written that Africans were ready for immediate self-rule:

> What kind of government are you saying you are ready to take over even today? Is it that of our ancestors filled with tribal warfare? The government in which the big fish swallows the small? No doubt you have in mind such a government. I tell you the days for such a government are gone.[24]

The metaphor of the fish was clearly an unfortunate one: as Omari suggests, 'the big fish swallows the small' could be interpreted as describing the relationship of the colonial power to the colonized.[25]

The 1950s were undoubtedly an important period in the history of the Tanzanian press. Readership was still small relative to the whole population, but among it were to be found most of those active in the leadership of TANU and other areas of African advancement. The Dar es Salaam-based Government papers, despite their partiality, did act as a valuable forum for public debate. Although at first TANU was at a disadvantage in not having its own daily paper, it probably benefited from the publicity, albeit negative, given by the Government press.

Another Government venture into the field of the press was *Baragumu* ('Trumpet'), whose first edition appeared in March 1956. This was an attractively produced weekly with a fairly evenly-divided diet of politics, leisure and sport. The paper's first two years of existence coincided with the United Tanganyika Party's campaign for African support, and it gave the party a considerable amount of publicity. When it became obvious that the UTP had failed, *Baragumu* stopped being political. In 1959 the paper was sold to East African Newspapers Ltd of Nairobi, publishers of the *Daily Nation*, and was then printed in the Kenyan capital for sale in Tanzania. Later renamed and amalgamated with other papers, *Baragumu* continued as *Taifa Tanzania* ('The Nation, Tanzania'). The fourth Public Relations Department newspaper was a weekly give-away, *Habara za Leo* ('News of Today'). Although these were Government newspapers supporting the colonial status quo, they all employed African journalists. In later years they were edited by Africans, though European officials in the Public Relations Department always had the final say. Whiteley wrote that the significance of these papers lay in the valuable service they performed of establishing Swahili as a means of communication in printed form. *Mambo Leo*, as the first major Swahili newspaper, played a particularly vital role in enabling many Africans to gain valuable professional newspaper experience.[26]

Omari argues, convincingly, that the Government press of Dar es Salaam produced the opposite effect to that intended by its sponsors. It failed to convince readers either of the case against nationalism or of that for the policies of slow African advance being put forward by the Government. Furthermore, by arguing the policy in detail through the correspondence columns and presenting opinions on all sides of the argument, the Government press, so Omari suggests, played an indirect part in increasing TANU's popularity.[27] If this is true (and it is not so far-fetched: if you carry on an intelligent argument with your readers in the columns of a newspaper, you cannot expect them to believe that the responsibilities of self-government are beyond them), then it would seem a good example of propaganda having the opposite effect to that intended. The popularity of a newspaper is not necessarily a guide to the opinions of its readers. It can be safely assumed that the overwhelming majority of *Mambo Leo* and *Mwangaza* readers were pro-TANU, in view of the size of the electoral victories in 1958, when that party was supported by sixty-seven per cent of an electorate in which Asians and Europeans were disproportionately highly represented.[28] *Mambo Leo* was popular not for its opinions but because it was well produced, entertaining and readable; nevertheless, its popularity did not mean that its readers either believed or trusted it. Leslie found in 1958 that the Government papers and radio were greatly distrusted: newspapers which were anti-government were avidly sought after but not always easy to obtain.[29]

The Government press of pre-independence Tanganyika left the country with an important legacy: a tradition of government involvement in the daily, weekly and monthly press which was to continue virtually unbroken.

(In this respect Tanganyika was not exceptional.) *Mambo Leo* was to be transferred to commercial ownership and to disappear shortly after independence, but other papers sponsored or produced by the Government took its place. Both colonial and indigenous rulers in Africa have been involved in newspaper propaganda since the beginnings of the press on that continent.

Tanganyika had only a limited tradition of an independent African press. Whereas the Government press could rely on a government subvention to support it for political or educational ends, private newspapers had to find private capital. Returns on such capital were uncertain at best and at worst nonexistent. The first in the field was *Kwetu* ('Ours'), subtitled 'The Key to Civilisation'. Founded in 1937 by Erica Fiah, African trader and leader of the African Welfare and Commercial Association,[30] the paper was initially a platform for that Association, and Fiah told his readers that effective improvement for Africans required them to have political power as well as economic and educational advancement. Fiah was perhaps the only African in Tanganyika who could be compared with those behind West Africa's press of the same period, men like Akikiwe, Danquah and Jackson. Like a number of his West African counterparts he had read the pan-Africanist writings of Marcus Garvey. He was also in touch with the British Independent Labour Party.[31] In its first year of publication, *Kwetu* had a circulation of one thousand, rising to three thousand by the early 1940s.[32] It was a paper produced by and for the radical, and generally non-tribal, urban Africans: in fact, it was very nearly involved in a libel case over criticism of Chagga chiefs. However, Tanganyika was not yet ready for the sentiments expressed by Fiah, and his paper did not survive the 1940s.

No further African newspapers appeared until the 1950s, when two small publishing ventures emerged in Dar es Salaam. Robert Makange started one of them, *Zuhra* ('Venus'). The paper was described by Leslie as follows:

> The editor gets one point which he wishes to put over, and he plugs it straight, hard and without qualification in the simplest terms which alone the semi-literate can understand.'[33]

Leslie contrasted *Zuhra* with the Government papers like *Mwangaza*, stating that the former was more sought after; *Mwangaza* was dull and heavy going. Unfortunately, no record of circulation figures for *Zuhra* can now be found. About the second, the anti-government newspaper *Mwafrika* ('The African'), more is known. Launched as a fortnightly in 1957, this paper had TANU behind it, and its first editor, Mr Bagdelleh, had been a member of TANU's Central Committee since the party's foundation in 1954. Yet party leaders did not want direct control, in case TANU was banned: they wanted the paper to be able to continue even in the event of this happening.[34]

Leslie noted that African newspapers like *Mwafrika* and *Zuhra* were unreliable and irregular in publication, but from 1957 *Mwafrika* was regularly sold on the streets. It was not the first African paper, although nowadays some Tanzanians think that it was; nevertheless it is the only one whose direct descendants are still in existence, and may be regarded as the first successful, viable paper (that term has to be used in a relative sense) edited and produced by Africans. In 1957 its circulation rose from four thousand to twenty thousand by its fourth issue.[35] TANU later severed its link with *Mwafrika* – evidently because of that paper's strident racial tone and what were regarded as poor editorial and reporting policies – and helped to found another paper, *Ngurumo* ('The Thunder'), in 1959.[36] This was published and printed from tiny offices in the centre of Dar es Salaam by R.B. Thaker, an Asian printer and stationer who had become committed to the nationalist cause and assisted TANU with its printing work on a number of occasions.

Meanwhile *Mwafrika*, which, despite TANU's departure still advocated the party's cause, became first a weekly and then, from 1959, a daily. Until 1960 it was, like *Ngurumo*, rather crudely produced, with a poor typeface, frequent errors, smudged printing and few pictures. Its main attraction before independence was that it provided an antidote to the Government propaganda of *Mambo Leo*, but it looked very shabby by comparison. The need for an improvement in *Mwafrika*'s appearance grew more relevant as independence became certain and there was therefore less point in attacking colonial policies. In April 1960 printing was transferred to the *Standard*'s modern presses, and was greatly improved. Nevertheless, financial problems continued to plague the paper, and in 1961 it was taken over by East African Newspapers Ltd, the Nairobi publishers of the *Daily Nation*, who wanted to get into the Tanzanian market. Having also taken over *Baragumu*, this company combined the two in mid-1961 as the weekly *Mwafrika na Taifa* ('African and Nation'), while continuing *Mwafrika* as a daily and keeping on Robert Makange as editor. Circulation fell, but *Mwafrika na Taifa* survived until 1965. The Nation group then reduced its press in Swahili to one daily paper, *Taifa Leo* ('The Nation Today'), produced in Nairobi for Kenya and two weekly papers, one for each country, *Taifa Kenya* and *Taifa Tanzania*, both also edited and printed in Nairobi. By this time, of course, *Mwafrika* and its successors had long since lost their former political stance. In Dar es Salaam and elsewhere during 1967 and 1968, one occasionally heard mention of *Mwafrika* as if it still existed, only to discover that what was being referred to was actually *Uhuru*, the official daily paper of TANU. This confusion was understandable: the *Mwafrika* of 1965 bore no relation to what people remembered of the old one, but the pattern set by the earlier *Mwafrika* and *Zuhra* seems to have been continued after independence by *Uhuru* and *Ngurumo*. *Ngurumo* resembled *Zuhra* in its slangy, irreverent tone, while *Uhuru* was more like the original *Mwafrika* – intensely nationalistic, but often rather heavy reading. One formed the impression that its editor gave his readers what he thought they ought to read rather than what they might want or enjoy.

Before independence, TANU had its own newsletter, *Sauti ya TANU* ('The Voice of TANU'), which it produced from its headquarters in Dar es Salaam. This had a limited circulation: mainly, it seems, through the party for which it acted as a channel of information about policies. *Sauti ya TANU* came into prominence in 1958 after its May 27th issue contained allegations by Nyerere that two district commissioners had used illegal methods against the party. Nyerere was found guilty of libel, and fined. However, this cyclostyled news-sheet was generally moderate in tone; in fact, it was often used by Nyerere when trying to cool down the more militant of his followers.

In Zimbabwe and Zambia (formerly the British colonies of Southern and Northern Rhodesia), the history of the press is closely bound up with that of South Africa, both colonies being linked to the South by economic ties, by transport and communications, and by the political pressures exerted by vocal white settler communities. In the same way that African opinion elsewhere found its voice in the press, so also did white settler opinion, which was frequently in conflict with the colonial authority. Southern Rhodesia soon became a self-governing colony, whereupon its settlers were directly represented in government: a situation different from that existing in Northern Rhodesia. In 1944 Roy Welensky, white trade unionist, campaigner for settler interests and later Prime Minister of the short-lived Federation of the Rhodesias and Nyasaland, founded his own paper. He used the *Northern News* to campaign for the establishment of a white-ruled Rhodesia independent of Britain. In 1948 another settler paper appeared, based in Lusaka: the *Central African Post*, edited by the retired medical practitioner, Dr Alexander Scott. Although his was a settler paper, Scott disliked Welensky. He began to oppose federation, and his paper was looked on favourably by African nationalists.

The South African Argus Group, which also had extensive interests in South Rhodesia, came north in 1951 and bought Welensky's *Northern News*, turning it into a daily in 1953. This group was later also able to buy Scott's *Post*, which it closed down in 1957. Not to be defeated, the following year Scott started a new paper, the *African Times*, which was even more strongly anti-Federation and aimed at liberal-minded whites and Africans. However, it failed financially and ceased publication. Scott could not succeed without outside finance, and soon this was supplied by David Astor, then editor of the London *Observer*, who put up half the money for a new venture, the *Central African Mail*, which began publishing in 1960. It was outspokenly anti-Welensky, opposed to white supremacy and campaigned for one man one vote and for independence. The *Central African Mail* had African editors: first, Titus Mukupo and later, Kevin Mlenga. Yet it remained weekly until after independence and was unable to compete on equal terms with the pro-Welensky, pro-Federation daily *Northern News*. By the time independence came, there had been no truly African press in Zambia.

The situation in Southern Rhodesia was scarcely different. There the settler interest was, of course, even stronger. The Argus group of South Africa brought out the *Rhodesia Herald* in 1892. Now one of Africa's oldest papers, it continues life in independent Zimbabwe as the *Herald*. The Argus group spread its interests, acquiring the *Bulawayo Chronicle, Umtali Post* and *Sunday Mail*. Other settler papers and a few mission-sponsored papers were in existence, the latter providing almost the only significant opposition to white rule and UDI in 1965. As in Zambia, the African press was virtually nonexistent. The *Bantu Mirror*, established in 1936, circulated in both Rhodesias, using African languages, but employed no African reporters: it merely used translations of news from Argus papers.

A small but important African press existed in South Africa. As early as 1884 the Xhosa editor John Tengu Jabavu launched *Imvo Zaba Ntsundu* ('Native Opinion'), which campaigned for African political rights. The effectiveness and influence of his paper were recognized by the Cape prime minister, Mr Sprigg, who attacked Jabavu in Parliament, describing him as:

> a highly educated native who publishes a newspaper in which he sets forth seditious articles . . . I am not sufficiently acquainted with the Kafir tongue to read the articles, but I am informed they are most libellous and seditious.[37]

Imvo survived into modern times but lost its original African nationalist leanings. There was also *Iswi la Bantu*, which was launched by Revd Walter Rubusana, a founder member of the African National Congress. The ANC had two other papers. One, *Ilanga Lase Natal*, was started in 1906 by Dr John Dube, later to become the ANC's first president. The second was the official ANC paper *Abantu Batho*. Its first editor, Dr Pixley Isaka ka Seme, used it in support of the ANC's early campaigns against the infamous Land Acts of 1913 which deprived Africans of the right to land outside the so-called reserves. Surviving until 1932, it proved to be the last newspaper published inside the country by that organisation. African, coloured and Indian papers have been silenced by successive measures taken by a white South African government which has consistently attempted to stifle the free expression of non-white opinion.

Fearful that an independent African press would be able to organize African opinion and campaign effectively against settler policies, white commercial interests sponsored their own ventures into African newspaper publishing. The Native Recruiting Corporation of the Chamber of Mines in South Africa attempted to divert African opinion away from what it regarded as dangerous channels by its *Umteteli wa Bantu* ('Voice of the People'), which first appeared in 1921. Nominally, it opposed the colour bar, but it also opposed any action against it as well as the formation of African trade unions. The Bantu Press newspaper group was a similar venture: part-owned by the Argus Group, it also tried in a paternalistic way to guide Africans in an approved direction. B.F.G. Paver, later to become chairman of the Rhodesia Broadcasting Corporation, had the idea of bringing several African newspapers under one management which could ensure unified policy and guidance. The aim was to have a 'Bantu paper in every province from the Cape to the Congo'[38] – a clear indication of the fact that white settlers in Southern Africa regarded their sphere of influence and authority over Africans as legitimately extending that far north. The Bantu Press established African language papers in Basutoland, Swaziland, Bechuanaland, Johannesburg, Durban, Salisbury and elsewhere. The *Bantu Mirror* and *African Weekly* of Salisbury were printed in a number of central African languages and put on sale in both the Rhodesias and Nyasaland. In urban South Africa, the group published the famous newspaper the *World*, which enhanced its reputation during the Soweto disturbances in 1976. That paper was later closed down and its editor, Percy Qoboza, went to work abroad. It should nevertheless not be forgotten that for most of its existence the *World* was despised by black political leaders. Although, like the other papers in the group, it had an African editor and staff, final editorial control was in white hands and there was usually close white supervision. The *World*'s correspondent was actually excluded from the ANC Congress in 1955. It is worth quoting from a comment made about another Bantu Press paper, *Lentsoe la Basutho*, by B.M. Khaketla, editor of the radical Basutoland monthly *Moblebani* ('The Warrior'). *Lentsoe* had the support of the British administration.

> The paper is called 'Voice of Basotho'. We call it 'The Voice of the Government, of Europeans, of Capitalists, of Exploiters, whose only interest is to squeeze the last penny out of the already empty purses of the Basotho.[39]

The powerful influence of the Bantu Press was to undermine most other African attempts at a truly independent press not only in South Africa but in the two Rhodesias as well. However, brief mention should be made here of the Indian press. The first of these papers was *Indian Opinion*, which began its long career in 1906, launched by Mahatma Gandhi. There have been many Indian papers since, mainly in Durban, which have, to a greater or lesser extent, opposed white supremacy. These have also remained independent of white control. The most noteworthy – established in 1953 and inspired by the Transvaal Indian Youth Congress – was the *Spark*, which helped bring together Indian, African, coloured and white opposition to apartheid. It had the added distinction of being edited at one time by Nelson Mandela, the ANC leader now in prison.

Some writers suggest that one can easily overestimate the significance and influence of the embryonic pre-independence African press. For example, the Kenyan scholar Ali Mazrui has written that the reason why the Swahili word for a newspaper is *gazeti* is merely that the first papers that East Africans came into contact with were government gazettes.[40] Another writer has said that 'the genesis of African journalism lay in dry official publications of colonial governments. The press in Africa began with publications owned and/or operated by officials.'[41] There is some truth in these comments. Certainly, in East and Central Africa official publications of one sort or another were more numerous than the sporadic and scattered indigenous African papers. Only in parts of West Africa was there anything approaching a deep-rooted tradition of an African press operating independently of colonial authority. Moreover, it was these official publications which were responsible for employing the very few Africans who gained journalistic and editorial experience. Such a legacy was hardly encouraging as far as the setting up of a free, unfettered press after independence was concerned. Controls during the colonial period varied considerably, but in most European colonies, including those in West Africa, measures of varying degrees of harshness were taken against those indigenous, privately owned papers which were considered troublesome. Nearly all territories operated strict laws governing the right of Africans to set up newspapers.

Colonial controls find their echo today in certain of the measures adopted by the post-independence governments. It was a commonly held view in colonial days that contrary opinions expressed in the press would mislead Africans, whom many European administrators looked upon as foolish and excitable. Thus a British colonial official in Nigeria commented as early as 1862 that press liberty was a 'dangerous instrument in the hands of semi-civilised negroes'.[42] In 1909 a Seditious Offences Bill was introduced in that country to punish publications which were designed to 'inflame an excitable and ignorant populace'.

The French took even stronger measures than did the British to discourage an African press. Until the 1930s a ruling was in force which forbade anyone other than a French citizen from starting a newspaper. Despite the fact that some *évolué* Africans were, of course, French citizens, the law hindered the development of an indigenous press. Similarly, in the Belgian Congo a 1922 decree made the publication and distribution of any journal subject to Government permission.[43]

Criticism was allowed in certain territories at certain times, but only on sufferance. The tradition of press freedom established in a number of metropolitan powers was not extended to the subject territories – although there were some rather clumsy attempts to do so as independence approached. Moreover, many of those laws on the statute books which empowered colonial administrators to control the printed media remained in force and were used by the new governments after independence.

Radio

Radio started in Europe shortly after the First World War, and the BBC began broadcasting in 1922. Two years later, broadcasting began in South Africa, to be followed in 1927 by Kenya. The first radio broadcasts from Salisbury came in 1932 and from Lourenço Marques in 1933. But these four stations on the African continent aimed their programmes exclusively at white settler communities; not until the Second World War was wireless broadcasting for Africans established.

Radio has made such rapid progress and become so fundamental a part of daily life throughout much of Africa that it is easy to forget just how recently it arrived and how fast it has grown. Today it is at the centre of things. Much important political or national news is likely to be announced over the radio. In the event of a *coup d'état* or any other kind of change in government, the radio building is always one of the first to be visited by the new administration, brought under control, and used to signal to the rest of the country and the world beyond what has taken place. Radio has taken on an especially important central role in situations where other communications facilities are either lacking or inadequate. Today, in most parts of the continent, radio far surpasses the press as the main source of regional, national and international news.

When radio arrived in Africa its potential was recognized by very few. Before the Second World War broadcasting was aimed almost exclusively at Europeans, from stations in Johannesburg, Salisbury, Lourenço Marques, Nairobi and Dakar. In 1936 the British began to plan colonial broadcasting for indigenous people, but these plans were shelved when world war broke out a second time. Yet the war also led to a degree of development of facilities. In the French territories, the Free French set up transmitters in both Douala and Brazzaville to counter the pro-Vichy broadcasts emanating from Dakar. Similarly, the London-based Free Belgian administration broadcast from Léopoldville in what was then the Belgian Congo to German-occupied Belgium as the voice of its country's legitimate government. In the Gold Coast, Kenya and Northern Rhodesia, the war saw the beginnings of African language broadcasting as the administrations there became concerned to inform the families of African soldiers about the progress of the war. Transmitters of varying quality, power and suitability were subsequently left behind to be used in the postwar development of radio for Africans. It should be noted at this point that all broadcasting in the colonial territories was initiated and administered by the colonial governments: the private entrepreneur has been virtually excluded from broadcasting on the African continent. Moreover, the burgeoning African political parties had no voice in radio until after independence.

First off the mark with African language broadcasting was Northern Rhodesia. The Director of Information in the colonial administration, Harry Franklin, started the Lusaka station in 1941 and ran it in his spare time. The few indigenous listeners availed themselves of community sets provided at chief's courts and administrative centres. An agreement was later made with the administrations of Southern Rhodesia and Nyasaland that Lusaka was to be the centre for broadcasting to Africans in the three territories. The introduction of the 'Saucepan Special' radio set has already been commented on: in the four months following its introduction in 1949, one thousand such sets had been sold. In 1950, five thousand were in African hands, and by 1954 the figure had reached thirty thousand.[44] With the invention of the transistor the 'Saucepan' became obsolete, but set ownership continued to grow. By independence ten years later, nearly half the African households along the line-of-rail had radio sets, and in the urban areas eight out of ten Africans had become listeners.[45]

Broadcasting also advanced rapidly in other British territories, particularly during the 1950s. It was official policy at the outset to broadcast as far as possible in African languages. In 1960, one hundred and nine African languages were being used by radio stations in tropical Africa, mainly in the British territories.[46]

The picture was somewhat different in the French territories. French was given priority in administration, education and broadcasting, little or no education being carried out in local languages. Moreover, the fact that France's African possessions stretched in an unbroken line from Morocco in the north to Gabon in the south led to the setting up of an entire series of relay stations transmitting centrally produced programmes and news bulletins. The majority of stations in French Africa were under the authority of SORAFOM (La Société de Radiodiffusion de la France d'Outre-mer), which from its establishment in 1956 was controlled directly by the French Minister for Overseas Territories in Paris. Those included were in Dakar, Niamey, Yaoundé, Bamako, Fort-Lamy, Conakry, Abidjan, Lomé, Cotonou, Douala, St. Louis and Brazzaville. When separate independence for the fourteen territories was conceded under de Gaulle, this vast network was abandoned and individual stations were established. Yet French influence continued in a number of ways. SORAFOM became OCORA and provided technical assistance to Francophone stations, for which it long remained a major source of material. (It had, incidentally, one of the finest collections of African music, much of which has been made available on commercial disc.) Another legacy of the French period of broadcasting is the fact that for a long time few such stations broadcast in African languages: radio services in the Ivory Coast are dominated by the French language even today. Elsewhere, especially in Niger, strong moves have been made to expand broadcasting in local languages.

The launching of radio in Tanganyika was a very modest affair. In 1951 an elderly transmitter of only 400 watts was purchased at the cost of seventy pounds and aerials were slung between two coconut palms. The single studio was extremely primitive, consisting of an attic room with two microphones, one turntable and a mixer. Broadcasting was on short wave only and at such low power that the reception area was limited, scattered and unpredictable. Regular programmes began in July 1951, when the station transmitted for one hour only, three days per week. According to estimates there were then a mere thousand radio receivers in the entire country.

A recurrent problem for the station was that of poor reception, even when the transmitting power was increased. Another major concern was the provision of listening facilities for Africans, the people for whom the service was primarily intended. At that time, radio sets were beyond the means of all but a very limited number of them. Inexpensive rediffusion sets (where one central receiver would serve a large number of speakers in different houses) were introduced in the Dar es Salaam suburb of Ilala and a few community listening posts elsewhere in the capital. More money was soon made available and a plan for expansion drawn up by an official from the BBC in London. A 1¼KW medium wave transmitter was installed to improve reception around the capital. In February 1952 the station began daily broadcasts of one hour.

With the arrival of more funds, further expansion was possible. A new 20 KW short wave transmitter was purchased and purpose-built studios were provided just outside the city. Although facilities were still very restricted, the station could now be heard throughout the territory. Reception was in many places extremely poor, but the new audience was enthusiastic and seemed not to mind the difficulty involved in tuning to Dar es Salaam. Import figures for radio sets showed that the audience was growing very rapidly: during 1954 and 1955 forty thousand sets were imported.

Despite the involvement of the BBC in its establishment, when broadcasting began in Tanganyika it came under direct government control through the Social Development Department. But in 1956 the Tanganyika Broadcasting Corporation was founded and, as a public corporation modelled along the lines of the BBC, removed broadcasting from the direct control of civil servants in the colonial administration. However, the Government was given reserve powers to

> prohibit broadcasting of any matter which may be contrary to the public interest, and the Minister responsible for broadcasting is also empowered to give directions of a general character, after consultations with the Corporation,

as to the exercise and performance of its functions in relation to matters concerning the public interest.[47]

All eight members of the board of the Corporation were appointed by the Governor,[48] and a director was made responsible for the day-to-day management of the service. At independence, the powers of the Governor and his administration were transferred to the President and his Cabinet but, as we shall see, these powers were not judged to be sufficient.

By January 1957, seven months after its establishment, the TBC was broadcasting six hours daily on weekdays. Swahili language broadcasts took up sixty-three per cent of the time, while the rest was in English. 1958 saw the arrival of a new director from the BBC. This was Tom Chalmers, who had already had a great influence on the development of broadcasting in Nigeria and was later also to have a major impact on the development of radio in Malawi, Zambia, Botswana, Lesotho and Swaziland. One of his main achievements as Director-General of the TBC (April 1958 to 1962) was to increase the effective independence of the organization, which severed its last remaining links with the Government's Public Relations Unit. Broadcasting hours were doubled to twelve hours on weekdays and plans made for separate networks: the TBC was to have a 'National Programme' in Swahili and a 'Second Programme' in English. Also discussed were plans for regional broadcasting. Concentrations of listeners – and potential listeners – existed in such regional centres as Mwanza, Mbeya and Arusha, where reception was poor. In addition it was felt that if regional studios were established as well as transmitters, these would be able to originate their own material for local transmission, which would help redress any cultural imbalance in programming. However, it was to be another fourteen years before the first permanent regional transmitter was opened in Mbeya in 1972.

In 1960 the TBC commissioned its first audience survey. Carried out nationally, this showed that almost ten per cent of urban African households now possessed radio sets; in the rural areas, the audience was far more scattered and the figure lower than one in fifty. Yet calculations based on the average number of listeners per set showed Tanganyika's regular radio audience to be probably just under half a million.[49] Great strides had been made in under ten years. The results of this survey were very encouraging to the broadcasters. Chalmers wrote a foreword to the report of the survey, expressing his confidence:

> The TBC is a young organisation, but its expansion is rapid and its achievements have been solid. It is in the happy position of having considerable capital funds at its disposal for further developments. It has a young and enthusiastic staff, mainly Africans, who are rapidly acquiring the up-to-date skills demanded by radio in 1960. It has, to serve the African audience, the most powerful short-wave transmitter of any territory in East Africa. Its growth of audience potential exceeds 10% p.a. Already the audience figures presented in this Survey need an upward adjustment.

This salesman-like language was exactly that: Chalmers was attempting to sell advertising time. The survey indicated that there were probably over seventy-two thousand sets in use but that only sixteen thousand of them were licensed. As the 1960 Annual Report said: 'If even half these (seventy-two thousand) set owners had paid a licence fee, the TBC's financial position would have caused the Board less anxiety'.[50] That anxiety was considerable. The TBC was intended to be self-financing, yet in 1960 it obtained only £5,002 from licences and £6,896 from advertising. The excess of expenditure over income was £83,604, and the TBC was obliged to rely on subventions from the government; that continued reliance was to be a significant factor in decisions that were taken later. In the meantime, the board had to try to increase revenue where it could. This pattern has been repeated in a number of African countries. Licence revenue has proved unreliable as the majority of listeners do not bother to purchase a licence, and radio stations have had to look elsewhere for funds.

In the first year of its existence the Corporation had earned only £898 from advertising. Two years later, receipts had gone up to £3,500, and after the audience survey, reached over £13,000. An office was opened in Nairobi in an attempt to sell advertising time to commercial companies operating from there, and a London representative was later appointed for the same purpose. The TBC's drive for increased revenue from commercial sources in order to free it from its dependence on government raised serious questions about the role of broadcasting. The Corporation was required by the law which established it to operate a broadcasting station as 'a means of education, information and entertainment for the public and to develop the service to the best advantage of the territory'.[51] The desire for advertising revenue, if pursued too vigorously, might well put those aims at risk.

> It was clear that careful consideration would soon have to be given as a matter of overall policy to increasing the space devoted to commercial programmes of one sort or another in Swahili, and to the effect they may have on the amount of informational and educational broadcasting. The conflict between God and Mammon in radio is as real as in other spheres of activity.[52]

This conflict was resolved after independence by the setting up of a separate Commercial Service in 1966. Ironically, in view of Tanzania's later advance along a socialist path, this proved to be the first entirely commercial radio service in English-speaking Africa.[53]

1960 saw a further expansion of broadcasting. The general standard of programmes improved, with increased variety of production and greater professionalism on the part of the staff. The output had now grown to 115 hours per week.

> At the end of 1960 it was possible to feel that, possibly for the first time, the TBC was playing an essential part in the life of the nation and had become an accepted and irreplaceable part of the lives of hundreds of thousands of people.[54]

The TBC took its responsibilities seriously. The main national network, which became known as *Idhaa ya Kiswahili* ('The Swahili Service'), had as one of its main aims 'informing and educating public opinion'. One innovation was a weekly commentary on current events intended to provide listeners with a background to the news of the day.[55] The Corporation was anxious to achieve a 'balance' of opinion on its programmes when controversial subjects were discussed. This policy continued but came under increasing government pressure after independence, so that the open discussion over the radio of certain issues became more limited: a point which is discussed further below. At that time the TBC held to its policy of standing 'above' politics, holding the view that the TBC,

> so long as it flourishes in an atmosphere of democratic idealism, must try to convey as fairly and as vividly as possible a wide variety of thought and action in Tanganyika.[56]

This notion of a pluralist democracy did not last long.

The mass media at the time of independence and beyond

The reason for separating this chapter into two distinct parts will become obvious. The accession to power of nationalist movements and parties – the taking of political power by indigenous Africans previously denied a voice in running their own countries – brought about a dramatic transformation in Africa's media. While the history of the press has been marked by cleavages between the rulers and the ruled, radio had been under the control of colonial administrators. New forces were now in charge. We shall look later in some detail at how independence changed the media of Tanzania and Zambia, but first it will be helpful to consider what facilities existed throughout Africa in that period of transition.

Independence was granted, either willingly or reluctantly, over a period of thirty years beginning with the cases of Ghana, Sudan and Morocco in the 1950s and ending with the somewhat exceptional one of Zimbabwe in 1980. As the majority of these nations became independent between 1960 and 1962, a fair bench mark to take for Africa as a whole would seem to be the year 1961, a time when the continent was beginning its modern period of self-rule. In that year two hundred and thirty-one daily newspapers served the whole of Africa, with a total circulation of three million copies, yet the majority of sales were at either extremity of the continent: in white-ruled South Africa and Rhodesia in the south, and Egypt in the north. The situation in black-ruled Africa was considerably less developed. No fewer than twenty-two countries were without any printed daily paper whatsoever.

What kind of press would the new Africa have? Which of the various legacies would most influence the post-independence press? Was it to be the relatively independent tradition of political argument, criticism and competition that characterized some of the English language papers of pre-independence West Africa? Or would African governments control the press and so prevent alternative voices from being heard? The subject is a complex one – as the account of media policies in Tanzania will make clear – but in much of Africa independent journalism soon died. In some countries it was never even born. As we have noted, many countries had no press to speak of at the time of independence, and in those that did the press has undergone a considerable amount of change. In Nigeria, the tradition of a politically independent press has been kept alive. Though eclipsed or subdued to some extent during the military period of 1966 to 1979, it has flourished again since, with each of the five political parties owning, or having an influence over, newspapers and radio stations. By 1981 some parties were planning to launch new papers or broadcasting stations. Nevertheless, the independence of the mass media elsewhere has declined: newspapers which had formerly been privately owned either disappeared or were taken over in, among other places, Ghana, Ivory Coast, Zambia, Cameroon and Malawi.

Many of the pre-independence laws enabling action to be taken against privately owned media have been enforced by the new African governments, despite the fact that most new leaders issued statements which committed them to the ideals of free mass media and free expression of opinion. In 1968, President Kaunda addressed the International Press Institute's annual assembly, then being held for the first time in an independent, black-ruled African nation: African countries, he said, had 'gone out of their way' to encourage the foreign press to report African affairs. He linked the freedom of the foreign-owned press in Africa to the general principle of press freedom, but remarked that its effects had been far from encouraging: the press had done things that he personally was very unhappy about. Despite this, he promised that his government would neither challenge press freedom nor take over the privately owned *Times of Zambia*. This, he said, was in recognition of the 'importance of an independent press, completely objective and free from influence of government'. However, in the same short speech, he made reference to what he saw as the enormous power of the mass media: the press was 'one of the major forces in shaping this world' – a situation he did not entirely welcome.

> Knowing what it is capable of doing or undoing, I would not be far wrong if I said that the International Press qualifies as one of the many invisible governments. At other times and in certain situations it can form a formidable opposition party where there is organisationally none.
>
> The press is capable of making or destroying governments given appropriate conditions; it can cause war or create conditions for peace. It can promote development or create difficulties in the way of development.[57]

Kaunda went on to argue that the image or interpretation given by the press of a particular government coloured attitudes to it internationally:

> It is largely true that a country is also what the press make it. Once they stick a label on it, what was a lie can slowly be converted into truth in the eyes of other members of the international community.

In this instance he was referring chiefly to the international press. But it soon became apparent in Zambia and other new countries that inexperienced and possibly unstable governments feared the ability of the press to provide conflicting or alternative 'truths', for this put enormous power into the hands of the press proprietors. This is undoubtedly the main reason why the last twenty years have seen a steady increase in controls over the mass media, either by government takeover or by censorship and suppression. In Zambia itself the ruling party, UNIP, took virtual control of the *Times*, but even before this the President had acquired the power to hire and fire its editor: a power he has used on a number of occasions.[58]

President Nyerere of Tanzania (as we shall see in greater detail later) has taken the view that, in a country faced with problems of poverty, ignorance, disease and underdevelopment on a gigantic scale, press freedom should be limited just as it has been in the liberal democracies in wartime. In his book on the African media, Dennis Wilcox remarks critically that the difficulty with this 'typical attitude' on the part of African leaders lies in their being 'both judge and jury of what was in the national interest'.[59]

This may be an easy point to win, but it fails to answer the question: is it part of the legitimate exercise of freedom for the press to speak out in opposition to a popularly elected government operating in a situation of uncertain stability, with the ever-present threat of division and disunity? If the new institutions of the state and government are weak, it is not surprising that those in command should try to prevent the press from undermining public confidence in them. This side of the argument concerning the freedom of the press in Africa is rarely put by those other than the governments concerned. Literature on the subject has chiefly been critical; for example, in a special review of the world press in 1973, *The Times* of London had this to say about the African press in what was a uniformly gloomy and disapproving report:

> In the years since independence one country after another has followed the same dreary pattern of suppression and victimization. A typical front page lead story is likely to be a speech by a minister to a local party meeting, or indeed a warning to 'agitators' not to stir trouble. It sometimes seems almost impossible to pick up a newspaper in Africa without reading that some group or other has been warned about something they should or should not be doing. Meanwhile the real stories, about corruption and mismanagement by people in power, seldom if ever get printed.[60]

In effect, what *The Times* was saying was that it knew what the 'real' stories were and that only dictators prevented such stories from being told. Although this account was not without some truth, it ignored the grave problems of poverty and disunity facing African governments then and now.

African journalists are generally better informed about their position and responsibilities; some are acutely aware of their dilemma. The distinguished Kenyan editor Hilary Ng'weno spoke on this subject at the IPI Assembly in Nairobi:

> The challenge to the press in young countries is the challenge of laying down the foundations upon which future freedoms will thrive ... anyone who has lived or travelled widely in Africa, Asia or Latin America cannot fail to be appalled at the enormous amount of poverty, illiteracy and disease that are to be found everywhere. Under some of the conditions in which vast numbers of Asians, Africans and Latin Americans live, it would be sacrilegious to talk about press freedom, for freedom loses meaning when human survival is the only operative principle on which a people lives.[61]

And he argued that, in conditions of such widespread disunity and tribalism as Africa suffered, the press had another responsibility, one which involved the very security of the State:

> In such countries the first duty of the press, as indeed of any other institution or individual, is to encourage greater national unity; for without a minimim amount of national unity all other human values in society become impossible. Freedom and justice become meaningless. Life becomes insecure. Where there isn't enough national unity, it is my view that the press should confine itself to the difficult task of helping to unify the nation and removing mistrust between communities or tribes. Just how this is to be done is a matter which must be left to the individual newspapermen and the conditions or times in which they work. Most likely it will involve restrictions on what can be published or commented upon; restrictions which ideally should be self-imposed but which may often be clamped upon newspapers by those in power.

But Ng'weno was clearly in two minds how to resolve this dilemma. A year later, he wrote:

> The trouble is that in most countries governments tend to treat themselves as the sole judges of what constitutes the national interest.[62]

Most governments in Africa today, whether civilian or military, democratic or dictatorial, look upon the media in general as something that should be instrumental in promoting national goals. The Zambian journalist Titus Mukupo put it like this:

> When governments need to explain policies, transmit their decisions, instructions, wishes, suggestions, or laws, or discuss new projects and ideas with their electorate, they must have a forum which is not antagonistic to the overall goals of national policy.[63]

Babatunde Jose, former chairman and managing director of the *Daily Times* of Nigeria, a distinguished and experienced journalist and editor, had frequent brushes with the authorities during his long career but understood the problem and was able to appreciate his adversaries' point of view. The points he made in an address to the Royal African Society in London in 1975 are worth summarizing here.

In his opinion African journalists, who often looked enviously at those in Europe and America, should understand why conditions were different at home. African newspapers were, in spite of their poor circulation figures, remarkably influential. Many people believed what they read to be the literal truth: it was even dangerous to use humour at times, because the underlying point was often missed and the joke taken seriously instead. The existence of this power resulted, ironically, in the fact that those African newspapers which had campaigned vigorously for the nationalist cause now enjoyed less freedom under the very governments that they had helped to create. At independence, the new governments had looked around for ways of publicizing their activities and seized upon the means to do so. Papers which had hitherto been forthright thus became slavish and sycophantic. Certain governments established their own papers and then saw to it that any opposition papers were starved of the advertising they needed in order to stay in business. Other newspapers were closed down either by law or by manipulation. This happened despite whatever the countries' constitutions may have said about freedom of speech. A few governments have done so quite openly and unpretentiously, by establishing laws of censorship as in Ethiopia, Niger and Cameroon: military regimes have generally had no qualms about controlling the press. Jose also pointed out that editors and journalists who had defied restrictions or offended powerful men had been punished, and he wryly quoted the memorable and often-repeated remark of the famous Kenyan editor George Githii:

> For governments who fear newspapers there is one consolation. We have known many instances where governments have taken over newspapers, but we have not known a single incident in which a newspaper has taken over a government.

Yet, said Jose, there was another side to the story. Today responsibilities existed which it was impossible to ignore. Things were very different from the way they had been in the colonial period:

> In the name of press freedom and nationalism we deliberately wrote seditious and criminally libellous articles against colonial governments. Today, at least ten years after independence, many African journalists still believe that a good press is one that is in a constant state of war with the government; that a progressive journalist is one who writes anti-government articles and a leading journalist is one who is in and out of prison for sedition.

The strategies used against colonial powers should not, he went on, be used against the new African governments. As an example he cited the case of the African journalist who wants to expose corruption in high places but is very unlikely to have the professional training for the painstaking investigation required. Undeterred nevertheless, he splashes the details of his serious allegations all over the front page, only to discover that

> a news item or an editorial concerning government that would raise eyebrows in London can incite inter-tribal riot or violent anti-government demonstration in an African country.

Therefore self-control was, in Jose's view, essential in all areas. African editors had to decide how to proceed: they could avoid politics, filling their pages instead with 'large pictures of lovely damsels', become mere megaphones of the political élite or, alternatively, adopt the philosophy of the Nigerian *Daily Times*, which he described as 'militancy without hostility'.[64]

Jose's point about the media's ability to incite trouble is borne out in one case which involved radio broadcasts. In 1966 a broadcast from a neighbouring country reported the killing of Hausas in the former Eastern Region of Nigeria. The news was followed by bloody retaliation in the north and a massacre of Ibos. When Tom Mboya was assassinated in Nairobi in 1969, the Government radio station Voice of Kenya chose initially not to report the news. It was feared that members of Mboya's Luo tribe would retaliate against the Kikuyu, the group who dominated the country's political life and of which the assassins were assumed to be members. There was in fact retaliation in any case, and it might even be argued that this silence on the part of the radio – which everyone knew to be under government control –

actually encouraged angry Luos to believe that a Kikuyu conspiracy existed within the Government.

Clearly, Jose was speaking from the perspective of a Nigerian journalist: much of what he said was true only of his own and a handful of other countries. As we have noted, only in comparatively few nations was the tradition of a vigorous opposition press established prior to independence. In many others, the new governments were faced with a situation of having either virtually no press worthy of the name or merely one in which the colonial government or settler point of view had been dominant.

Personally, I am sceptical about Jose's view that the press has such power to mislead and to be always believed. In 1980, the first full year of the new civilian constitution in Nigeria, newspapers supporting one or other of the country's five political parties began reporting allegations against their rivals. For example the *National Concorde*, launched by the millionaire Chief Abiola to support the NPN government, took to printing stories alleging that Chief Obafemi Awolowo and his UPN supporters had hatched a plot to subvert the constitution and were about to launch this plan over the radio by courtesy of a foreign radio station. The Kaduna-based Hausa language newspaper *Gaskiya ta fi Kwabo* ('The Truth is Worth More than a Penny'), took this allegation further by quoting from a leading Kaduna State politician:

> The secret aims of the UPN continue to be exposed in relation to the plot and intrigue to destablise the Federal Government of this country, to create disturbances, strife and civil war which will please Odumewgu Ojukwo, former Biafran secessionist leader, no end.

> The Deputy Leader of the Kaduna State House of Assembly, Alhaji Maccido Muhammad made this statement in Kaduna recently. He said that, as things stand at the moment, the UPN has sought assistance from organisations outside this country in a plan to prevent the Federal Government of this country from importing foodstuffs and to plot to create strife between the different communities of the country.[65]

In Jose's own words, 'eyebrows' may have been 'raised', but I have seen no evidence to support the idea that this or other stories like it have by themselves led to demonstrations. Many Nigerians seem to regard such allegations with amusement, dismissing them as part of the party political game which should not be taken too seriously. On the first anniversary of the return to civilian rule President Shehu Shagari vigorously condemned party bickering in the papers and said that he hoped it would end. Some of the allegations that have been made have led to libel proceedings. The question of rumour and unsubstantiated allegation is a much broader one. It is sometimes said by government officials – I have heard it said by leading members of the administrations of Tanzania, Nigeria, Sierra Leone and Zambia – that African journalists are not sufficiently experienced to tell when an interested party in a dispute may be attempting to put over a particular point of view or discredit a government policy by using the press or radio. For example, Zambian government officials claimed that a story (in the *Times of Zambia*, June 23rd 1970) to the effect that clothing factory workers believed they might lose their jobs as the result of a new duty on imported cloth, was the work of clever lobbying by clothing manufacturers and retailers. Similarly, on June 29th 1970, the same newspaper reported Portuguese troops as having crossed the border from Angola in order to kidnap the inhabitants of a remote Zambian village. In a country the size of Zambia, with few telephones in rural areas and few reporters based anywhere outside the few major towns, it is impossible to check such a story speedily. When eventually the story was checked it was found to be false, evidently initiated as part of an intercommunal feud by a tribal group which held a grudge against the government.[66]

In 1975, Wilcox listed seventy-one newspapers in independent black African countries, of which all but twenty were in the hands of governments or ruling parties. Seven of these twenty were Nigerian.[67] Since Wilcox produced this analysis a number of the independent papers have either closed down – voluntarily or under compulsion – or been taken over. Alternatively, in some countries previously without a daily paper it has been the government which has started one: there would probably be no daily newspaper in the Central African Republic, Botswana, Niger, Mauritania or Chad had each of these countries' governments not decided to finance one. Some governments operate policies forbidding outside or indigenous investment in the press. Yet starting a daily paper anywhere other than in a few large cities is scarcely an attractive investment. For this reason, and in the wake of a succession of nationalizations in Ghana, Uganda, Tanzania, Mozambique and elsewhere, the foreign ownership of Africa's newspapers has declined sharply. Even in Nigeria, Africa's most densely populated country, with the largest urbanized, literate readership, most of the fifteen daily papers on sale in 1981 were running at a loss.

In the field of broadcasting, government ownership and control is almost complete. In 1975, Wilcox counted only five privately owned radio stations in Africa (excluding the Arab north and white minority-ruled territories of the south);[68] today, some seven years later, I can find only three. Some radio stations are run by public corporations with a degree of operational autonomy from government, on paper at least – as in Malawi, Ghana, Nigeria and Zimbabwe – but in each case a greater degree of government control exists than is true of the BBC, which provided the model for the corporations of these countries.[69]

All African broadcasting stations rely on governments for a large proportion of their income, insufficient funds being raised either from advertising or the licence fee. Broadcasting is regarded as a public service, and in many countries the difficult task of collecting the licence fee has been dropped. The link between government and broadcasting is often very close, generally closer than with the press. Senior executives of radio stations are frequently drawn from the ranks of the political élite rather than from the professional corps of broadcasters. When journalists and broadcasters are recruited for an established media organization – a newspaper, radio or television service – there is already an existing tradition, a set of values, professional codes and ethics, into which they must fit. The process of selection and socialization into a media organization is well documented.[70]

Things are somewhat different when the institution or profession is itself new. When, for example, the BBC began in 1922, a great deal more than simply the use of the new technology had to be established. It took the influence and personality of one man, John Reith, to mould the organization in the early years. But he did have a long-established base on which to build – and that was the British class system. Reith's BBC adopted the culture and, broadly speaking, the social outlook of middle-class southern England.

In African countries there was less certainty as to what to do. Very often the tendency was to look abroad, mostly to Western Europe, for a model. The pre-independence newspapers that campaigned for self-government knew what they were aiming for; their journalists, contributors and backers came from the new, educated élite united by common aspirations and interests. After independence, things were less clearly defined. Everyone might agree on the need for national unity, development, and the rapid elimination of poverty, ignorance and disease, but what institutional framework would be workable for the media? What values should be promoted? And what did national political freedom and the end of colonialism mean to African-run papers and radio stations? Could media content continue to be exciting and enjoyable now that it was concerned with the mundane problems of national development in place of the heady business of attacking colonialism?

It was common for African political parties and governments to organize seminars and conferences for media personnel on this very subject. There was frequently a conflict of opinions. Many of the broadcasters and journalists had been trained either in Europe or locally by Europeans, and many also looked to Europe as their guide to what broadcasting and journalism were for. The former director of broadcasting in Tanzania complained to me that the politicians did not understand the professional methods of broadcasters. By this he clearly meant the professional codes established by the BBC, which had fathered the original Tanganyika Broadcasting Corporation. (The argument that went on in Tanzania at this time is referred to in some detail in the next chapter.) The BBC was influential in the setting up of broadcasting in no fewer than seventeen African countries, and the French had a similarly extensive involvement. Influences on the development of the press were, as we have seen, a little more mixed. On the one hand lay those who had trained in or followed the European tradition of independence and free investigative journalism; on the other lay a tradition that was also important and which has perhaps been the more lasting. As we have seen, in a large number of colonies the authorities had been involved in publishing newspapers. Using both the colonial and local languages, they had tried to put over the official point of view, often in an attempt to forestall or counter alternative interpretations and opinions. This tradition of government involvement has continued in many countries after independence. Occasionally there existed a press independent of the State but representing white settler interests; this, however, was plainly not a suitable model for the post-colonial period.

Moreover, a major qualification needs to be made to the view that broadcasting in the ex-British territories was everywhere cast in the BBC's image. It was only towards the end of the colonial period that the notion of a public corporation was raised. It may be overly cynical to suggest two things. The first is that broadcasting was placed in the care of public corporations independent of the government of the day only when the prospect of African government loomed large. The second is that the British colonial rulers did not genuinely believe in independent, publicly owned public service broadcasting because when in government they made sure that they had full control and tolerated the idea of a corporation only when their rule was coming to an end. Cynical perhaps, but this was certainly the pattern. Only when independence under majority rule seemed assured were statutory corporations established by the departing British in an attempt to distance broadcasting from the newly Africanized political and governmental arena. A less difficult choice existed in the French territories. Under French rule broadcasting had no pretensions to autonomy and so made a fairly smooth transition from being an arm of French colonialism to being an arm of the new African governments.

Yet there is more to the dilemmas of media tradition and ideology than the question of control. Irrespective of the type of control, what are the press and broadcasting for? What are they to do in the changed circumstances? And, remembering that mass communications depend on individuals making choices, what do people look to the media to provide?

The Australian writer and journalist Lloyd Sommerlad observed that it was innappropriate to apply western-based criteria to the media worldwide. Attitudes to the media might vary a great deal even in the case of Africa, whose media have their origins in western contact and rule.

> In the West, the very idea of government publishing newspapers is anathema – it is incompatible with the independent, objective, critical role of the press. But in the new nations it is considered a logical and proper function of governments to produce newspapers.[71]

Sommerlad might well have added that, although such an idea might have been anathema at home, nothing prevented the colonial authorities from publishing newspapers in Tanganyika, Kenya, the Rhodesias, Sierra Leone and many of the French territories.

Western academic literature is found to be far from helpful in providing an understanding of Africa's media and their role. In a well-known work on the general subject of the press within various types of political system, three American writers listed and described four main types of press philosophy: *authoritarian, soviet-communist, libertarian* and *socially responsible*.[72] Nevertheless, the typology does not fit the African scene at all adequately. The *authoritarian* philosophy, according to the authors, sees the press as something to be controlled because it is a potential nuisance; there is little or no conception of the press as a possibly positive contributor to human progress and development. The *authoritarian* philosophy can be traced back to sixteenth-century England, where strict controls were imposed on the publication of what were regarded by the king and his advisers as seditious pamphlets and journals. The outlook is one of negative control by the means of censorship, anti-sedition laws and the obligatory posting of large bonds as security against misbehaviour – all aimed against a press which was privately owned. Elements of this view are to be found in Africa today, as in Cameroon, where censorship and other laws have defeated efforts to form a critical, independent press. However, the term does not describe, even in the most general way, any press philosophy current in Africa.

In contrast, the *soviet-communist* theory of the press involves the state ownership of all media, which are then harnessed to the achievement of national goals as defined by the ruling party and government. The modern mass media fit very well into communist notions of society as a collectivity, the name given to the 'masses' of workers and peasants whose interests are best served by a vanguard political party. This idea finds an echo in many African countries but assumes a Marxist-Leninist view of the economic and social order found in only a handful of African ruling élites. It may be a fairly accurate description of press philosophy and practice in Ethiopia, Mozambique and Angola, yet few other countries have engendered such an ideologically coherent, centralized role for their media. Elsewhere there is greater flexibility, less certainty and a more liberal approach to economic and political diversity.

The *libertarian* theory of the media is based on western liberal democracy. It envisages a press which flourishes amidst industrial prosperity and a high level of development and education – relatively diverse and run by commercial enterprises, some of them very large indeed. However, none of these conditions prevail in Africa. The capital necessary to support an independent press is lacking. Nigeria and South Africa are the only obvious exceptions.

The fourth type of press theory put forward is that of *social responsibility*. The idea arose from fears expressed in western industrialized countries that the free market of ideas was being threatened by the fact that the prohibitive costs of entry into media ownership prevented the involvement of anyone other than rich individuals or large corporations. This situation meant freedom of expression only for the wealthy and already powerful. It was suggested that some form of social or governmental control could be used to ensure access to the media for all viewpoints. The idea, which originated in a 1947 United States Commission on the Freedom of the Press, found an echo more recently in Britain, where similar ideas were put forward by some leaders of the Labour Party. The philosophy (with the arguable exception of the Netherlands) is not actually practised anywhere in the world, although the concerns that give rise to it have led to a continuing debate in some western industrialized democracies about ways in which the monopolistic nature of the capitalist press might be usefully modified. Again, this is a philosophy that does not really fit the African scene.

The absence of any coherent and agreed philosophy for the media in many African countries is a matter which is of obvious concern to many of that continent's politicians as well as its media professionals, and a number of African leaders have addressed themselves to the problem. Kwame Nkrumah, who had himself used the press to mobilize support for his party and its nationalist demands against the British, developed strong views about the role of the media in the post-colonial period:

> The African journalist [has] . . . the duty of gathering information carefully and disseminating it honestly. To tamper with the truth is treason to the human mind. By poisoning the well-springs of public opinion with falsehood, you defeat in the long run, your own ends. Once a journal gains a reputation for even occasional unreliability or distortion, its value is destroyed.[73]

The irony of this statement would not have been lost on any Ghanaian journalist working in the period under Nkrumah from 1957 to 1966, for this was exactly what happened to Ghana's newspapers: they became sycophantic, uncritical mouthpieces for the President and his view of that country, Africa and the world. Nkrumah also claimed to be against the existence of a privately owned press. His concept of the press was very close to the soviet-communist view outlined above, in which the ruling party knows what truth is and falsehood equals anything which happens to challenge that view.

> Within the competitive system of capitalism the press cannot function in accordance with a strict regard for the facts . . . the press therefore should not be in private hands.[74]

The reason, according to Nkrumah, was that the motivation of the capitalist press was profit and the news-gathering and reporting functions were merely secondary.

> The journalist . . . is forced into arranging news and information to fit the outlook of his journal. He finds himself rejecting or distorting facts that do not coincide with the outlook and interest of his employer or the medium's advertisers. Under the pressure of competition for advertising revenue, trivialities are blown up, the vulgar emphasised, ethics forgotten, the important trimmed to the class outlook. Enmities are fanned and peace is perverted, the search is for sensation and the justification of an unjust system in which truth or the journalist must become the casualty.[75]

Such ideas, he said, were permeating Africa's media and had to be resisted. The 'true African journalist' sets his sights on higher things:

> His newspaper is a collective organiser, a collective instrument of mobilisation and a collective educator – a weapon, first and foremost to overthrow colonialism and imperialism and to assist total African independence and unity . . . His satisfaction is in his integrity, in work performed for the betterment of his fellows and the society of which he is a worthy member . . . The true African journalist very often works for the organ of the political party to which he himself belongs and in whose purpose he believes. He works to serve a society moving in the direction of his own aspirations.[76]

It is not difficult to understand why so many journalists and broadcasters fell foul of Nkrumah's government. It was not for them but for the ruling CPP to decide what best promoted the goals Nkrumah outlined.

In most African countries, government involvement in, and even supervision of, the press may not rest on such ideological precepts: sound pragmatic and economic reasons exist for that involvement. Botswana is just one country whose only daily paper is owned and run by the government, without whose assistance it would probably have no national paper at all. In other countries where readership is similarly very limited and where the high cost of imported newsprint and machinery and the paucity of advertising revenue combine in much the same way to exclude the private investor, the government has to become involved if a local press is to exist. Journals or papers designed to be sold in a number of African countries can succeed commercially, as some have shown in recent years, but these are directed at a limited, élite readership. It is quite a different matter to produce a weekly or daily paper aimed at the widest possible audience, with the aim of informing it about national and local, as well as African and international, news.

Two further reasons have been given for the establishment of government-owned newspapers or for the taking over of existing privately owned ones. One was given by Kenya's first Minister of Information in 1963:

> Commercial newspapers aim primarily at making profits, so that they are not likely to undertake the publication of newspapers for small linguistic groups. The government will have to fill that vacuum.[77]

Mr Achieng Oneko might well have added, using the same argument, that the capitalist private press is unlikely to serve other minorities and tends to favour socio-economic groups which have the highest spending power and therefore attract the most advertising. Privately owned papers which are unprofitable do exist, but this is because they receive backing for other purposes – political, in most cases. To return to Oneko's main point, however, there have been a number of government ventures into minority language papers, notably in Zambia and Liberia.[78] The other reason most often given for government ownership is that government needs a voice of its own and cannot rely on the privately owned press. This is why in some countries with privately owned papers the ruling party, or even the government, has decided to launch its own.

Far less argument has taken place on the subject of broadcasting which is almost entirely government-controlled and where that control is usually direct. The main area for discussion has been the extent to which there should be close day-to-day supervision of television and radio. Should the broadcasting station be placed under a government department under a politically appointed boss? Or should it be able, despite being owned by the State, to distance itself somewhat from political authority? The question was argued out in Tanzania, as we shall see from the case study. That argument is now highly relevant to Nigeria, whose five political parties each control one or more of the nineteen state governments. State governments are responsible for the radio broadcasting services of the area under their jurisdiction, whereas television is still mostly federally controlled and financed. (The Federal Government also controls a national radio service.) Should these state governments be permitted to use their radio services to promote the interests and policies of the ruling parties? Some Nigerians say that this is already happening. If so, then this is perhaps a unique case of oppositional broadcasting in Africa. The problem is, however, that state radio stations are not intended to be used for the purpose of broadcasting beyond state frontiers; indeed, it was decided in 1978 to forbid these stations from using short wave transmitters with sufficient power to reach other states. Opportunities for Nigerians living within a single region to receive alternative views on their own sets are therefore limited.

Wilcox provided a useful analysis of African press philosophies in thirty-four independent sub-Saharan black states, of which twenty-seven have a press that is predominantly government-owned. The reasons given for involvement follow a clear pattern: 'mobilise the masses around precise objectives', 'unifying the country', 'to help educate the masses and rally support for the government', 'to mobilise the people behind the president and party', and so on.[79] The same arguments, and others which we will come across in the case studies, have been used in favour of control of broadcasting. Nigeria apart, the universal trend has been one of increasingly centralized political control.

Notes

[1] Sydney Head, *Broadcasting in Africa* (Philadelphia, 1974).
[2] Information on the early days of Africa's press here is drawn mainly from Rosalynde Ainslie, *The Press in Africa* (London, 1966), and William Hatchten, *Muffled Drums* (Ames, Iowa, 1961). Ainslie's book contains the best and most thorough history of Africa's press yet published, but sadly it is out of print.
[3] Kwame Nkrumah, *The African Journalist* (Dar es Salaam, 1965), pp. 2-3. The booklet consists mainly of a speech given by Nkrumah, then President of Ghana, to the Second Conference of Pan-African Journalists in Accra in November 1963.
[4] Dennis Austin, *Politics in Ghana: 1946-60* (London, 1964), p. 119.
[5] Abiodun Aloba, 'Journalism in Africa: 1. Nigeria', *Gazette*, V, no. 2 (1959-60), pp. 245-8.
[6] Virginia Thompson, 'The Ivory Coast' in (ed.) Gwendolen Carter, *African One Party States* (Ithaca, 1962), p. 272.
[7] Ainslie, *The Press in Africa*, p. 132.
[8] Gabriel Almond and James Coleman, *Politics of the Developing Areas* (Princeton, 1960), p. 352.
[9] Ainslie, *The Press in Africa*, p. 134.
[10] Tom Hopkinson, 'The Press in Africa' in Colin Legum (ed.), *Africa: A Handbook*, revised edition (London, 1965), p. 445.
[11] Mohammed Abdulaziz, 'Tanzania's National Language Policy and the Rise of Swahili Political Culture' in *Language Use and Social Change* (London, 1971), pp. 160-178. Also Wilfred Whiteley, *Swahili* (London, 1969), p. 60.
[12] Ainslie, *The Press in Africa*, pp. 99-100.
[13] *Ibid.*
[14] United Nations Trusteeship Council, *Report of the Visiting Mission to Tanganyika*, 1954, p. 66.
[15] *Tanganyika Standard*, 26th January 1955.
[16] There was a startling example of this shortly before independence. Self-government was achieved on 1st May 1961, seven months before full independence. On 29th April the new Cabinet – Tanganyika's first – was announced. The *Tanganyika Standard* headline the next day read: 'Compensation on Instalment Plan: Scheme for Expatriates Announced'.

17   'An African Press Survey: Part 3, East and Central Africa', *New Commonwealth*, 28, No. 4, August 1954, pp. 169-71.

18   Whiteley, *Swahili*, p. 60. Note that, unless otherwise stated, all journals with Swahili titles are given in the Swahili language.

19   Literacy figures are notoriously difficult to establish with any degree of reliability. No official figures or estimates are available for 1961. In 1968 one source estimated a literacy rate of 15 to 20 per cent. AID, *Selected Economic Data for the Less Developed Countries* (Washington, 1963), p. 6.

20   J.F.R. Hill and J.P. Moffett,(eds.), *Tanganyika: A Review of its Resources and their Development* (Dar es Salaam, 1955), p. 116; Gerald Sayers, (ed.), *The Handbook of Tanganyika Territory* (London, 1930), p. 381. There were 100 cents to one shilling, twenty shillings being worth one pound sterling.

21   I.M. Omari, 'The Kiswahili Press and Nationalism in Tanganyika 1954-58', *Taamuli*, II, no. 2 (July 1972), p. 37.

22   *Ibid*, p. 40.

23   Hill and Moffett, *Tanganyika*, pp. 116-117.

24   *Mwangaza*, 14th July 1956, quoted in Omari, 'Kiswahili Press', p. 41.

25   *Ibid.*, p. 42.

26   Whiteley, *Swahili*, p. 63.

27   Omari, 'Kiswahili Press', p. 43.

28   Sophia Mustafa, *The Tanganyika Way* (Dar es Salaam, 1961).

29   J.A.K. Leslie, *A Survey of Dar es Salaam* (London, 1963), pp. 195-200.

30   John Iliffe, 'The Age of Improvement and Differentiation (1907-1945)', in *A History of Tanzania*, ed. I.N. Kimambo and A.J. Temu (Nairobi, 1969), p. 148.

31   *Ibid.*, p. 147.

32   Duncan MacDougald jun., *The Languages and Press of Africa* (Philadelphia, 1944), p. 68.

33   Leslie, *Survey*, pp. 198-199.

34   Martin Lowenkopf, 'Political Parties in Uganda and Tanganyika', M.Sc.(Econ.) thesis, University of London, 1961, pp. 180-181.

35   *Ibid.*

36   Hugh W. Stephens, *The Political Transformation of Tanganyika 1920-1967* (New York, 1968), p. 109.

37   Ainslie, *The Press in Africa*, p. 48.

38   *Ibid.*, p. 51.

39   Quoted in Ainslie, *The Press in Africa*, p. 52.

40   Ali Mazrui, 'The Press, Intellectuals and the Printed Word' in *Mass Thoughts*, ed. Edward Moyo and Susan Rayner (Kampala, 1972), p. 162.

41   John Williams, 'The Press and the Printed Word in Africa', *Overseas Quarterly*, December 1963, p. 243.

42   Quoted in Fred Omu, 'The Dilemma of Press Freedom in Colonial Africa: The West African Example', *Journal of African History*, 9, no. 2 (1968), p. 288.

43   *Ibid.*, p. 293.

44   Peter Fraenkel, *Wayaleshi*, p. 135.

45   *Radio Listenership Survey of Zambia: Main Urban Areas, 1965* (Salisbury, 1965), tables 2 and 11.

46   Arno Huth, *Communications Media in Tropical Africa* (Washington, 1960).

47   Tanganyika, Laws, Statutes, etc., *Ordnance No. 4*, 1956.

48   Two were members of the Governor's Administration. Of the eight, four were Europeans, one was Asian and three were Africans. One of the latter was Rashidi Kawawa, later to become vice-president and prime minister in independent Tanzania.

49   Market Research Company of East Africa, *Tanganyika Broadcasting Corporation*

Audience Survey Report May 1960 (Nairobi, 1960), pp. 1-2.

50 Tanganyika Broadcasting Corporation, *Annual Report, 1st January to 31st December 1960*, p. 3.

51 TBC, *Report 1956-57*, p. 6.

52 TBC, *Annual Report 1960*, p. 4.

53 When the Commercial Service was launched it used a purpose-built 100 KW medium wave transmitter, then the most powerful in East Africa. In the same year, two 50 KW short wave transmitters, built by the Chinese, were completed for Tanzania's External Service aimed at South Africa. As this was on the air only during the evenings, the broadcasting authorities had no hesitation in using one of the Chinese transmitters to improve reception on the Commercial Service in Tanzania during the day.

54 TBC, *Annual Report*, 1960, p. 2.

55 *Ibid.*, p. 5.

56 *Ibid.*

57 Kenneth Kaunda, address to IPI Assembly, in Nairobi, Kenya, 4th June 1968.

58 At the time of writing (1982), Lonrho still owns the paper. UNIP is due to take over as the full owner, but this will probably make little difference editorially. Lonrho is likely to have a management and printing contract.

59 Dennis Wilcox, *Mass Media in Black Africa* (New York, 1975), p. 21.

60 *The Times*, London, July 23rd, 1973.

61 Hilary Ng'weno, 'The Role of the Press in a Developing Country', address to the IPI Assembly in Nairobi, 4th June 1968.

62 Hilary Ng'weno, 'The Nature of the Threat to Press Freedom in East Africa', *Africa Today*, 16 (June-July 1969), p. 4.

63 Titus Mukupo, 'What Role of Government in the Development of an African Press?' *Africa Report*, 11 (January 1966), p. 39.

64 Alhaji Babatunde Jose, 'Press Freedom in Africa', address to the Royal Africa Society in London, April 10th, 1975. Note that at this time Nigeria was still under military rule.

65 *Gaskiya ta Fi Kwabo*, 26th September 1980.

66 Vernon McKay, 'The Propaganda Battle for Zambia', (unpublished typescript).

67 Wilcox, *Mass Media in Black Africa*, p. 38.

68 *Ibid*, p. 78.

69 The case of Nigeria is a little unusual. While the federal government is responsible for the Federal Radio Corporation of Nigeria (FRCN), each of the nineteen state governments has its own broadcasting corporation. The twenty public radio corporations in Nigeria do provide some variety of interpretation of events and therefore, to some extent, enhance the degree of diversity and weaken central control.

70 Jeremy Tunstall, 'News Organisation Goals and Specialist Newsgathering Journalists' in Dennis McQuail (ed.), *Sociology of Mass Communication* (London, 1972); Philip Elliott, 'Media Organisations and Occupations' and Krishan Kumar, 'Holding the Middle Ground: the BBC, the Public and the Professional Broadcaster', both in James Curran, Michael Gurevitch and Janet Woollacott (eds.), *Mass Communication and Society* (London, 1977). See also Peter Golding, 'Media Professionalism in the Third World' in the same volume.

71 Lloyd Sommerlad, 'Problems in Developing a Free Enterprise Press in East Africa', *Gazette* 14, no. 2 (1968), p. 77.

72 Fred S. Siebert, Theodore Petersen and Wilbur Schramm, *Four Theories of the Press* (Urbana, Illinois, 1956).

73 Nkrumah, *The African Journalist*, pp. 5-6.

74 *Ibid*, pp. 5-6.

[75]   *Ibid.*
[76]   *Ibid,* pp. 9-10.
[77]   Quoted in Frank Barton, *The Press in Africa* (Nairobi, 1966), p. 39.
[78]   The Liberian experiment of simplifying the production of small local papers in minority languages has been reported in Robert de T. Lawrence, *Rural Mimeo Newspapers,* UNESCO Reports and Papers on Mass Communication, no. 46 (Paris, 1965).
[79]   Wilcox, *Mass Media,* p. 111.

5
Three case studies: Zambia, Tanzania and Nigeria

I carried out field research in both Zambia and Tanzania. My research in Tanzania took place in 1967 and 1968 and in Zambia from 1970 to 1973. Although I did not conduct field research in Nigeria, I visited that country in 1975, 1978 and 1981. The three case studies illustrate different aspects of mass communication and society.

Zambia

The pioneering work of radio in Zambia has already been referred to. The medium expanded rapidly during the 1950s and 1960s, both in terms of facilities and set ownership. When the Central African Federation was dissolved, the three territories concerned developed separate organizations and facilities for broadcasting. The Zambia Broadcasting Services (ZBS) transmitted two networks nationally and simultaneously. In the early 1970s these two services together broadcast 240 hours per week in seven Zambian languages and English. Television was introduced before independence in 1961 – as an extension of Rhodesian Television Ltd. – to serve the large white mining and commercial community on the Copperbelt in the north. Independence three years later meant that this arrangement had to be altered. In 1966 the headquarters moved to Lusaka, and television was incorporated into the ZBS, broadcasting being conducted entirely in English. During the 1970s television was on the air between thirty-five and forty hours a week.

The history of the Zambian press is also brief. In December 1964, shortly after independence, the *Northern News* (owned by the South African Argus group) was sold to Lonrho. Lonrho had just bought out the brewing concern Heinrichs, which in 1964 had started another daily, called the *Zambia Times*, and a weekly, the *Zambia News*. Both Heinrichs papers having lost a lot of money, Lonrho amalgamated the *Zambia Times* and the *Northern News* into the *Times of Zambia* while continuing to publish the *Zambia News* as a Sunday paper. It later became the *Sunday Times of Zambia*. These two, shorn to some extent of their settler and pro-Federation image, grew in circulation and, for a while, the *Times of Zambia* remained the sole daily paper.

Meanwhile, the survival of the *Central African Mail* seemed in doubt: David Astor of *The Observer* in London wanted to withdraw. The new government decided it wanted its own paper and so bought the *Mail*, which became a bi-weekly in 1967 and went daily in 1969. In the mid-1970s it was selling around thirty thousand copies compared with the *Times*'s sixty thousand. The *Zambia Daily Mail*, as it was now known, received a subsidy from the Government. Among the other problems encountered was its failure to attract the scale of advertising enjoyed by the *Times*. It had fewer reporters, fewer offices and relied more heavily than did the *Times* on official press releases from the Government and its news agency, ZANA. Neither paper maintained any correspondents away from the line-of-rail. Although the *Times* and *Sunday Times* did not become official UNIP papers until 1975, the editor of the former had been appointed by the President even before this date. Since 1975 the major news media of Zambia have been either party or government mouthpieces. This does not mean that they speak with one voice – the press has often either been critical or published critical opinions – but there is clearly a limit to government tolerance. In 1980 an editorial shake-up occurred following the detention of several dissidents alleged to have been involved in a plot.

During the 1970s both daily papers showed a heavy reliance on foreign material, and not only for non-African news. It was quite common to read in either paper a feature article about another African country written by a journalist in London: on the day after Nkrumah's death, both ran stories and obituaries written by European news agencies. The *Mail* had a regular page for women which would not be out of place in an English daily, where it may well have originated:

> Judging by the pictures in the papers of late more than just a few brides are scorning convention and getting married in hot pants, knickerbockers and all sorts of weird things. Now, I'm all for new departures but I honestly think that the timeless trend of the long classic, style-less but simple wedding gown is better . . .

And, in the same edition:

> With my thoughts turning to holidays, I hope you'll forgive me for saying that never a year goes by that I don't find myself laughing at some female's expense. Honestly, you see some frightful sights by the sea occasionally! Which is a pity. Because good grooming is just as important on the beach as it is at a cocktail party. Believe me, you should never buy a swimsuit without trying it on first and studying your reflection from every angle in a long mirror.[1]

These and similar articles on women's and other pages were syndicated from agencies in Britain. There was also a regular *Mail* fashion column by Queen Elizabeth's dress designer, Norman Hartnell.

This sort of material appeared less frequently in the *Times* but quite often in its sister paper, the *Sunday Times of Zambia*. Apart from regular 'cheesecake' or 'girlie' pictures of the sort that help boost the circulation of the popular press in Britain, there were syndicated pieces similar to those bizarre examples quoted above, though perhaps not quite so glaringly irrelevant. The culture of the features used was overwhelmingly middle class and European: the cookery columns, for example, assumed the reader lived in a house with a gas or electric oven. The press in Zambia had broken its links with the South only to forge new ones with the British press and its allied agencies. The material used was cheap, readily available – very often with attractive photographs or other illustrated matter – and took up space unfilled by the papers' own journalists.

Actual news coverage in the press was nevertheless more comprehensive than that on the radio and television. Both papers carried at least two pages of local news, not including sport, and generally had one or two pages of foreign news. The latter was taken almost entirely from the wire services of Reuters and Agence France-Presse, although the *Times* obtained stories from its sister papers in East Africa and the group's London correspondent. The *Times* also occasionally sent journalists abroad to get special stories.

For the coverage of local news, both suffered from a shortage of trained reporters. One consequence of this was that many stories were not really *about* events but merely reports or rewrites of speeches made by leading politicians *at* events. The context of the event and the event itself often went unreported, simply because the journalist assigned to the 'story' covered only the opening speech. At such opening ceremonies and speeches all the paraphernalia of the mass media would be present: movie cameras, floodlights, still cameras and tape recorders. Typically, as soon as the minister or other speech maker had finished on each occasion, the media would leave, and the following day all that was reported was an edited version of the speech. This was generally true of much news reporting in Zambia, not just in the press but on radio and television as well: journalists followed the president, ministers and district governors around. Few stories about their activities went beyond the editing-down of a long speech – except, perhaps, to relate that the occasion was attended by 'leading party and Government officials'.

A directory I compiled in 1971 listed one hundred non-daily Zambian periodicals, ranging from the fortnightly Zambian language government newspapers to annual journals. The list included the 'house' magazines of leading companies and organizations, newspapers published by mining companies, journals of professional organizations, religious papers, and literary and academic journals. There was one educational comic for children.[2] A large number of periodicals survived for a few issues and then disappeared: ten ceased or suspended publication during 1971. Those published during 1971 claimed sales of around two hundred and fifty thousand.

The non-daily periodical with the highest circulation, of forty-two thousand, was *The Miner*, published weekly on the Copperbelt. It was followed by the educational 'comic', *Orbit* (published by the Commission for Technical Education and Vocational Training), which was sold through schools and came out three times a term. The Government's information service ZIS had six Zambian language fortnightly newspapers, of which only one, *Mbila*, in Bemba, exceeded twenty thousand in sales. Similarly, the Ministry of Rural Development published *Progress* in four Zambian languages, but its circulation was very low: although intended for peasant farmers, it was almost impossible for them to obtain. In contrast to certain other African countries, Zambia had remarkably few periodicals published by churches or religious organizations; the few that were published all had small circulations. Recently, some Zambian churches have combined to produce the weekly *Zambia Mirror*, which has met with a degree of success.

In Zambia, as in every other African country, radio is the most widespread news medium. However, as in many other countries, its importance has not been fully recognized. Most books on Zambia hardly mention broadcasting at all, and in public and political debate within the country, discussion of radio and public policy towards this type of broadcasting is curiously lacking. Radio broadcasters have to be content with a low status, and the medium has been starved of funds. Yet its importance and impact are beyond question. It expanded at a rapid rate, the early 'Saucepan' sets being replaced by cheap transistor sets which could be operated with less expensive batteries. ITT opened a radio assembly plant in Livingstone which produced sets that sold for about K12 in the early 1970s (then about £8 or $20). The advent of the transistor brought rapid expansion in set ownership. In 1954, about thirty thousand African households had radio sets.[3] A survey conducted in 1965 showed 42% of African households along the line of rail to have sets.[4] My own national survey of 1970-3 revealed that 50% of households in the urban line-of-rail centres and 24% of rural households had radio sets. This meant that approximately two hundred and sixty-two thousand households in the country as a whole had radio. Each day 45% of urban and 16% of rural inhabitants listened to ZBS programmes, and over half the total population listened at least once per week.[5]

The audience, potential and actual, for television was considerably smaller. Television transmitters were set up only in Lusaka, Kabwe and on the Copperbelt. The television sets on sale required mains electricity, available only in certain parts of Zambia's towns; they were also costly to buy and to maintain. In those areas where it was possible to receive transmissions only 9% of households had a set, and only 8% of our sample watched television daily. One surprising fact emerged from the survey results. Although it might be expected that only the better-educated and wealthier sections of the community would watch television, the existence of the extended family system meant that the television sets owned by prosperous Zambians were also watched by a number of relatives who were less well off. My 1970-3 survey showed that 26% of the TV audience consisted of adult males earning less than K450 per annum. This income group constituted 30% of the sample.[6] The total audience was still very small.

These figures, when comparable data for newspaper readership are also taken into account, demonstrate the influence of radio. 17% of urban adult and a mere 2% of rural Zambians read the *Times* or the *Mail* every day. In fact 77% of those interviewed never read a daily paper at all, and 75% read no weekly or other non-daily paper.[7]

A number of factors contributed to the prominence of radio. First of all, it overcomes the problem of illiteracy. Also, radio sets do not require mains electricity. Reception was, and still is, poor in many parts of the country, but with ingenuity and a certain amount of patient tuning it is possible in any area to pick up services from transmitters in Lusaka, Kabwe, Livingstone and the Copperbelt. Radio in Zambia broadcast not only in English but also in seven Zambian languages; therefore, unlike television and most newspapers, it was able to communicate with a large proportion of the people in their own language or at least in one they could understand. It is difficult to quantify the number of languages in Zambia. Many tribes speak languages which, although substantially different from one another, are still mutually comprehensible. Data obtained in the 1969 Census (to which I have had access but which, to my knowledge, remain unpublished) suggest that only 15% of the population spoke a mother tongue which was not closely related to one of the seven African broadcast languages. Thus radio spoke to a large proportion of the population, both urban and rural, either in a language spoken at home or at least in one closely related to it.[8]

The allocation of broadcasting time to the various languages was a delicate and controversial issue. Equal time was not allotted to each. The ZBS argued that language groups varied greatly in size. The two largest ones, Bemba and Nyanja, made up 34% and 17% of the population respectively. Each of these languages had become the lingua franca in significant parts of the urban areas of Zambia. One or other is spoken by many more individuals than had learned either language at home as children. In my national survey of 1970-3, 56% claimed knowledge of Bemba and 42% of Nyanja. Of the time devoted to Zambian languages, the ZBS allocated 23% to Bemba and 21% to Nyanja. The smaller language groups were allocated proportions ranging from 16% for Tonga to 8% for Kaonde.

This allocation was a frequent subject for complaint in letters to the ZBS. Certain chiefs and other prominent members of small language groups felt they were disadvantaged: the ZBS's recognition of a language and its use on the radio gave that language and tribe a status superior to certain other languages and tribes. Members of those groups which had been left out of broadcasting altogether felt aggrieved and often campaigned vigorously for recognition. Those belonging to language groups such as Kaonde, Luvale, Lunda and Lozi, which were recognised but received proportionately less time, also protested, saying that all the recognised languages should in fairness receive equal time.

The criteria for allocation had been devised in an attempt to find a balance between having too many languages to do justice to any of them in limited broadcasting hours and discovering which languages were comprehensible to the largest number. But this fact was not widely understood. I have read a number of letters to the ZBS arguing in roughly the following terms: 'The national motto of our country is "One Zambia One Nation". And yet we see that this is not so in reality. One or two tribes have been given much more time on the radio than others. Does this mean that people from those tribes are better Zambians than us?'

Nonetheless, the language allocation decided upon was strictly adhered to. Largely established during the colonial era, it hardly changed at all after independence. The seven languages recognised for the purposes of broadcasting in addition to English were also used in primary school education, at political rallies and in local newspapers published by the Zambian Information Services.[9]

Zambia Broadcasting Services are a department of the Ministry of Information, all broadcasters being therefore civil servants. This was not always the case. In its first year of independence, Zambia, like other ex-British territories, had a public broadcasting corporation on the lines of the BBC. However, as in most other ex-British territories, this arrangement was not popular with the authorities. The Zambia Broadcasting Corporation was dissolved.

There is not necessarily a direct correlation between government ownership and the degree of government control. Malawi has kept a public corporation, and yet there has probably been more direct interference by the government in broadcasting there than in Zambia. Incorporation into the civil service nevertheless creates many problems. First of all, the service operates strict rules concerning recruitment which are not always suited to radio. Broadcasting talent is not something easily tested by civil service examinations or recruitment procedures. The profession requires people of an artistic and creative ability which may be alien to the needs of the civil service. Moreover, the bureaucratic regulations imposed by the service are inappropriate to radio. In broadcasting, decisions have to be made quickly: a broadcast cannot wait while some minute or other is pending in a civil servant's in-tray. In Zambia, such procedures have delayed the purchase of essential new equipment. For a large part of 1975 a major transmitter in Zambia's Copperbelt was off the air because of the lengthy procedures involved in the purchase of a small spare part. Similar regulations and procedures have delayed both the promotion and dismissal of staff and have hampered the ZBS by failing to provide it with adequate transport when needed at short notice. The pay structure is equally unsuitable. Civil servants are paid according to criteria which should not apply in a creative profession. Zambian broadcasters found themselves a long way down the civil service hierarchy and were accordingly poorly paid, some earning the meagre salary of a junior clerk; certain technical studio operators received little more than messengers did. Due to the low pay offered the likelihood was that anyone with creative talent would be attracted to a better-paid job elsewhere. Some of the most gifted broadcasters of the past are now no longer with the ZBS. Certain staff who might have shown a real aptitude for broadcasting found themselves discouraged by civil service rules on promotion and pay. No provision was made for the payment of special rates in order to retain the services of particularly talented people.

When broadcasters were promoted they found themselves in administrative posts: talented people were rewarded with jobs which meant that they broadcast no longer. Given the structure of broadcasting in Zambia, it was impossible to promote employees by any other means. No one retained a broadcasting role and at the same time enjoyed a good salary. Finally, the civil service status of the ZBS resulted in confusion as to the role and function of broadcasting. Was the ZBS to be the official voice of the Government? Clearly it could not be – every comment, piece of advice or statement on the radio could hardly be regarded as official policy – and yet the broadcasters' feeling that they were 'a part of the Government' certainly acted as an inhibitor on the manner in which some matters were handled on the air. Many broadcasters felt that they were expected not to say anything on the air which was in contradiction to Government policy. This meant that important contemporary issues, such as labour relations, 'shanty' towns, political disagreements within the ruling party and many similarly controversial or sensitive subjects, were neither fully discussed nor featured on the ZBS.

The existence of a subsidized television service became, to some extent, an anomaly. Government spokesmen expressed a desire to spread television to rural areas. In May 1972 the Minister of State for Information, Broadcasting and Tourism called for a complete 'rethink' about the role of television in the country. He said that it should not be regarded as a luxury but used for education, rural development and economic reform: the time had come, he said, 'for television to change its outlook in this country in order to suit the requirements of a developing country like Zambia'. He would 'recommend a stronger transmitter be bought for the benefit of the rural areas'.[10] Yet it was estimated in 1967 that to cover the country no fewer than thirty-three TV transmitters would be needed at a cost then of about K12 million.[11] The economic situation in Zambia then and since has prevented any such ambitious project from being carried out.

Television also received a disproportionate amount of public attention in the press and parliamentary debate. The political élite paid it more attention than it did radio, even though the latter had a greater importance insofar as size of audience was concerned. Members of Parliament did complain about poor radio reception in their constituencies, and some made occasional allegations of political interference and bias in the radio news. (Similar allegations in 1971 led to one MP's being suspended from the House.) In 1971, a Minister of State for Rural Development, Mr Otto Vibetti, made a strong attack on the performance of TVZ:

> We either make up our minds to sink a lot of money to get results, or we scrap television altogether and then concentrate on Radio which in fact everyone consumes in this country. To me ... at the present moment Television is a luxury this country cannot afford.[12]

He went on to recommend a temporary suspension of TV services until these became more Zambian in content, then making a remark which – though a wild exaggeration – was not challenged by any other member, not even by the Minister. He said that only 0.04% of TV sets in Zambia were owned by Zambians.[13] Taking the official figure of twenty thousand TV sets, this would have meant that only eight sets belonged to Zambians! The main part of his argument was nevertheless beyond dispute. Production standards in Zambian television were poor and the service relied heavily on imported material.

Zambian television also received considerable press attention, while radio was almost completely ignored. During 1970 and 1971 a series of articles and editorials appeared in the *Times* on the poor quality of TVZ transmissions, particularly on the Copperbelt. Reference was also frequently made to the low standard of programmes, the high incidence of breakdowns during transmission, and other technical and production weaknesses. The *Times* made its strongest attack, one of the strongest ever made by that paper on a government department, in an editorial in February 1971:

> Take the flickering pictures off the air until such time as those responsible for the transmission can find suitable personnel to man and maintain the equipment properly; plan programmes and stick to schedules; find camera men who are not cross-eyed; monitoring men who are not half blind and deaf; and interviewers and continuity staff whose intelligence is above nursery school level.[14]

Yet the paper made no reference on this and other occasions to the overwhelmingly foreign content of TVZ programmes, neither did the weekly column of TV criticism in the *Sunday Times* question the desirability of this situation. The writer both of that editorial and the weekly *Sunday Times* TV feature was an expatriate who seemed unaware of the cultural gap between the content of TVZ programmes and the environment of Zambia. Few Zambians other than Mr Vibetti questioned the use of government finance to subsidize a communications medium whose main output was then mostly imported and often in conflict with the values both of its audience and of the government that financed it.

Radio was only rarely mentioned in the columns of the daily press. The *Mail* in 1971-3 did not give the radio schedules, while the *Times* usually printed the wrong day's schedules and then only for the General Service (English), omitting altogether the Home Service (Zambian languages) to which the majority of its readership listened most of the time. The press ignored the fact that the radio was the major communications medium in Zambia. This was significant in that it tended to be the press which informed and influenced political debate. The editorial in the *Times* of February 1971 appeared just before the debate in Parliament referred to and was specifically mentioned by one MP in that debate, which was dominated by the subject of television.[15] The Minister for Information, Broadcasting and Tourism, Mr Sikota Wina, after rejecting calls for TVZ to be suspended, made the following remark, which is significant as a statement of government policy on the television service:

> Every country has got to start from somewhere and you have got to accept that when you learn to walk you have got to stumble from time to time. The popularity of Television, Sir, apart from the educational value it has got, is that it is reaching the people who are opinion formers. These are the young people from the universities, the people in key jobs who are in a position to influence public opinion *et cetera*, so that although their number may be small, I think in the national context their influence should be extremely big, if only the Television services were properly improved.[16]

The question of radio reception was raised later in the same debate by the then Minister of State, Mr Masiye, who gave reasons for poor reception. He pointed out that the SOFRECOM recommendations for a VHF-FM system would be the only way to achieve national coverage, but that this would be very expensive: a mere K537,000 had been allocated for capital expenditure,

The world's new media often report the same stories. Cameramen, newspaper journalists and radio and television reporters surround Idi Amin at the OAU Conference, Kampala, 1975. (*The author*)

The death in 1952 of Edwin Mlongoti, one of Northern Rhodesia's best known broadcasters, was an occasion for spontaneous national mourning. The funeral procession was reported to stretch for at least 2 miles. (*Zambia Information Service*)

The first popular mass-produced radio set in Africa, the 'saucepan special', in Northern Rhodesia in 1950. (*Zambia Information Service*)

Portable tape recorders, introduced during the 1950s, made interviews with people in their homes possible. (*Zambia Information Service*)

Television purchased in a package.   A complete television station in container, ready to install on site, purchased for one of the many new stations in Nigeria. (*Marconi*)

Television studio in Ghana in 1966 at the end of a period of fairly high spending on the mass media by the government of Kwame Nkrumah. (*Marconi*)

Television control room in Nigeria, 1964. In 1959, Nigeria was the first country in Africa to have television. (*Marconi*)

The new technology: satellite earth station at Mt. Margaret, Kenya, providing international telephone, telex and television circuits via a geo-stationary satellite above the equator. Many African countries now have this facility. (*Marconi*)

The author with a radio listeners' club in Kano, Nigeria. Listeners' clubs are a popular type of social activity in Northern Nigeria. (*The author*)

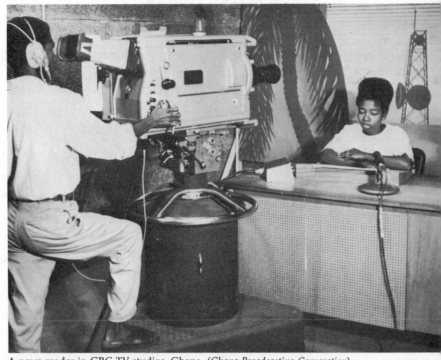

A news reader in GBC-TV studios, Ghana. (*Ghana Broadcasting Corporation*)

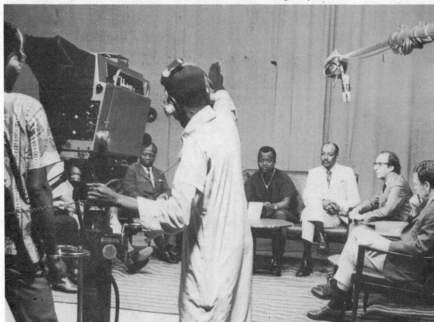

A public affairs television programme in Lagos, Nigeria. (*Commonwealth Broadcasting Association*)

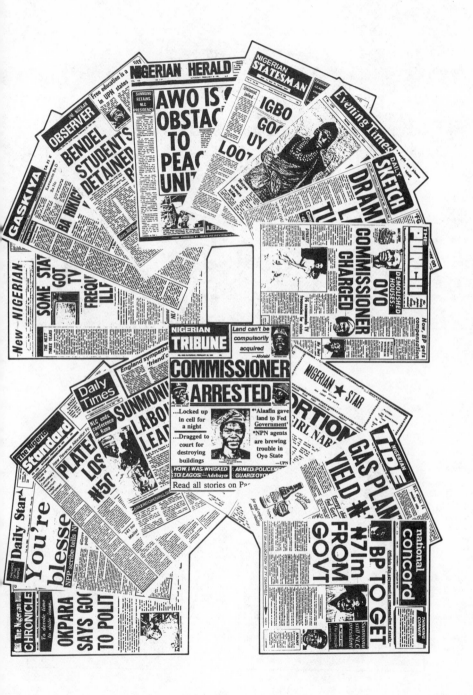

Nigeria's newspapers – the most diverse in Africa

Africa's newspapers – circulations ranging from a thousand to hundreds of thousands 'just a drop in a sea of water'.

> Our expenditure on Broadcasting as far as I am concerned is chicken feed. I wish to say that it is grossly unfair to provide little money for the development of Broadcasting and at the same time begin levelling attacks at us for not carrying out our job properly.[17]

Yet few Zambian politicians ever called for increased funds for broadcasting. The allocation was decided at the highest level of government, and radio broadcasting had long been low on the list of priorities. Economic difficulties experienced in Zambia since this 1971 debate have delayed still further any substantial improvements, although a new studio centre has been built. For the most part, only lip-service has been paid to the importance of radio broadcasting. It has been starved of funds, and leading politicians with the power to do something about it have done little or nothing, apparently content as long as the radio reported what they wanted it to report. This may seem an excessively cynical view; nevertheless, it was one held by many Zambian broadcasters and did seem to have some basis in fact.

But what role did radio play in Zambia? It is, of course, impossible to generalize satisfactorily about the role of broadcasting in the lives of its audience. In one sense, there are as many roles as there are people in the audience: no one person derives exactly the same information, entertainment or instruction as another. Individuals use their radio and television sets in different ways and for different purposes, and expect different things of them. Nevertheless, certain clear patterns emerge from interviews conducted in Zambia in 1972. It must be remembered that it is often difficult to get people to express themselves freely, that there is a tendency in any survey for interviewees to say what they think they are expected to say, and that individuals frequently find it hard to express subjective views on an aspect of their life which they might never have consciously considered before.

During 1972, three colleagues at the University of Zambia interviewed radio listeners in various parts of the capital city, Lusaka. Those listeners who also had television sets were asked about their viewing.[18] These few typical examples will help to illustrate the role that radio – and, to some extent, television – play in some Lusaka homes:

Ngombe Compound: Woman aged 35-40, from Petauke, Eastern Province. Listened to Nyanja programme, and enjoyed Julius Chongo's *Pocheza M'madzulo*, because he 'tells good stories'. She also found the women's programmes useful in learning about child care. She had heard the programme *Nation and Humanism*, but was not interested. She did not know what it meant. She did not listen to the news very often, because it came on when her husband came home for lunch. She had heard about restrictions being imposed on unaccompanied women walking in the towns at night, and felt that this was good because women needed protection.

Kalingalinga: Man aged 40 from Mumbwa, Central Province. He belonged to the Watchtower sect. His mother tongue was Lenje. He remembered a programme he had heard in the Kaonde language which advised 'loafers' to go back to the land. This was a good programme because its message was related to his own experience. When he had enough money saved, he would buy a plough and go back to the rural areas. He liked very much to listen to rural development programmes, which had taught him something about gardening. He liked the music, both popular and traditional, on the General Service. He had heard on the news that Zambia was to change its political system but did not know what this meant.

Ngombe Compound: Two sisters, aged 17 and 18 years, from Kabwe District, Central Province. The younger girl spent most of her time at home 'waiting to get married'. She listened to the radio a lot during the day. She listened to the programmes in the Tonga, Nyanja and Bemba languages, and enjoyed the Tonga play *Malikopo*, because 'it teaches people not to drink beer'. She also found it interesting to hear the main character fighting with his wife after he had been drinking! Both sisters said they enjoyed this play. From the news they remembered about the action to be taken against girls found loitering in the towns at night. This restriction they both felt to be good. But other news had not been understood. They knew nothing about the proposals for a one-party democracy, nor that Zambia was changing to the metric system. Most of the time they listened to the music on the radio, and often switched off when there was no music. They both claimed to have got a better understanding of the Nyanja language from the radio. Their own mother tongue was Lenje.

Ngombe Compound: Woman, age not known, but a grandmother, from Chipata District, Eastern Province. Her radio was bought two and a half years before. She said it had made a great difference. Before, she said she did not know what was going on in Zambia and the world. And she also enjoyed listening to music, especially to 'rhumba' music. In spite of what she said about hearing the news she was unable to remember anything, but her grandson aged fifteen who had finished Grade Seven had remembered quite a lot. He said that he had heard about the Americans in Vietnam, and about President Nixon going to Russia. He said that some people had demonstrated and 'wanted to shoot him', so he was given a bulletproof car. He had also heard about the round-up of defective taxis in Lusaka. The woman had listened to the health programmes and to the instruction given on metrication but could remember nothing. Both enjoyed listening to Julius Chongo's *Pocheza M'madzulo* in the Nyanja language, their own mother tongue.

Kalingalinga: Woman from Petauke District, Eastern Province. Married with four children. They had bought a radio to hear the news and the music, and also for the stories on *Pocheza M'madzulo*. She also enjoyed listening to the advice given on *Ndidzatani*. She listened to programmes in Nyanja and Tonga, and also tuned to Malawi and South Africa. She particularly remembered a story told on Malawi radio about a man who would not give money to his wife, so she wrote him a letter pretending it was from relatives. He found out and summoned her to court. The programme she said taught people to be honest and not to go writing false letters. She found *Nation and Humanism* boring and usually switched it off. 'Before we got the radio we did not know what was happening in the country but now we know.' But she knew nothing about the proposals for a one-party democracy. She was critical of ZBS in some respects, and thought that the way some programmes were presented was bad. Also some of the moral advice given on *Ndidzatani* she found unacceptable. She thought that the problems of people living in places like Kalingalinga, a shanty area, should be discussed. When she did not like what was on ZBS she tuned to Malawi.

Matero: Man aged 22, from Chisamba, Central Province. Educated to Form Five level and had a job with a bank. He had a radio but listened only to the news in English in the morning and evening. He had a record player and said that was why he did not listen to the radio at other times, except for sports commentaries. He watched television sometimes at a friend's house for entertainment. He seemed to be more interested in getting news from the papers and read both the *Times* and the *Mail* regularly.

Matero: Man aged 19 from Luapula Province. Educated to Form Two level, still at school. He liked to listen to music programmes, and to *Kabusha Takolelwe Bowa* in Bemba (advice on listeners' letters like *Ndidzatani* in Nyanja). He said he liked to hear news from other countries. His blind brother aged 21 was also at school. Radio was more important to him, he said, because he could not read the papers.

Matero: Man aged 45, from Kasama District in Northern Province. After he finished school at Standard Three, he participated in the freedom struggle and lost an arm. He bought a radio three years ago, and listened to both General and Home Services from the early morning. He particularly enjoyed the historical programmes in Bemba which he said told about people who came to town a long time ago, and who look back on the past and how things were changed as a result of colonial rule. He said that this sort of programme was important on the radio and should be on more frequently so that the children of today should learn. He said that in many ways the old life was better. He found *Nation and Humanism* interesting but not as good as it was when David Yumba was in charge. He also listened to and enjoyed *Malikopo* in Tonga. He thought that radio could teach young girls not to go walking about the streets after dark.

Kaunda Square: Man aged 30, from Mongu District, Western Province. Completed school to Standard Six. Had a radio set for a long time, but it was being repaired. Listened to programmes in Lozi, Nyanja and English. He sometimes disagreed with his wife about the advice given. He found he could not listen to *Nation and Humanism* because he got tired of it and used to fall asleep. As far as the news in Lozi and Nyanja was concerned, he thought there was too much uninteresting local news and not enough foreign news.

Kaunda Square: Woman aged 18 years, from Chipata District, Eastern Province. Educated to Grade Seven. She had had a radio for as long as she could remember. She particularly enjoyed *Happy Returns* (a record request programme) in English and Julius Chongo's *Pocheza M'madzulo*. Also she found the programmes for women very useful and interesting. She had a child and claimed that she had learned about child care from the radio. She had also learned how to make soup which she did not know before. She also listened to *Ndidzatani* but felt some of the moral advice to be wrong. She said the moral always seemed to be 'keep your husband happy'. The women were always found guilty. She did not agree with that.

Matero: Divorced woman aged 30, from Mumbwa District, Central Province. Her mother tongue was Kaonde. She had bought a radio six months earlier and listened mostly to music. Sometimes she listened to the advice programmes. She remembered one of the items. A rich man died, obviously poisoned by his wife. The relatives came and took all the property away. The message was, she said, don't kill your husband, the relatives will come and take his property anyway. She remembered another story about a man who went to a field and stole some maize. But when he got it home he found he couldn't get it off his shoulder. He went to see a local 'doctor' who advised him to go back to the field and return it, and the maize would fall off. The man did this and so it happened. She said this was a good story teaching people not to steal.

She also found the women's programmes interesting and helpful. But she did not listen to many other programmes. *Nation and Humanism* she found either too difficult or too dull, and she did not listen to the news much. She too knew nothing about the introduction of a one-party democracy. She listened to *Personal Call* (a programme put out in all languages informing listeners about deaths and funeral arrangements). She said she had been able to attend two funerals after hearing about them on the radio.

Lilanda: Woman of unknown age, a grandmother living with her son. She was from Luapula Province and spoke only Bemba. She listened to the radio and found it to be interesting. She had not listened to the radio before coming to Lusaka about a year previously. Since coming to Lusaka she said that she had heard many things she had never heard before – about Zambian humanism, about the one-party state, about drunkenness and accidents. Now she knew about these from the radio. She also found it interesting to hear the advice given on *Kabusha Takolelwe Bowa*, but found that she was in disagreement with a lot of it.

Her son had a television, which she found 'very strange'; 'I have seen people fighting'. But she found it difficult to understand when there was a lot of talking and her son was not always there to translate.

Lilanda: Woman 18 years old from Mongu in Western Province. Educated to Grade Seven level. Before she came to Lusaka five years ago, she lived in a village where there was no radio. She liked the music programmes best of all, and then the programmes in Lozi and Nyanja. She preferred the General Service with its more western popular music. She had enjoyed a recent play on the radio in Lozi and could remember a lot about it. She thought radio could teach young mothers like her more about child care. She claimed to have learned something from the radio from the women's, health, and nutrition programmes. Like very many others interviewed, she said that she particularly remembered a programme advising people to keep food covered.

She watched television and liked some of the imported entertainment. She did not like talk-programmes because she found them too difficult to understand. What difference had watching television made to her? She said that she could now see other countries, for example when the President went on a visit. Also she said it kept her at home when she might otherwise have gone out.[19]

What people want and expect from the radio is not necessarily what those who control broadcasting want to give them. In the national audience research survey I conducted in 1970-73, listeners were asked to state their favourite programme or programmes. Again, news bulletins and those programmes offering practical help in farming, health and child care, advice on moral and social issues or providing music, stories and plays proved the most popular. There was less interest in programmes on political subjects and an actual dislike of political propaganda programmes such as *Nation and Humanism*. Most listeners who had something to say about the last-named found them either boring or incomprehensible. Listeners expected the radio to be relevant to problems as they saw them. This did not mean that they were wholly resistant to new ideas – that was clearly not the case because many spoke of the helpful advice and information given on the farming, nutrition, health and child care programmes – but they seemed to resist anything which either conflicted with views they already held or seemed to have no relevance to their experience.

At the time my survey was carried out, the social fabric of Zambia was undergoing great changes. These changes had been occurring, at a varying pace, for most of the present century and affected individuals in a number of ways. As a result, people have looked to the radio to provide explanations, give advice and act as an arbiter of social morality. The radio was thus given a traditional role once entrusted only to wise old men and women. Inevitably, this did not please everyone, and the ZBS postbag was often full of complaints. Letter writers frequently regarded the ZBS as representative of the new social order – the new nation – and wrote to it with that in mind. The radio was seen as possessing authority on standards of moral and social behaviour:

> **Ndola:** Is it good to marry a girl from a different tribe? Why do our parents not want us to marry anyone except from our home villages? When I went home on leave, I was told to get engaged to a local girl, but I told them there were no beautiful girls there that I could marry. They said 'You want to be like your elder brother who married a girl from a different tribe in town'. Well, I am engaged to a girl of a different tribe and I have already paid some money. When my parents get to hear of this what do you think they will do?

> **Lusaka:** I am just asking why most parents, when they quarrel, the husband often talks of bewitching the children. Does it mean that the children are responsible always for domestic disputes? My parents want to kill me and my young brothers. What shall we do?

> **Lusaka:** Please tell me. This thing pains me a lot. Why does our TV service use only English? Do you think that all our people in Zambia understand English? Even things that are not supposed to be said in English, you use English. Is English our language? Why I have said this is that when you are watching TV with people who do not understand English, they keep asking you what is being said. The mouth becomes sore.

> **Mkushi:** Why is it that you announce something which the majority of your listeners do not want to listen to? For example you say 'Go to Happy Grocery where you will find wigs at K18' and many other things like this for women. How do you expect people to dislike such things when you keep on announcing them on the radio.

A large number of letters like this last one noted a conflict between the advice given on the radio in political programmes and some of the commercial advertisements. Some listeners wrote about problems with their jobs:

Mpika: We here in Mpika are working on the new railway. Some are working as carpenters, some as plumbers and some as labourers. We know our jobs well. But there is always a chance of promotion if you do well. But this does not happen here at Mpika. We have been working here for nine months but only the newcomers are given the good jobs. These are usually their [the bosses'] relatives. Because they drink beer together, they get promoted.

Nevertheless, the great majority of the letters involved marriage and love problems. These seemed to arise from the process of urbanization, the breaking down of traditional practices, and what was seen as a conflict between the old morality and the new.

Chililabombwe: Why is it that when you are looking for a marriageable girl most of them refer you to their parents? What is usually with the parents?

Lusaka: I am married to a Nsenga girl. I am a Bemba. I love her very much and we understand each other well. But here is the snag. I want to go and live at Mandevu compound, but her grandmother won't allow her, because she says that I might run away with her to Kasama (a town in the north, in the centre of Bemba country). She goes on to say that if I love her very much I should remain in Misisi. But there is piped water in Mandevu whereas we get water from wells here at Misisi.

Such letters concerning difficulties in love and marriage came almost exclusively from people living in towns. Rural listeners sometimes considered the questions and the answers given to them to be improper:

Chishi Island, Samfya: The people who ask these questions just do it for fun. It looks as if they want to disagree their wives or husbands just be getting advice on the air. Because a good many people listen to it. Most of the problems asked about are: how a woman or man runs away from home, how the mother-in-law does not like him or her, how girls wear miniskirts when they should not. Are these questions fit to be asked on the radio? I think it is disgraceful.[20]

The social tensions evidenced in many of these letters found an echo in some of the music played over the radio. The great cultural diversity of the country, and the conflicts which this gave rise to, found expression in popular song. There were conflicts within individuals who found themselves looking nostalgically to their own tribal past while at the same time wanting to be part of the newly emerging social and economic order.

In Zambia, as in most other parts of Africa, music has been the vehicle for the communication of a variety of such emotions and comments. Praise songs were composed for revered and respected figures, and tribal or village history was preserved through song. Songs provided instruction and advice on social, sexual and economic problems. Singers in Zambia were very skilled at improvisation, and the same skill seems to be common in many other parts of Africa. I have been present at occasions of celebration when poets and singers – there is often no distinction since poems tend to be sung or chanted – have made up verses on the spot and provided a seemingly endless number of embellishments. Everyone is expected to join in the chorus. Songs can teach, can reinforce the norms of the society and can often provide reassurance of order and continuity in confused and troubled times.

Moreover, music can act as a form for the expression of satire or mocking protest when such expression may be neither possible nor wise in other more direct ways.

The conflict between the old and the new was a common theme. In the 1950s, the novelist and writer Stephen Mpashi, a man who very much represented success in the new social order, composed a popular song expressing this conflict. In the song, a newly urbanized man feels somewhat guilty about his and others' deviation from the ways of their ancestors:

> Oh, the restless wanders!
> He has forgotten his tribe and his family.
> He picks up any woman of the town.
> He sucks the lollypops of Ndola.
> He has forgotten the taste of the sweet wild fruit of the bush.[21]

At the same time, singers also sang of the new delights of detribalized urban life:

> We are the smart men about town. We eat from tables.
> We are the smart men about town. We've got *the* girls.
> We are the smart men about town. We put on shoes.
> We are the smart men about town. We look like teachers.
> We are the smart men about town. Wonderful wires stretch into our houses.
> We are the smart men about town. We have electric lights and tin roofs.
> Now come and see what hell-of-a-fellows we are.[22]

Town life does indeed bring the good life to some. Yet marital relations were a constant theme of controversy, discussion, humour and, of course, song. Many men found girls in town with whom they lived without necessarily getting married: there were numerous songs about town women and how they compared with those from the rural areas. According to popular, male mythology the worldly, urban woman was continually demanding more material possessions and, if she did not get them, might desert her man. Many urban liaisons were between partners from different tribes, and such marriages were rarely entered into in the proper, traditional way. The traditional *lobola* payments were rarely made and no contract drawn up between the families. Some of these relationships were lasting; others broke up because the man wanted to return to his home village. A woman from another tribe might not easily fit into her partner's home environment, where she would not know the language and where the local women might not accept her. A marriage occasionally broke up because the wife asked for too much. This is the theme of one of the most beautiful modern songs from Central Africa, whose composer and singer, Alick Nkhata, is probably the most popular commercial recording artist Northern Rhodesia or Zambia has yet produced.

> Good-bye! Now I go back to my home where I came from.
> Don't forget your duty. Look after our children.
> Even though I go, I will help you support them.
> It is you who have made the mistake.
> You want too much wealth which I can never possess.
> I, poor man, must return to my home.[23]

Peter Fraenkel, writing in 1956, noted the absence of any songs on the very important subject of kinship and the traditional ties binding the extended family together. Such ties have been placed under great strain as the result of urbanization and the arising of great inequalities within society, inequalities which have been mirrored within society, inequalities which have been mirrored within many families. Men or women who achieved success through education, business or political office found they were expected to support a seemingly ever-growing number of relatives, especially nephews. In traditional society this would not be regarded as sponging or parasitism, for it was felt that one's relationship to one's own son was no closer than that to the sons of siblings, and most people had more nephews than sons. In recent times the demands made by traditional society have no longer always been welcomed. They were often talked about but not sung about: 'We do not sing about such things. It wouldn't be decent. Grumbling about them – that is private. But singing is public.'

Fraenkel's view was that kinship ties were still held in high regard, and I believe this to be still true, however irksome people may find them. However, almost nothing else was considered a taboo subject. Songs about sex were often very explicit – far more so than would be acceptable in many other cultures. The following song was broadcast on the radio and was on sale in the record shops, yet the wearing of miniskirts a few years later was denounced as improper and an example of western sexual decadence and permissiveness!

> Let me tell you about town wives . . .
> All day long she is never satisfied.
> She threatens 'I'll not stay with you'.
> Yet . . . she remains, for I satisfy her at night.
> All night I fondle her.
> Her body becomes our playground.[24]

The period written about by Fraenkel preceded independence. The following years saw a decline in local music production so far as commercial recording was concerned. The traditional music of the villages continued much as before, but less Zambian music was produced in the towns, where young musicians tended more and more to copy the popular music of Britain, the United States and Zaire. Formerly, Alick Nkhata and men like him had adapted the western popular music of the time, particularly country and western music, which they married with traditional melodies and themes. But during the 1970s, urban Zambian musicians adopted rather than adapted western popular music styles. Why this has happened I am not competent to say, but it could be a fruitful and fascinating subject for research.

Radio and television news was supplied by the national news agency, ZANA. It received the wire services of Reuters and AFP, which it retransmitted to its customers, including the *Times* and the *Mail*. It also carried out its own news collection from offices in Lusaka, Kabwe, Ndola, Kitwe and Livingstone. Other news was provided by district information officers at district capitals around the country. Poor communications meant that very little news from outlying districts appeared in ZANA output, the only notable exception being when the President went on one of his tours of the country and a journalist from ZANA accompanied the party. Similarly, when a Cabinet minister or district governor went on tour, a ZANA journalist would usually go with him, sending stories back to Lusaka. An analysis of news originating anywhere away from the line-of-rail showed that it frequently came from such a tour, which shows what difficulty the news media had in getting rural news. Only when transport was made available for some other reason did journalists – meaning, as a rule, Government journalists – get a chance to report news from Zambia's rural areas. At other times they did not have transport and so did not travel.

Local news tended to be dull and repetitive, as the following typical example shows:

> The Minister of State for Southern Province, Mr. Zongani Banda, has called for hard work among the people and also urged them to work cooperatively to achieve self-sufficiency in political, social and economic development.[25]

There was heavy emphasis on leaders' reported statements at the expense of the event or situation in which the remarks were made:

> The assistant General Secretary of the Zambia Congress of Trade Unions Mr. Raphael Mang'ambwa has warned workers and employers to be on the alert of (sic) foreign powers trying to divide the masses in what he called the second scramble for Africa.[26]

The context of a growing rift at that time between trade unions and the Ministry of Labour was not mentioned.

Bulletins in Zambian languages were identical in subject matter and from 1245 to 1335 were broadcast every day in Lunda, Luvale, Tonga, Bemba, Nyanja, Lozi and Kaonde in that order, all being translations of the same basic bulletin. The English news, inserted at 1315, was more up to date, having been prepared in the late morning. The bulletins used for the Zambian languages were prepared in the early morning, because ZBS staff required time for translation.

Zambian language bulletins concentrated on Zambian news: in the period studied, 81.1% was Zambian news and a further 11.7% from other African countries south of the Sahara. Only 2.6% of the news used in these bulletins was other foreign news as compared to 14.3% of the English language bulletins. This was a deliberate policy: it was felt that anyone with sufficient education to understand or be interested in foreign news could be expected to listen to and understand English. Because these Zambian language bulletins were short they were very limited in content. About half (53.3%) of the average English language news bulletin was concerned with Zambian affairs, but because there was three times as much news in English there was in fact twice as much Zambian news content in English in real terms. Looked at from all angles, a member of the minority of the total listenership which spoke English well was likely to be better informed.

Another problem for the listener who relied on Zambian language bulletins was the fact that much of the translation was of a very low standard. The staff of ZBS were fluent in the language in which they broadcast, but their knowledge of English was frequently inadequate. Many admitted to not fully understanding the bulletins they were supposed to translate. Their translations were often either incorrect or contained a word left in English for which the translator could find no equivalent in his language. An example of mistranslation occurred when President Kaunda returned from the Singapore Commonwealth Conference in 1970, where he had clashed with the British Prime Minister over British arms sales to South Africa. ZANA reported him as saying on arrival in Lusaka that his fight was with Mr Heath only, and that he wanted the people of Zambia to 'leave the British people here alone'. The implication was clear to anyone who understood English well: the President was anxious that Zambians should not make Britons in Zambia take the blame for the policy of the Heath government. But the Bemba language translator used the word *ukubstanduka*, which means 'to boycott them', so that Kaunda was quoted in Bemba as saying that Zambians should shun or have nothing to do with Britons in Zambia.

Such mistranslations occasionally had their amusing side, as when 'State Ball' was translated so as to give listeners the delightful picture of the President playing football with a visiting group of dignitaries at State House. And when a car collided with a stationary vehicle, listeners were told it had encountered a van full of envelopes and other items of stationery!

About 12% of radio time in Zambia was taken up by news in the various languages. To determine how important radio was as a source of news I selected some news stories and tried to find out if and how Zambians in various parts of the country had learned of these events. A variety of news items were selected at different times during the three years of the survey. As was to be expected, town dwellers were better informed than rural people. Those who had heard about major items of foreign news – such as the Amin coup in Uganda, the deaths of Nasser in Egypt and Nkrumah in Ghana, or the proposed resumption of British arms sales in South Africa – had for the most part received the news from the radio. Generally, about one half of the urban people had received these items of news, compared with between ten and twenty-five per cent of those living in rural areas. In both cases, most of those who had heard the news named the radio as their source.

We also asked questions about some important events in Zambia itself: the change in the vice-presidency in 1970, the conference of non-aligned countries held in Lusaka in the same year, the price control measures introduced a year later and the increased prices being paid to farmers for maize in 1971. The results here were quite surprising. We found many people, including a large number of radio listeners, who were ill-informed on these matters. The change in the price of maize was intended to encourage increased maize production at a time of shortage when the country had to import large supplies from Rhodesia: a politically humiliating thing to have to do. In two important maize-growing areas, fewer than half of those interviewed had heard of the increased price, and in an area where the Government was keen to encourage a substantial increase in local production, less than one in ten had heard of the new prices.[27]

Access to the media was clearly a very significant factor. Radio listeners and newspaper readers were generally far better informed, but investigation showed that a great deal of news was either misunderstood or not listened to because it was incomprehensible. If news bore little or no relation to a person's experience, then it might not be remembered. Yet this does not explain the lack of knowledge about the price of maize. It may be that the announcement was not repeated frequently enough. It is also possible – and in my view more likely – that even this news was not understood. Press releases given in technical language, with a large number of figures and percentages, were not easy to listen to and understand when broadcast. Translation often made matters worse, since this tended to be the responsibility of people whose knowledge of English was inadequate for the task: as has already been noted, phrases or words in the original text were frequently left in English. Another factor working against effective communication may well have been the air time given to Zambian language news bulletins: these were only five minutes long. News in Bemba broadcast at lunchtime was rarely repeated in the evening Bemba news. Very few listeners listened to all three news bulletins in their own language each day, and so it was very easy to miss important items. Also, news bulletins concentrated heavily on the speeches and activities of leading politicians, particularly the President. On days when he was particularly active, other items of news which might have appeared in the ten-minute English language bulletins were squeezed out of those in the Zambian languages.

However, the radio did play an important role in the dissemination of certain types of news, and it was clearly more influential than the press. News of major disasters, like the tragedy at Mufulira mine in 1970, spread rapidly around the country by radio and by word of mouth. Listeners paid attention to, and remembered, those items that seemed significant to them. I noticed that they frequently lost interest during bulletins when political activities and speeches were reported or some official announcement was made. At times the broadcasters themselves did not really understand the significance of what they were broadcasting, so it was hardly surprising that their listeners took the same view: enthusiasm, and the lack of it, are equally infectious.

Those listeners who were mothers of young children often spoke of their appreciation of health and nutritional programmes; they found advice and information on the radio that was relevant and easily understood. While this should not, of course, be taken to imply that female listeners lack intelligence, it does suggest that radio is not perhaps a suitable medium for putting across complex ideas or instructions. The broadcaster who gave a complicated radio talk on a technical subject was wasting his time, for no one listened to him – a point which came over in interviews so often that it became indisputable. For example, President Kaunda's philosophy of humanism was not widely understood, and the reason seemed quite clear: the programme *Nation and Humanism*, designed to promote understanding of that philosophy, was often very dull. The participants talked in abstract and theoretical terms, rarely relating the subject to the listeners' experience.

Radio achieved its greatest impact when it related most clearly to the experiences of listeners, who expected it to reflect and comment on life as it was, give advice on difficult contemporary and age-old problems and make life more enjoyable by providing entertainment. This is what accounted for the enormous popularity of Julius Chongo's *Pocheza M'madzulo*, especially in Lusaka and in Eastern Province. Because of his considerable talent as a story-teller, Chongo was able to entertain his audience and the same time to encourage it to think about moral problems, sometimes in a new and challenging way. The radio cannot demand that we listen to it: even if we leave it switched on, this does not mean we are listening. We listen and pay attention when it says something in such a way as to attract our attention. Although most professional broadcasters know this, governments tend to ignore the point – and many radio stations, like the ZBS, are under government direction and control.

Tanzania

Political attitudes towards press and radio in independent Tanzania are in many ways typical of those in newly independent African nations. At independence in 1961 and during the period immediately afterwards, the new TANU government was concerned that it had no direct voice in the press. *Ngurumo* supported it, but was still a private, independent paper. The colonial administration's paper, *Mambo Leo*, had, like its stablemates, been turned over to private hands. Though highly political in the later years of colonial rule, *Mambo Leo* was now largely apolitical, and its coverage of national affairs tended to be non-controversial. The *Standard* supported the government, but not out of any fundamental conviction. *Mwafrika* was now a commercial rather than political paper. No other newspapers of major significance were in existence. In 1959, TANU had tried to launch its own National Times Press with Nyerere as chairman, the ambitious plan being to publish a Swahili daily, an English daily and a Gujerati weekly. Insufficient capital was raised for the project, which proved abortive; yet TANU leaders remained determined to have at least one daily paper, and preferably two: one in English and one in Swahili. Eventually, some finance was provided and a weekly paper called *Uhuru* ('Independence') made its first appearance on Independence Day, 9th December 1961. It became a daily on its fourth anniversary in 1965. In addition, a decision was made during 1962 to launch an English language daily. Ainslie interprets this decision as a response to a difficult situation, particularly internationally:

> Already the Tanganyika leaders were finding that the demands of nation building, and of the strongly anti-colonial policy to which they were increasingly committed, imposed on them policy decisions that led them into conflict with interests in the territory, and with many of their former 'friends' abroad. Nyerere's warm support for Kenyatta (only recently released from detention) alarmed many of those who had looked upon him as a reliable friend of 'the West'; and so did his Government's active support for the African liberation movements in Southern Africa. It was clear that these policies should be presented to the public by Government itself.[28]

TANU's English language daily, the *Nationalist*, first appeared on April 17th 1964, thus preceding its sister paper *Uhuru* as a daily by twenty months. In Ainslie's opinion, this came about because of its greater international impact as an English paper. The international aspect continued to be of importance and was one of the reasons why the *Nationalist* – a very costly venture – was kept going even when its existence could no longer be justified on any other grounds. But why was the party so keen to have two national daily newspapers published in Dar es Salaam when it was clear that they would use up much-needed funds in the initial investment and could not guarantee to pay for themselves? Jointly they represented a heavy financial burden which, as it turned out, became the responsibility of the Government rather than the party. The emphasis placed on the press by the Government and TANU was to continue long after independence. Although it has since been modified and greater attention paid to radio, it is still manifest in some of the Government's actions in the field of mass communication. There were, I believe, five main reasons why the national daily press was stressed at the expense of radio and local newspapers.

Firstly, the radio, represented by the Tanganyika Broadcasting Corporation (TBC), was constitutionally 'above' politics at the time of independence. TANU wanted a medium that would be totally committed to its goals. The radio was accessible to TANU but nevertheless independent of political direction. Besides, TANU members had been involved in the press, while they had not been involved in radio. Broadcasters were supposed to be outside the political arena, and held attitudes different from those of their colleagues in the press, many of whom were political campaigners. The radio had been virtually closed to TANU's campaign for independence, whereas the same period saw the emergence of a modest, but nevertheless committed, nationalist press.

Secondly, I think few realized in 1961 just how sizeable the radio audience had become or how rapidly it would expand. A far larger number of sets were in use than licence figures would suggest, but during and especially at the outset of the campaign for independence the number of newspaper readers exceeded that of radio listeners. Not until after independence was the really massive growth in the radio audience to occur.

The prestige of the written word, considered by TANU to be of particular significance, was the third reason for the emphasis on the press. Those in power wanted the voice of newly independent Tanganyika to express itself forcefully in a printed medium that could be received not only nationally but also abroad. There was a frequently reiterated belief that for Tanganyika to be understood properly in the international community it needed to have a strong English language press in which TANU policies would be stated clearly.

Connected with this attitude was the fourth reason for dedication to the establishment of a national TANU press. In the early days, few people talked about decentralization. As has been noted earlier, TANU's cadres felt that nation-building could be achieved only through the control of the centre – a view which extended itself to the press. Tanganyika's local press, which flourished in the pre-independence period with government support, collapsed soon after independence, for the simple reason that, unlike the colonial administration, the TANU government spent all the funds available for the press on supporting its own papers published in the capital.

The fifth reason was that mixed feelings seemed to exist about the mass media generally and radio in particular. It should not be assumed – though in the literature on the subject it often is – that political élites necessarily desire an effective means of *mass* communication or have any clear policy on how to use it. They may want to control the media capable of reaching large sections of the population, yet at the same time be suspicious of the power these media possess: power which is ultimately beyond their control. Political activities such as party meetings and rallies can be observed and supervised, but there is no way of controlling what an individual listens to on his radio set. Thus while those TANU members concerned to achieve effective communication for the purpose of education and development preferred the press to radio, whose full potential they failed to recognize, there may have been others who realized that radio had powers to reach people which TANU had not. TANU had succeeded in coping with a nationalist political movement, but could it cope with the demands of people whose national political consciousness might be further aroused by messages coming from outside the party's framework of control? In the early days of independence, TANU and the Government appear to have been anxious to lower the political temperature, following the excitement of the previous three years. This may have accounted in part for their reluctance to promote the growth of radio while at the same time encouraging the development of a press based in Dar es Salaam. In Africa the press, like television, tends to serve the political, social and economic élite: these are the people who can read, can afford to buy a newspaper and are likely to be living where newspapers can be bought. Press and television in Africa are generally allowed more freedom of expression than is radio, and one suspects that the reason is that already mentioned: the elitist fear of uneducated people listening to radio and being 'misinformed' or 'confused'.

It is difficult, perhaps impossible, to establish exactly how much was spent on the two papers, *Uhuru* and the *Nationalist*, in the years between 1964, when the *Nationalist* was launched, and 1972, when it merged with the *Standard* to form the *Daily News*. However, I was able to obtain fairly detailed information on the situation in 1968, when the subvention had to be increased substantially. A confidential Ministry of Information report, written in April 1968, revealed that the two papers owed Sh.900,000/- to the printers, who threatened to discontinue working on them altogether unless this amount were paid and an assurance received from the Treasury that printing costs for the rest of the financial year would be met. These amounted to Sh.450,000/-. The financial problems of these papers were acute. The Sh.800,000/- voted by the Ministry of Commerce and Co-operatives in the 1967-68 estimates was then able to meet less than half the two papers' annual operating deficit. A further Sh.1,050,000/- had to be found if they were to survive, and no extra money had been voted by Parliament.

The *Nationalist* and *Uhuru* were not commercial propositions, neither were they intended to be – they existed to give TANU and its government a mouthpiece both within Tanzania and in the outside world – but both were losing money more heavily than anticipated. Publishing costs accounted for more than Sh.3,000,000/- per annum, whereas revenue amounted to only just over Sh.1,000,000/-. Two reasons can be given for this, the first being their low circulations. The *Nationalist* claimed sales of 7,000; in fact its print order during 1967 and 1968 rarely exceeded 4,000, and numerous copies remained unsold. *Uhuru* was somewhat more successful, with a print run of around 12,000 and sales of 10,000. Secondly, neither paper attracted much advertising, probably because of their restricted circulation. It is also possible that many advertisers were put off by the political tone. The *Standard*, read by the better off, was considered the prestige paper, and when advertising in Swahili most firms preferred the Commercial Service of Radio Tanzania, with its mass audience.

Various attempts were made to increase the sales and advertising revenue of the two party papers, though the measures taken were at best mere palliatives. It is probable that *Uhuru* could have been commercially successful on its own, unlike the *Nationalist*, which certainly was not. Moreover, the papers were run as political ventures; there were none of the commercial, management, planning and sales activities that were to be found at the *Standard*. The government subsidy made it likely that the staff of the two papers were less worried about pushing up sales than were their counterparts on the then Lonrho-owned *Standard*. This paper's remarkable success in increasing sales between 1965 and 1969 not only showed what could be achieved by a powerful sales campaign (which also brought in advertising at higher rates) but also indicated that new purchasers of newspapers were not attracted to the party press, whose sales remained relatively stagnant. Between January and June 1965 and the same period in 1969, the *Standard*'s sales rose from 11,844 to 19,496 copies daily.

My own estimates, based on Ministry sources, suggest that *Uhuru* and the *Nationalist* cost the Government Sh.7,000,000/- in subsidies between the financial years 1965-66 and 1968-69. This sum is equivalent to about one third of the Government grant to Radio Tanzania for the same period, and to more than the entire sum allocated to the development of information and broadcasting services in the first Five Year Plan.[29]

In mid-1968, a time of financial difficulty, while urgent discussions were taking place at the highest level on ways to save the party newspapers, the Ministry of Information was trying to find ways of cutting back expenditure on broadcasting and information services. The saving of the party newspapers at this time was given priority over matters related to broadcasting and other information services. In effect, the Government had decided that the heavy subsidy given to the readers of the *Nationalist* and *Uhuru*, who lived mostly in towns (half the sales and probably half the readership of both newspapers were in Dar es Salaam) should take precedence over, for example, the building of satellite radio stations to improve reception in remote areas or the provision of community listening points. Both these projects were provided for in the Five Year Plan current at the time but were shelved for lack of funds. The closure of the party newspapers, on the other hand, was then unthinkable.

The crisis was resolved by the vote of extra money by Parliament, and no break occurred in the publication of either newspaper. Yet recognition of the difficulties in which the two papers found themselves had the apparent effect of making the Government and the party think more clearly about mass communications. The Ministry of Information and TANU began to organize seminars and study groups on information services and the mass media and their place in socialism, nation-building and development. The first series of these was held at Radio Tanzania between May 22nd and August 19th 1968. Participants included senior radio personnel, editorial staff from the party press and the TANU publicity secretary; there were no participants from non-governmental or non-TANU media. Out of this and out of a more general TANU mass media seminar in 1968 was eventually to come TANU's mass media committee, which has now become an important influence on Tanzania's mass media as a whole.

Whilst large sums of money were voted by Parliament to establish and keep *Uhuru* and the *Nationalist* going, MPs always showed extreme reluctance to extend that generosity to radio. Even before independence, the Corporation's shaky finances drew criticism and demands for more direct control of broadcasting. In February 1961 Parliament was asked to approve the grant of an extra £12,000 in the Supplementary Estimates. Licence fees had failed to meet expectations, and more funds were needed to keep broadcasting going. Backbencher Mr Sijaona stated that the TBC was uneconomic and recommended that a committee of enquiry be set up to examine possible alternatives. He made clear what he had in mind:

> A broadcasting system is a very powerful instrument and it can be a very dangerous instrument if those who are responsible for running it happen to hold different views from those of the Government and great harm can be done to this country by giving emphasis to the wrong thing and paying very little attention to those things which need special attention. It is my view . . . that to avoid this powerful instrument being used by people who may not have the interests of the country at heart, this instrument should be taken over by the Ministry of Information Services and run as one of the Government Departments. (Applause)[30]

Another Member, Mr Kasambala, made the same point, adding:

> As the Scots say, we are paying the bagpiper, and we have the right to call for the tune. This TBC has got to bear in mind what this House has got to say on it.[31]

One backbencher disagreed; Mr Tunze said that he wanted

> to repudiate a point that the TBC should be controlled by the Government. I think the Government is one of the bodies which would not give balanced information to the public, and we never know, it might be government of TANU today and the government of Congress (an opposition party not in Parliament) tomorrow.[32]

It was by all accounts a fairly heated debate, with interventions from the Government benches, including two from Nyerere. Except for Mr Tunze, all seven African backbenchers who spoke were highly critical of the TBC and advocated more direct control over the way it handled its finances, the news it chose to broadcast, and even the type of entertainment it presented. The emphasis in these speeches was on the need for unity and the avoidance of dissent in radio programmes. The view was that radio should always speak with the same voice as the Government, aiming to educate and improve rather than entertain the public. An image of national unity should be portrayed even if this was not a true reflection of reality.

Within a year there had been a shift in the Government's attitude towards the Corporation. In the debate on the annual budget in June 1962 the Minister of Education, who was then responsible for broadcasting matters, gave a review of the TBC's achievements during the previous year. He spoke as if the Government now regarded the TBC as being within its sphere of activity. It was clear that the Government now saw itself as taking a greater part in determining TBC policies, and this was confirmed by the addition of an External Service to the TBC's responsibilities. In his speech, the Minister referred to the Corporation's 'year of fulfilment' and included the TBC's activities in his review of Information Services as a whole, pointing to their 'valuable work . . . in the publicising and classifying of the momentous political changes which have taken place'.[33]

Backbenchers mostly made the same points that they had made over a year earlier. Some of them added that they thought the TBC paid too little attention to the speeches of politicians: this was to be a frequent complaint. Perhaps the most significant contribution to the debate was that made by a member of the TBC board, the former *Mwafrika* editor Mr Bagdelleh. The TBC, he said, had got to be an arm of the Government

> so that the Government information, Government activities can be communicated to the people at large . . . Let us forget about this independent corporation business. It has never worked in Ghana and it will never work in any other country in Africa.[34]

He wanted more money to be spent on broadcasting and a separate Ministry to be set up to direct and co-ordinate all information policy: this was the only way a minister would be able to deal with all the criticisms levelled at the broadcasters. Although at the time the Minister rejected this suggestion as unacceptable, the Government soon agreed to most of the MP's suggestions. In 1964 a separate Ministry of Information and Tourism was established under a minister in the Cabinet. The new Minister, Idris Wakil, who had only recently come from Zanzibar to join the new Cabinet after the union of Tanganyika and Zanzibar,[35] explained the reason for the new Ministry:

> The Union Government emphasises strongly that people should get good news concerning the country's development especially now we are underway with our Five Year Plan . . . News, through the press, the radio, film or any other means, is one of the strongest tools that can be used in building the country. Ignorance caused by knowing nothing is one of the big enemies of progress and people who do not know what is happening in the world, in the country they live in, are the people who are always frightened with suspicions, who can believe anything that is said whether it is rumour or falsity.[36]

A new trend in official thinking was evident. From now on, the news media were to be accorded greater importance. The Government and TANU, at the centre, wanted to talk directly to the people and were becoming increasingly aware of the communications gap between the centre (the capital) and the periphery or grass roots, given the remoteness from Dar es Salaam of so much of the country. The weakness of TANU as a communications channel was well known. The army mutiny of 1964 had created fears about the country's stability and produced a greater intolerance of dissent. Tordoff noted that the mutiny forced Nyerere to take a tougher line, as was evidenced by his use of the Preventive Detention Act; it also accelerated other trends which increased government control over such alternative power focuses as the trade unions, the co-operatives and the armed forces.[37] The Government wanted to speak directly to the people without having to compete with other voices, to give its version of events, of its own policies and activities, without having these questioned. It seemed worried about the power of alternative media, beyond its control, to give interpretations different from those it wanted put over. Though backbenchers were not unanimous in supporting this line, a significant proportion of them did so. It would shortly be the turn of another group to state the opposite view, but in the meantime majority opinion was in favour of increased centralized political control.

Another reason given for increased central control – and one which I have heard frequently in Tanzania – was that there was a danger of confusing illiterate peasants if the media did not speak with one voice. It was concluded that the media had no business either relaying bad news about government and party policies and activities or suggesting that alternative measures might be better. The logical result of this attitude was, of course, the takeover of the most prominent media, which would involve placing them under more direct control, a corollary of this action was the suppression or limitation of any privately owned media that might either be critical of TANU and the Tanzanian Government or campaign for alternatives. When communications were inadequate and weak, it was argued, the country could ill afford the luxury of competing media.

In Mr Wakil's first speech to Parliament he referred to the Five Year Plan, in which an expansion of broadcasting was projected. The message of the entire Plan had to be put across:

> We cannot wait until everyone is literate before planning development matters. . . We want development now and one means we can use right now to inform all the people is radio. In . . . America and Europe where people have ways of getting food and shelter then this radio can be used for entertainment, but in our country where we . . . are fighting a war to raise our people's standard of living we ought very much to be using radio for the benefit of all the people. For this reason we cannot leave the studios in the hands . . . of a group of wealthy people who could use it as a shop for business only ('Hear, Hear,' and applause), without minding the needs of our Republic ('Hear, Hear,' and applause). The Government ought to have power in these studios (applause) and I and my Ministry will do everything we can to see that our radio is working for the benefit of this country (applause).[38]

Nevertheless, the Minister did not think at this time that it was necessary to end the corporate status of Tanzania's radio service. The existing ordinance gave him enough power. The Corporation was in charge of day-to-day administration 'on my behalf', but, he stated:

> If I find the powers I am given are not sufficient for fulfilling my work, then I will
> not delay in coming back to you to ask for greater powers (cries of 'Hear, Hear,'
> and applause) for educating the people on development, especially on the Five
> Year Plan which must be successful. This is the main pillar for the success of the
> whole plan.[39]

Plans for broadcasting in the First Five Year Plan included the setting up
of community listening points, the building of regional and satellite stations,
the replacement of transmitters and the provision of a tape transcription
service for the better preservation and use of recorded material at
Broadcasting House. The capital allocation of the Plan to broadcasting was
Sh.4,640,000/-.[40] The Ministry was to spend considerably more than its total
allocation for the period 1964-69. It exceeded its investment target by thirty-
nine per cent,[41] but most of the money went towards tourism.[42] At the end of
the five-year period, no money had been invested in projects for broadcasting
except for a new medium wave transmitter in Dar es Salaam. The plan had
been ambitious.

> Among the aims of the information and broadcasting services are (a) the
> development of a communications system capable of welding citizens dispersed
> widely throughout the expanse of the country into a unified community; (b)
> assistance in educating and training persons who so far have not had the
> opportunity provided for them; and (c) generally providing links between town
> and country and one Region and another.[43]

The capital development of the broadcasting services during this five-year
period improved the ability of radio to reach remote parts of the country and
beyond but did nothing to improve two-way linkages between Dar es
Salaam and the regions and districts. And ironically, in view of the Minister's
remarks about business interests in broadcasting, the main beneficiary of
this expenditure was the Commercial Service and the companies using it to
advertise their products. When the new transmitter was installed, the
Commercial Service produced a brochure for prospective customers which
boasted, with some justification: 'East Africa's Most Powerful Advertising
Medium'.[44] It sometimes seemed that the Government was less interested in
broadcasting from the point of view of fulfilling the three aims mentioned in
the Plan than in what it could and should do to publicize its own policies and
activities. The Commercial Service publicized the Government *and* brought
in much-needed revenue: a combination which pleased both politicians and
Treasury officials.

During 1964 a backbencher asked about the amount of news broadcast by
TBC, saying that he thought that the Voice of Kenya broadcast more. The
Minister agreed that the broadcasting of news still needed improvement but
was glad to note that, in addition to world news, plenty of news was
broadcast about Tanganyika and Zanzibar. Significantly, he went on:

> All important speeches by the President, Ministers, Parliamentary Secretaries,
> Regional Commissioners and other TANU and Afro-Shirazi leaders were
> considered first before news from neighbouring countries and of Africa as a
> whole, and before other important news.[45]

No mention was made of the place of other Tanzanian news within this Ministerial pecking order. Indeed, at this time radio bulletins began to contain less and less of any kind of Tanzanian news other than the speeches and activities of the President, ministers, commissioners and so on. This policy was eventually modified and finally reversed some eight years later. It is highly unlikely that TBC personnel would have agreed to such criteria for news without heavy pressure from the Minister or someone else prominent in the Government. Even before it was dissolved the TBC had effectively become an arm of the Government under the Ministry of Information and Tourism, and the Minister was clearly determined to impose controls.

Mr Wakil's short answer above brought supplementary questions. Why, another member wanted to know, were the speeches of the President often cut short to make way for the programmes which follow? This was not so, said the Minister: the President's speeches were being broadcast in instalments, on different days, so that nothing should be lost. However, Nyerere was said to be personally opposed to this kind of personality cult, and eventually the policy was changed.[46] In the meantime, radio broadcasters felt obliged to give prominence to his speeches and activities as well as to those of his Ministers and other prominent officials. No one in Parliament objected: the assumption seemed to be that this was what a publicly owned radio service ought to do.

It was perhaps to be expected that during this post-independence period TANU and its politicians in Parliament would want to see the nation establish itself in a symbolic sense. Radio might help to instil a feeling of national glory and pride, even if the substance did not amount to much as yet. There was a strong belief that radio should not merely give prominence to the national leadership but also take measures to reduce foreign influence and content in its programmes. Radio had been established by foreigners and much of its programming planned by them: there was a need for everyone to feel that it was now thoroughly Tanzanian. MPs demanded a reduction in the amount of foreign music on the air. One member wanted hotels in Dar es Salaam to stop playing such music over their loudspeakers and play TBC news bulletins instead. That raised problems, said the Minister. There was always the question of what people wanted:

> The honourable member has said that it was time now to make people feel nationalism. This matter of the kind of music played is difficult because very often people request this [foreign] music . . . That is why there are request programmes. If someone wants to hear certain music then he sends in a request. . . and this is played for him. But . . . if we suddenly stop certain music I do not know whether people will approve or not. No doubt we will get many letters . . . then we will see what the people want. But at the same time we will not ignore the suggestions given by the member. But perhaps we can meet half-way, if we reduce this [foreign] music a little. Let us not make people angry.[47]

The same case could, of course, have been made about listeners' attitudes to the number and length of speeches to which they were now to be subjected. No one pointed out at the time that radio, like other media of mass communication, leaves the audience with the choice of looking elsewhere. While in the case of the press alternatives were difficult to find, in that of radio other stations existed that could be listened to if the national station was found to be boring or did not cater for listeners' tastes.

The nominal independence of the TBC was ended in 1965. By this time the only real difference was that broadcasters lost their separate status along with certain privileges in pensions and related matters, and became civil servants. As far as control was concerned, the Government had already taken over. The TBC Dissolution Bill was debated and passed into law in March 1965. Introducing the measure, Mr Wakil said:

> Radio is an important basis for the country's progress. In Tanzania, where most people are illiterate, who cannot read or understand what is happening in their own country, it is the radio alone which can educate all the people ... therefore the radio is an important asset for us and the only way to use this asset properly is to bring it under Government control.[48]

The Minister explained that the Corporation had been a British creation. In Britain the party system made it necessary for there to be an independent corporation, since broadcasting had to remain outside political conflict. In Tanzania the political system was different, and broadcasting policy should reflect the fact:

> Tanzania today embodies a one-party state. Our policy is of a special kind of *ujamaa*. The aim of TANU, its brother the Afro-Shirazi Party and the Government is to use the radio to direct people in development matters and especially in political matters as well. To any Tanzanian, TANU, the Afro-Shirazi Party and the Government are very important instruments on which his whole life depends. Therefore there is nothing to fear about what is going to be taught by the radio.[49]

There was no opposition to the measure, and Radio Tanzania Dar es Salaam (RTD) became a department of the Ministry of Information, Broadcasting and Tourism on July 1st 1965.

But it was not long before the dominance of news about ministers and politics at the centre drew protest from MPs, who said that news from their respective areas of the country was not being heard. The Minister of Information, Broadcasting and Tourism's customary reply was that communications difficulties prevented the collection of news from all parts of the country. On one occasion a member complained that no news was ever heard from Kigoma, and wondered why. The Minister denied that this was so, but his reply gave a further indication of the way news reporting was officially regarded:

> Radio Tanzania has no bias for regions because its duty is to inform the whole nation. But also the Hon. Member should remember that it would be difficult for the radio to announce on the same day every event or word which the Regional or Area Commissioner or an MP is involved in, when you come to think just how many there are.[50]

Yet there was no discussion of whether the listeners wanted to hear so much about regional and area commissioners and MPs: few politicians ever questioned the assumption that what they said and did should form the basis of daily news. In a supplementary question, another member told Parliament that many regional commissioners were 'crying out' for news of their activities to be broadcast.[51] A few days earlier, someone else had asked: 'Why don't the Information Officers follow the MPs when they tour their constituencies?'[52] The Minister replied that the duty of information officers was not only to follow commissioners and MPs but also to report on other matters. He made a similar reply to another member who insisted that radio should give better publicity to what MPs said in the House: it was not, he said, the job of his Ministry to build up the reputation of individual MPs. Immediately, another rose to his feet:

> Mr Speaker, Sir, doesn't the Minister know that much more broadcasting time is taken up with music than with educating the people? Research shows that 50 per cent is taken up with music and 41 per cent is used for informing the people in what is happening in the country. Doesn't the Minister think that the time has come for the reverse to be the practice?[53]

This time it was the then Second Vice-President, Rashidi Kawawa, who intervened:

> There is a limit to the amount of educational and development programmes people will listen to. If you force too many of these programmes on them, then eventually they will not listen at all. It is necessary to entertain the nation as well as to educate it. (Applause).[54]

But as the policy of giving a great deal of attention to politicians had become established, complaints were inevitable: certain individual politicians were given more publicity than others, which led to jealousy. Broadcasters themselves were also aware that it was easy to overdo the attention given to politicians and political news; it might make some politicians happy, but not the audience. Eventually the Government realized this, and in early 1967 there was a banner headline in the *Nationalist*: 'People's Efforts Make News'.[55] Announcing a change in policy, Idris Wakil said that from now on what ordinary people did should make the news. His remarks reflected the general alteration in TANU policy which was to be embodied in the Arusha Declaration a few days later. The idea was to move away from an elitist and centralist view of things, yet it was to be a long time before such changes were implemented in the Government's media, and it might well be argued that they have not progressed very far to this day.

There was in fact a mixture of elitism and anti-elitism in the mass media policies of the Government, which had consistently refused to introduce television on the mainland, in contrast to action taken by the Revolutionary Council of Zanzibar and the governments of most other independent African states.[56] In 1965, on being asked when television would be introduced, the Minister replied that Tanzania was not yet ready to afford such a luxury. The Government's first intention was to expand radio so that everyone would be able to receive it easily. Mr Wakil drew attention in Parliament to 'quite a few other developing countries' which had embarked on television in some haste and already found it too costly; Tanzania, he said, would have the sense to learn from their experience.[57]

Two points were considered to be crucial. One was that television should not first be introduced to Dar es Salaam and only later to other areas. However, existing technology, combined with economic considerations, made that seem inevitable. There was some optimism that experiments with direct transmission to receivers via satellites might eventually provide great opportunities for countries like Tanzania, which had a scattered population. The second crucial point was that Tanzania should not have television until it was really ready to make full use of it. Tanzanian ministers had seen Kenyan and Ugandan television and been struck by the extent to which these stations relied on imported material such as *Rawhide, Bonanza, The Lucy Show, Steptoe and Son* and the like. Mainland Tanzania would not, it was decided, have television until it could produce the bulk of the programmes itself. Little imported material was broadcast on the radio, and there were fears of cultural transference from the West to those sections of society who were, in any case, already well catered for in entertainment and information.

The Government's policy on television in mainland Tanzania could be seen as anti-elitist; the same could not be said of its policy on the press. The local press, which had flourished during the last years of colonial rule, had been allowed to die. Instead, the Government had supported a daily press in Dar es Salaam, which catered for a relatively small and mainly urban readership. Ben Mkapa, then editor of the two party daily newspapers, argued in 1967 that there was good reason for this. His two papers, *Uhuru* and the *Nationalist*, had an important educational function. The role of his papers, he told me, was to shake people in key positions out of their 'colonialist attitudes': too many of those in responsible positions had 'jumped into the shoes of the departing expatriate and taken over his whole approach to the job'. He saw the *Nationalist* as the more appropriate paper for this task. With *Uhuru*, the job was broadly the same, only here the audience was different and the object was to try and 'disabuse people of their expectations of Government'.

> We have all the time to do the explaining for the Government. Explaining price increases, the falls in the price of coffee, how much money there is in the Treasury, what needs to be done, and so on. People must be told the necessary facts which affect their position.[58]

The editor and others working on *Uhuru* were well aware that their audience was mainly urban, and they wrote accordingly. It was, perhaps, an inevitable kind of elitism.

Radio was, as we have seen, put under direct Government control only a short time after independence. But what of the press? The senior staff of the TANU press felt that, while they might not always be in agreement with everything the Government and its various ministries did or said, they were committed to its goals; the same, they believed, could not be said of the *Standard*. Though from time to time the editorial columns of both *Uhuru* and the *Nationalist* called for the Government to take the paper over, and a few MPs supported them, the *Standard* was not nationalized until February 1970. Many people took the opposite view, holding that Tanzanians should be able to read opinions and interpretations independent both of the party and the Government. The argument was partly about nationalism – there were those who resented the fact that the country's most prestigious and successful newspaper belonged to a foreign company and was edited by a European – but, more importantly, it was also about the degree of freedom which could or should be permitted. Some spoke of the need to have a press and a broadcasting service which discussed alternatives within broadly agreed policy frameworks. For example, Government- or TANU-employed journalists who had given thought to the matter told me that within the provisions of the Arusha Declaration and its main socialist objectives there was a wide range of issues concerning implementation to discuss. Some went further and stated that the press must be free to say whatever needed saying; not surprisingly, opponents of this school of thought pointed out that this gave freedom only to those who had a newspaper at their disposal. In the political framework and atmosphere of Tanzania in the post-Arusha period, it was obvious that the press was going to be controlled: 'By whom?' and 'How?' were the main questions.

In 1968 the Government introduced the Newspaper Ordnance (Amendment) Bill, which empowered the President to order a newspaper to cease publication when he considered it in the public interest to do so.[59] This Bill was gazetted only two months after the closure of one of Tanzania's few private political newspapers – the last paper which could be considered to have been in open opposition to the Government. The new law was prompted by events at the end of 1967. In that year Oscar Kambona, former Foreign Minister, TANU Secretary-General and close political associate and friend of the President, left the Government and, shortly afterwards, the country. The full story of what happened has never been reported, but it seems that Kambona had lost in a power struggle with other key figures in the Cabinet and TANU. While originally he had been fully in support of the Arusha Declaration and allied policies, later he began to attack the Government from London. In particular, in the closing months of 1967, he appears to have attempted to use a newspaper edited by his brother Otini Kambona to express his views. That paper was *Ulimwengu* ('The Universe'), a four-page weekly owned by the Tanzania Co-operative Press. This had no connection with the Co-operative Union of Tanganyika; despite the name of its owner, *Ulimwengu* was a private paper. The Government possessed no legal power to close down this paper, nor indeed any other paper at this time: its powers were restricted to refusing the initial registration of a paper, and *Ulimwengu* was registered. What had offended the Government was an issue of the paper which came out two days before Christmas 1967. Few copies ever reached the streets: it seems that most copies were seized. The editor was detained along with another Kambona brother, Mattiya, and *Ulimwengu* never appeared again.

On Thursday, 21st December 1967 another ex-minister and colleague of Oscar Kambona who had left the country at around the same time returned to Dar es Salaam: the former Zanzibar Vice-President, Kassem Hanga. He was detained on Saturday, 30th December, the same day that Mattiya and Otini Kambona were picked up and at the same time as the closure of *Ulimwengu* was announced. The press was at first unhelpful in either explaining or interpreting the events. The *Sunday News*, sister paper to the *Standard*, quoted the Government as saying that it welcomed criticism but would crush any attempt to change government by unconstitutional means.[60] Three days later the *Standard* announced that Oscar Kambona would be making a statement in London. It said that Kambona had claimed that his brother Otini had been arrested for writing an editorial 'in favour of human rights and the liberty of the individual'. This, according to the *Nationalist*, was nonsense: all the paper had done was to 'extol Kambona's ego'; the article 'excelled in lies and innuendo'.[61]

The closure of *Ulimwengu* could have been challenged in the courts had anyone felt willing, or been at liberty, to do so. Five months later the Minister of Information was asked in Parliament, during the debate on the Newspaper Ordnance (Amendment) Bill, why this new Bill was necessary if the Government had been able to close down *Ulimwengu* was it somehow to legalize what had been done already? The Minister replied:

> There are many things a proprietor of a newspaper is required to do under [the existing Newspaper Ordnance] . . . Ulimwengu erred in not fulfilling some of the conditions provided therein. Many letters were written to the owner of this newspaper reminding him that his affidavit was not complete . . . He did not comply with the Newspaper Registration under this law, and so we closed it down. If we left it free, then it would have been publishing things illegally. We tried to warn the Honourable Editor, Mr Otini Kambona, but he didn't want to listen. So we decided to close it down. If he had complied with or responded to what the Government had told him we would not have banned his newspaper because it was not our intention to do so.[62]

Part of what the Minister said may have been correct. Nevertheless the episode had shown the Government that it had no authority to ban newspapers published in Tanzania which were properly registered and also that it might have been in difficulty had it not discovered a technical irregularity in the case of *Ulimwengu*. Even with this explanation, one is not necessarily convinced that *Ulimwengu* was in the wrong, since we have only the Government's side of the story.

As things stood, although the Government was able to refuse registration to a newspaper on the grounds of some technicality or other, nothing in law prevented a person from using one of the existing, properly registered newspapers to put over a particular political line. One possible political opponent was the workers' paper *Mfanya Kazi*, published by the trade union NUTA. The union had already shown some opposition to aspects of Government policy, but this had always been voiced in a guarded or indirect way in its newspaper. Another possible opponent was *Ngurumo*. Although the latter was in the hands of people who rarely expressed anything but praise for the Government and TANU, neither of these institutions had editorial control, and there was always the possibility of its political line changing: after all, *Ulimwengu* had formerly been a firm TANU supporter. It seemed to me at the time that the Tanzanian Government feared that papers could be used as mouthpieces for dissident political groups anxious to advance their own positions. However, this was not the main argument used by the Government during the debate on the Bill in Parliament, where it met with determined opposition.

The Minister for Information and Tourism, Hasnu Makame, said that there was a need for a provision in the law for the President to ban a newspaper should this be necessary. Freedom of speech was guaranteed in the constitution and was also basic to the TANU creed; such freedom could nevertheless be abused:

> Someone can also express subversive ideas with the intention of hindering the development of the country. If such views are published and circulated in a newspaper they can bring danger to the country.[63]

In seemed that the Minister expected little opposition in Parliament, where all MPs were members of TANU. He may not have been prepared for what followed. Twenty-four backbenchers took part in the debate, most of them making speeches opposed to the Bill. One claimed that it would intimidate the press. Were members to pass it as it stood, this would be an arrogant move indeed: they would be considering themselves to be more sensible than people outside.[64] Another speaker made the point that the House was being asked to give power over the press to the presidency, not merely to its present incumbent, President Nyerere, who, he said, could be trusted not to abuse his power. There must, he said, be a place where people are free to say what they like. Nowadays a large number of the population listened to foreign radio stations and read foreign newspapers: once the Government had the power to conceal the truth within Tanzania, would it also be necessary to try to stop people sending their views to the foreign media?[65] Yet despite the extent of the opposition the Government was quite uncompromising. The Second Vice-President took over defence of the Bill in the House and turned the discussion away from considerations of press freedom to a critique of newspapers like the *Standard*, which were owned by capitalists. He asked why MPs wanted to leave the *Standard* in foreign hands. Had they forgotten the Arusha Declaration? Had they not supported it when it called for the major means of production to be taken over? How could freedom of expression be put at risk merely by the Government's saying to any one individual (the Second Vice-President was here referring to foreign capitalist press owners) that 'what you have said is of no relevance in this country and will stir up trouble and mar the peace'?[66] Mr Kawawa repeated more than once his view that the Arusha Declaration not only permitted the takeover of capitalist concerns but actually called for 'the masses' to have control of the information media.[67]

A number of important points emerged from the Vice-President's speech indicating the creation of more coherent Government attitudes to the press: these concerned its role, the limits there should be to its activities and the relationship it ought to have with the Government. Firstly, said the Government, it did not want to stifle all criticism of the way its policies were carried out. It wanted newspapers and the radio to be able to report where things went wrong, especially if this led to matters being put right. What it was not prepared to tolerate was any questioning of the basic tenets of party and Government policy. (One formed the impression that the Government was genuinely anxious about the precariousness of its policies at this time and was afraid that determined opponents might be able to sabotage these policies by questioning them through the news media.) Mr Kawawa referred to the 'confusion' which would result from people being given information which contradicted what they were being told by their own government through Government and party channels.

Secondly, a press which probed deeply and reported news that the Government wanted left unreported – for example, defence matters or other highly sensitive issues – would equally not be tolerated. No censorship would take place beforehand, but it was made quite clear that on these issues the press was expected to censor itself, to know what ought not to be reported.

Thirdly, the Government took a near-Marxist view of arguments about the freedom of the press. The idea that this was a necessary part of freedom of speech was rejected. Freedom of the press was a powerful privilege that could actually be used against other freedoms which were the property of the people as a whole. In the nature of things, only a tiny minority had the control of, or access to, the press and were thus able to exercise this freedom. In Tanzania, the Government had control of most of the media and claimed to exercise this control on behalf of the workers and peasants in order to enhance their freedom rather than to restrict it. The Government refused to accord the privately owned press the right to claim absolute freedom of expression, since this right could be used against the majority who were voiceless. The proprietors of the privately owned press, however benevolent, were nevertheless wealthy and unrepresentative of the people as a whole. The possibility that, in spite of this, an independent commercial press might act as the safeguard of people's rights against a capricious or dictatorial government was rejected out of hand. The rhetorical question was asked: 'How could a TANU government, a government elected by the people which drew its power from those people, act against the people's interests?'

The danger, from the Government's point of view, was that a well-entrenched, privately owned press would support the interests of those opposed to socialism and whose cause could be served by development along capitalist lines. The Government needed control over the media, or to have that control in reserve, not only in order to prevent such support of minority interests but also to ensure that the vitally important class of entrepreneurs and middle-level professional executive people – whose loyalty was vital to the success of any government policy – should be won over to the cause or, at the very least, not be encouraged to oppose government policies. The problem was that this class evidently preferred the 'moderate' tone of the *Standard* to the more intense political hectoring of the *Nationalist* and tended overwhelmingly to read the English language press.

Fourthly, although the Second Vice-President had outlined clearly why he felt the Government could, and even should, take over all newspapers, it neither did so nor was, at this time, intending to do so. In spite of what Mr Kawawa said about the inevitability of capitalists' misusing their press in a country like Tanzania, no plans were made at that time to take over the *Standard*. While Mr Kawawa gave many reasons why they should take over the newspaper, he gave no reasons why they did not. It was doubtless because the government was then concerned about possible foreign reaction to a takeover. Sensitive to criticism from abroad, it was endeavouring to create a more favourable impression with investors, following what this group regarded as the upheavals of the Arusha Declaration.

Lastly, the Government was obviously concerned about the way the press and radio could, by their manner of reporting, either build up or damage the reputations of political figures. Opinions may differ as to the extent of the media's influence in the field of politics and their role in the formation of public opinion, but it would be difficult to argue against what Mr Kawawa said on the subject of politicians and the media:

> Newspapermen have various tricks. They can even decorate and embellish your speech. Your speech may be a very bad one yet you can find it so wonderfully presented on the front page with some attractive and pleasing headline... the newspaper owner can work on it very nicely because he likes it – he likes the words of the speech because they help him. This is the truth and we cannot deny it... Through this skill a good speech can also turn out to be a bad one.[68]

No doubt the Second Vice-President had in mind the days when the TANU paper the *Nationalist* used to 'embellish and decorate' the speeches of Kawawa's rival Oscar Kambona whilst doing less than justice to the speeches of other ministers. There was an unspoken fear that political figures could use the press, even papers controlled by the party or government, to their own advantage or that editors and proprietors could promote certain political figures by creating a good 'image' of them in the press. As a corollary to this, there was perhaps the suspicion that some of the opposition to the Bill came from politicians who wanted an alternative press in order to enhance their own political future.

Kawawa's intervention succeeded in rallying most backbenchers to supporting the measure, and the Bill was passed. *Ngurumo's* editor commented that the new Bill did not really alter anything. Newspapers tended to get into trouble with governments, something which had happened before independence and since. There was a feeling in Parliament that the Bill would prevent the press from saying anything controversial – it would 'gag the press' – but *Ngurumo's* feeling was that prevailing practices would continue whether the Bill was passed or not.

> As newspapers our obligation is to bring hope where there is despair, and other matters like this... Parliament has passed a law which empowers the President to close any newspaper which prints undesirable news, and at once different translations were given that, Ah! Now this is the death of freedom of speech. I say No! This is not the death of freedom of speech, because if that was the aim then those who brought the Bill before the House would be the first to be caught in the trap.[69]

In other words, there was no need to fear for the freedom of speech in Tanzania: such freedom was guaranteed. If people did not exercise their rights, that was no fault of the law:

> If people don't express their opinions, ah! When a thirsty horse who has reached the water hole refuses to drink then the one who brought the horse cannot drink the water for him.[70]

The official attitude to the press reflected a lower level of concern about broadcasting. During 1967 and 1968 no one knew how many radio sets there were in Tanzania. Various statistical sources giving figures for the number of receivers show the country as having 120,000 sets. The true figure was almost certainly four to five times as great, but both Government and RTD officials conceded that there might be as many as 160,000 to 200,000 sets. None of them imagined the number was in fact as high as 500,000. They expressed surprise at the figures I produced, and they were to be even more surprised in 1973 when a survey far more extensive than mine gave the number as 1,737,000. Had it been realised just how large the audience had become and how fast it was growing, greater attention might have been paid to broadcasting during 1961 to 1968. As it was, RTD received far less investment than it needed to improve reception. Money was required not only for more powerful transmitters but also for the building of regional studio centres to make programmes for the entire country, so that RTD output would not be so Dar es Salaam-orientated. Broadcasters were conscious of their obligation to serve the whole country not only by reaching people in all areas but also by playing local music, recording local views, experiences and so on. RTD, in other words, wanted radio to be less centralized and to have a real two-way contact with its audience. But the politicians and civil servants could not agree that further expenditure on the development of broadcasting should be given priority:

> They admit radio is important and they want to control it. But they don't seem to see what further expansion is needed. 'What more do you really need?' they ask me. 'The programmes go out. The news is read. You get thousands of listeners. What more do you need?' It is difficult to convince them of the need to develop further.[71]

RTD succeeded almost in spite of itself. Unlike the press, it engaged in little self-promotion, but commercial companies helped through their advertising of transistor radios. In addition to local production by Philips at Arusha, low-cost sets were imported from Japan, Hong Kong, West Germany and the Netherlands.[72] During 1967 and 1968 a small, serviceable set with both medium and short wavebands could be obtained for as little as Sh.200/-. If the figures below from audience surveys in 1960, 1967 and 1973 are reliable, then the number of households with radio sets was growing by an average of more than 100,000 per year. This figure would have been much smaller in the early 1960s and higher at the end of the period. The growth of radio between 1950 and 1973 is shown opposite.

TANZANIA: The growth of radio and its audience
1950-1973

Year	Number of transmitters		Number of imported receivers	Licences sold	Contemporary estimates† of actual number of sets in use
1950	1 SW		n.a.	–	1,400
1952	1 SW	1 MW	n.a.	–	
1954	1 SW	1 MW	19,045	–	
1955	1 SW	1 MW	21,225	–	
1956	2 SW	1 MW	11,418	–	60,000
1957	2 SW	1 MW	14,685	–	
1958	2 SW	2 MW	10,721	20,480	
1959	3 SW	2 MW	12,486	18,176	
1960	3 SW	2 MW	12,479	18,000	72,232
1961	3 SW	2 MW	14,488	34,404	
1962	3 SW	3 MW+1*	22,520	37,620	
1963	3 SW	3 MW+1*	27,892	62,280	
1964	4 SW	3 MW	86,502	144,581	
1965	4 SW	3 MW	58,351	139,010	
1966	5 SW	4 MW	26,009	124,057	
1967	5 SW	4 MW	n.a.	113,000	500,000
1973	5 SW	4 MW + 3 regional	n.a.	–	1,787,000

*Experimental regional transmitter, later closed.
n.a. Not available.
† From surveys.

Notes:
Import figures are for imports coming from outside East Africa. They do not show how many sets were re-exported to Tanzania from Kenya. Some retailers, especially in the north, obtained supplies through Kenyan traders. Local production started in Arusha in 1965 and soon reached an annual output of more than 60,000 sets. Radio licences were introduced in 1957 and abolished in 1968.

Sources: Interview with S.H. Saidi, Senior Licensing Assistant, RTD, 28th November 1967; *Annual Trade Reports*, Tanganyika/Tanzania (1958–1966); UNESCO, Statistics on Radio and Television: 1950–1960 (Paris, 1963); Stephen Mlatie, RTD. Letter 6th May 1972; Tanganyika Broadcasting Corporation, *Annual Reports* (1956–1963); Market Research Company of East Africa, *TBC Audience Survey Report May 1960* (Nairobi, 1960); Associated Business Consultants, *Radio Audience Survey in Mainland Tanzania December 1973 – January 1974* (Beirut, 1974).

The role of the mass media in Tanzania, or any other country for that matter, is clearly defined in large measure by its content. What image of Tanzania and the world did they present to their audience? To what extent did the mass media follow interpretations of events, both national and international, which originated elsewhere? The almost total dependence of the media on the western news agencies Reuters and AFP meant that the image Tanzania received of events in Africa and the rest of the world was largely determined by those organizations. Did this affect the image Tanzanians were given of their own country? How much foreign material was actually used in the press and on the radio, and did this clash with Tanzanian cultural and political realities? What attention did the media pay to other countries which faced problems and constraints similar to those of Tanzania? And what image did the media give Tanzanians of their country as a cultural entity? I shall deal with this last question first, since I think that approaching the subject of content analysis from a cultural and qualitative perspective can be more informative than using quantitative methods which involve counting column inches and sitting with radio and stopwatch.

In his inaugural speech as President, Nyerere announced that he was setting up an entirely new ministry, that of National Culture and Youth. It represented a conscious effort to offset colonial influences and to promote a national culture which would reflect the new nation.

This, said Nyerere, was very important to nation-building:

> A country which lacks its own culture is no more than a collection of people without the spirit which makes them a nation. Of all the crimes of colonialism there is none worse than the attempt to make us believe we had no indigenous culture of our own; or that what we did have was worthless – something of which we should be ashamed instead of a source of pride. Some of us, particularly those of us who acquired a European type of education, set ourselves out to prove to our colonial rulers that we had become 'civilised'; and by that we meant that we had abandoned everything connected with our own past and learnt to imitate only European ways... When we were at school we were taught to sing the songs of Europeans. How many of us were taught the songs of the Wanyamwezi or of the Wahehe? Many of us have learnt to dance the 'rumba', or the 'chachacha', to 'rock'n'roll' and to 'twist' and even to dance the 'waltz' and the 'foxtrot'. But how many of us can dance, or have even heard of, the *Gombe Sugu*, the *Mangala*, the *Konge*, *Ngang'umumi*, *Kiduo* or *Lele Mama*?[73]

The President went on to ask how many had forgotten about African musical instruments and the kind of excitement which came from performing music and dance that was truly indigenous.

> So I have set up this new Ministry to help us regain our pride in our own culture. I want it to seek out the best of the traditions and customs of all our tribes and make them a part of our national culture.[74]

One feels that Nyerere was specifically addressing educated people like himself, who had come from different backgrounds, absorbed European culture and manners, discovered a common nationalist cause and gone through a political campaign successfully together, yet still knew relatively little about one another's cultural traditions. Tanzanians were brought up with their own musical, dance and oral traditions but at school or college were taught the language, culture and even the history of the colonial power. It was common, even after independence, for schools to be teaching more about the history and geography of the British Isles than about those of Tanzania or East Africa. And it took longer for schools to begin to teach Tanzanian or African music and literature. If the colonial culture was to go, there had to be something with which to replace it. It was feared that an emphasis on individual tribal culture might increase or encourage separatism: was it possible to find common ground out of which would emerge a truly indigenous *Tanzanian* culture? Along with many others, Nyerere believed that it was possible, but he emphasized that this should not involve the rejection of outside influences:

> A nation which refuses to learn from foreign cultures is nothing but a nation of idiots and lunatics. Mankind could not progress at all if we refused to learn from each other. But to learn from other cultures does not mean we should abandon our own. The sort of learning from which we can benefit is the kind which can help us to perfect and broaden our own culture.[75]

Demands were to be made for a complete ban on foreign music on the radio and the exclusion of particular styles of western dress, but these outbursts of cultural nationalism were felt to be an inevitable part of a cultural renaissance.

The task of establishing and encourging national cultural activities was pursued with some vigour by the new ministry. The National Dancing Troupe was immediately established, and made a study of Tanzanian dance and dance mime throughout the country; it was soon performing regularly both at home and abroad. Its members came from different parts of Tanzania and performed traditional dances from all the regions, as well as choreographing new works. Thus it was a small but important beginning.

Nevertheless, it was radio which played the greatest role in the development of music. RTD had built up a collection of Tanzanian regional music. Although its potential was never fully realized, RTD was still the single most important source of cultural material (mainly in the form of music) from the different areas. With the co-operation of music groups organized by such pan-tribal or national organizations as the TANU Youth League, the police and the National Service, RTD also promoted new music which was an amalgam of various traditions, both local and foreign.[76] However, the mounting of a recording safari in remote areas proved an expensive operation, and money was scarce, although the importance of this work was recognised. Commercially recorded music proved to be more readily available. When restrictions were placed on the amount of foreign music that could be played, more of the new urban music, which had been recorded commercially, was broadcast.

RTD's output remained heavily influenced by its geographical situation in Dar es Salaam. The listener was given only a limited picture of life outside the capital and one which was seen through urban eyes. This was perhaps inevitable, given the nature of the medium. Radio demands particular technical skills, and a person required a minimum standard of education before being accepted for training as a broadcaster – a standard that was progressively raised. The urban bias of radio was thus increased: it was virtually impossible for people who had not become urbanized to some extent to be appointed as full-time radio broadcasters.

The extent to which educational skills are needed in broadcasting can nonetheless be exaggerated. Some of the best broadcasters in Africa have had little in the way of schooling: there is a place in radio for good story-tellers, musicians and other men and women with knowledge and wisdom gained from experience rather than from formal education. But the civil service structure of broadcasting did not allow such people to be employed on a full-time basis, and when funds were short the fees paid to freelance contributors of this kind were often the first items to be cut. Unfortunately, the educational background of many radio staff may well have been to blame for the overly formal tone of many programmes, which frequently caused them to sound stilted and unnatural. Educational and factual programmes sounded dull and lifeless, when they might have inspired. There was always a marked difference in impact between those programmes where people spoke freely in an impromptu, unscripted way and those where the same subject was dealt with in scripted form. The former were usually lively and interesting; the latter, almost equally likely to be very dull indeed. If radio is to contribute effectively to the national culture, its material needs to be presented in an attractive manner. Should the message be unfamiliar and its manner of delivery unappealing or otherwise distant from the recipient, its relevance or value are unlikely to be accepted.

In the early days of radio the major part of its audience was to be found in the urban areas and among the better educated, and programmes tended to be created with this in mind. Greater emphasis was placed on urban than on rural events, a practice which did not alter substantially, even though that audience became increasingly rural and uneducated. The extent to which radio is able to cater for the tastes and interests of an urban, educated audience at the expense of a rural and less well-educated one is easily overlooked. Two factors contributed to this bias. The first lay in the fact that letters to RTD from educated people in urban areas far outnumbered those received from the less well-educated. For obvious reasons, the person with minimal education who wrote to a radio station was an exception. While radio can overcome the problem of illiteracy in reaching a mass audience in a country like Tanzania, a large part of that audience may be unable to 'talk back' to the radio because they cannot write. One of the record request programmes on RTD was *Hongera* ['Congratulations']. During 1967 and 1968 it received some one hundred and fifty cards or letters every day. The overwhelming majority of these came from Dar es Salaam and the few other urban centres around the country: a group which constituted only a minority of listeners. Nevertheless it was this group that determined which records would be played on request programmes. It was also from members of this group that comments on and criticism of radio programmes came. The second reason for urban bias was the fact that the radio broadcasters themselves lived in the towns: the people who spoke to them and commented on their programmes were living in the same environment. The politicians and officials who expressed public criticism of their work or brought pressure to bear, for whatever reason, did so mostly from an urban standpoint. All this, inevitably, showed in RTD's output.

The impact of all these divisions in Tanzania – urban-rural, tribal, educational and economic – was greatly reduced by the national language, Swahili. Without Swahili, the history of nationalism in Tanzania might have been very different. The use of a widely understood and increasingly popular language which was neither identified with any one tribal group nor with the colonial power was a great asset to the nationalists. From the earliest days, TANU promoted the maximum use of the language in political activity. This enabled the party to put across its message more efficiently and effectively than would otherwise have been the case, and helped compensate for the other serious communications difficulties within the country. Nyerere has always used Swahili at his public meetings; he once declared that he had used interpreters on only two occasions.[77] Perhaps he assumed a little too readily that his audience understood what he had to say. Nevertheless, he was probably better able to communicate directly with his people than were most other African leaders – more so, for example, than neighbouring nationalist leaders like Samora Machel in Mozambique, Milton Obote in Uganda or Kenneth Kaunda in Zambia.

Writing in 1957, Whiteley identified over a hundred language groups in mainland Tanzania, many of which were extremely small. The thirty or so largest groups accounted for about seventy per cent of the total population in the 1948 census.[78] Yet the Bantu languages of East Africa, of which Swahili is one, are closely related and have a large core of common or similar words. For these and other linguistic and cultural reasons it is relatively easy for the speaker of one Bantu language to learn another and develop a high level of competence in it. This has contributed to the widespread adoption and acceptance of Swahili.[79] For the vast majority of Tanzanians it is a second language, being the mother tongue of relatively few. In 1969 Whiteley estimated that not more than one million people in Tanzania and Kenya combined were mother-tongue speakers of the language.[80] However, he thought it was probably the second language of no fewer than ninety per cent of Tanzanians.[81]

Swahili began to spread during the nineteenth century. The language used by the ivory and slave traders as well as by European explorers like Burton, Speke, Stanley and Livingstone, it spread along the trade routes: inland from Bagamoyo, Kilwa and Mboamaji to Tabora and then south towards the gap between Lakes Tanganyika and Malawi, west to the town of Ujiji on Lake Tanganyika, north-west to Karagwe and north to Lake Victoria. By the time the Germans arrived, Swahili was well established as the language for all travellers, traders and intruders to use.[82]

There was never much doubt about which language the colonial rulers would use in local administration. By 1914, the Germans had found that they could conduct most of their correspondence with village headmen in Swahili,[83] and the British also found this a great advantage. Colonial officers were expected to learn Swahili; they could then be posted and reposted anywhere in the territory. The use of one language simplified administration, and it also simplified communication between Africans, which became increasingly important. As the use of Swahili grew, communication became easier on a territory-wide scale.[84] Furthermore, it made the emergence of a countrywide nationalist movement possible.

Not all the Christian missions felt the same about using Swahili. The Universities Mission to Central AFrica (UMCA) started using the language from the 1890s. At their centres in Zanzibar, Tanga and elsewhere, they produced hymn books and other religious literature in Swahili and started the first Swahili newspaper in 1898. The Lutheran Church, Benedictines and White Fathers also favoured the use of Swahili wherever possible, depending on where the mission was stationed; it met with a certain amount of resistance in the provinces around Lake Victoria and in the north. Some missionaries in the Sukuma, Nyemwezi, Chagga and Haya language areas preferred to use these languages in evangelism and religious literature. At some of the mission schools literacy was also taught in local languages. However, resistance to Swahili did not last. The Chagga of Kilimanjaro were perhaps the group most fiercely opposed to the increased use of Swahili, but when they elected their paramount chief in the early 1950s they were unable to agree on which of the Chagga dialects to adopt as their common language, and they, too, adopted Swahili.[85] It was a language with little or no tribal identity.

The challenge to Swahili came less from local African languages than from English. For a long time after independence, English was the language of the educated élite, just as it had largely been that of the colonial administration. TANU's campaign – and the adoption by Nyerere and his ministers of the Swahili language for most great state occasions – gave the language a status it had not previously enjoyed; but secondary education, the University College in Dar es Salaam, Parliament, the higher law courts and other important institutions still used English, which was not to be easily displaced. However, between 1961 and the present day, the progress of Swahili in these fields has been steady. It soon became the language of Parliament, then of the Cabinet and of most areas of the civil service; the law courts also began to use it. The amount of English on the radio was reduced, and government documents, which had previously been printed almost entirely in English, began to appear in Swahili during the mid-1960s.

The Government promoted Swahili as a national language not only because it was useful in administration but also because it was seen as an instrument 'for uniting the people of the nation's different tribes'.[86] Some attached an even greater importance to it:

> The Minister for Community development and Culture . . . Mr Mgonja said that the language heritage and the study of Kiswahili as a national language was part of the cultural revival. He told members that Kishwahili was a great national heritage and all was being done to enrich and spread it.[87]

But languages are not culturally neutral. Swahili's cultural heritage was by no means the cultural heritage of all. Mgonja and others have sometimes ignored the fact that Swahili was originally the language of the coastal people and not spoken in the country as a whole.[88] There were, and still are, many other regional cultures which are not Swahili but are nonetheless Tanzanian. This is certainly a problem which mitigates against the widest acceptance of the language, though the number of people resisting its use today is probably very small, composed of the older and the less well educated. My survey revealed that a few people in Sukuma-speaking areas still had difficulty in answering questions in Swahili; others who understood Swahili nonetheless asked to be interviewed in Sukuma. Moreover, despite the widespread day-to-day use of Swahili in the areas visited, many still did not use the language in their own homes. Yet its adoption as the language of primary education, and the increased mobility of people living in the country, means that the use of Swahili will spread. Despite undoubted problems in certain regions its presence as a widely-spoken African language has contributed greatly to furthering national communication in Tanzania.

Tanzania is one of the very few countries in Africa that broadcasts in only one African language plus that of the former colonial power. Swahili has been the dominant language since broadcasting began, but the widespread acceptance of it as the national language did not mean that no controversy was involved. Before independence, a daily half-hour in Asian languages had been introduced in 1959 to cater for the territory's substantial Asian minority. An audience survey showed that Asians were keen listeners to radio: in 1960, out of approximately twenty-one thousand Asian households nearly eighteen thousand (86%) had radio sets. Yet it was known that, although most Asians knew Swahili, English or both, there were still some who spoke only one of the languages of the Indian subcontinent.[89] Programmes were therefore introduced in Gujerati and Hindustani. The Tanganyika Broadcasting Corporation defended its decision by saying that, despite the fact that many Asians could speak English and Swahili, 'the language of childhood and of the home is Asian'.[90] But of course the very same argument could have been used in favour of broadcasting in any of over a hundred African languages. Swahili was the language of the home and of childhood for only a minority of Tanzanians. A Masai MP, Chief Edward Mbarnoti, used this argument to promote the use of his people's language. The use of Masai in broadcasts should be introduced for a time but should not, he said, become 'a permanent privilege'.[91] His plea was nevertheless unsuccessful. Most politicians were opposed to the idea of any special treatment for language groups, and pressure was put on the TBC to drop Asian language and even English broadcasts. Mr Sijaona, an influential and outspoken backbencher who later became a minister, said this in 1961, and it was a theme taken up by others on a number of occasions:

> Here in Tanganyika we are trying to build a nation, a nation in which all of us irrespective of colour or race shall regard ourselves to be Tanganyikans. I do not think it helps at all to foster that spirit of nationhood if the minority groups are given special treatment. Kiswahili is our national language and everyone who regards himself, or herself, to be a Tanganyikan ought to be proud to use the language of that country to which he or she belongs.[92]

In 1962, TBC policy changed. Its board had been largely Africanized, and it adopted the view expressed by Mr Sijaona.

The 'Hindustani/Gujerati Half Hour' . . . was discontinued during the last quarter of 1962 . . . It was felt that the two languages, English and Swahili, were sufficient as a vehicle for reaching unified Tanganyika and that a multiplicity of languages was likely to damage the existing unity.[93]

Further attempts were made by Asian leaders to have Asian languages reintroduced, but these were resisted. The same argument was later employed against the use of English on the radio. English language broadcasts remained but were made part of the country's external radio services. The separate English Service was ended in 1970 and incorporated into the External Service, which could be heard both inside and outside the country. The logic of this move was that, as Tanzanians understood and spoke Swahili, English language broadcasting was for non-Tanzanians. The local transmissions of the External Service were for the many expatriates working in the country who understood little or no Swahili.

Nigeria

The history of the mass media is longer and more complex along the west coast of Africa. The press in English-speaking West Africa grew up in a nationalist tradition: newspapers were the mouthpieces of emerging, campaigning, nationalist politicians. One writer has made the observation: 'To study either nationalism or the press in British West Africa is to study the other.'[94] This is very true of contemporary civilian politics in Nigeria, where the mass media occupy a central place in the new democracy. So far in our case studies we have examined only those media in one-party systems; the contrast between these and a multi-party political situation is immediate and obvious.

Just as the press gave African nationalism its primary means of dissemination and propaganda, so today, along with radio and television, it gives politicians their prime means of reaching national audiences and of attempting to secure a national following. Despite the entry for a time of media conglomerates such as the Mirror Group and Thomsons into the West African press, I think it is still fair to say that the primary motivation for producing a newspaper in Nigeria is political rather than commercial. As we shall see, Nigerian newspapers are able to command quite large circulations, but high overheads and stiff competition for limited advertising support mean that few would survive on commercial grounds alone.

During 1980-81 Nigerian spending on development projects was at the rate of about $30 million a day. A significant proportion of this expenditure found its way in to the mass media field. In these circumstances any analysis of the Nigerian news media can quickly become outdated; however, this does not mean, that an account of trends to date will not guide us towards a better understanding of present practices.

Nigeria has become the world's fifth largest oil exporter. It is unusual among oil producers both in being a democracy and in having a very large population on which to spend its wealth. In October 1979, Nigeria's hundred million people returned to democratically elected civilian rule after thirteen years of military government. The country is a federation of nineteen states, and in 1979 there were five separate national political parties, each with a degree of power, effectively controlling at least two states. Each party also has members in the Federal National Assembly. The leading party, the National Party of Nigeria (NPN), forms the Federal Government but does not have a majority in either the Senate or the House of Representatives. President Shehu Shagari, who was then the NPN presidential candidate, did not win a majority of the popular vote.

There is a considerable amount of heated dispute in Nigerian politics. Much of this is conducted through the news media, where the political atmosphere is reflected quite clearly. In 1980-81 the major media were the fifteen daily papers, twelve or so political weeklies, twenty-five radio stations and twenty television stations. A Nigerian politician who has no access to, or is not reported by, any news medium is at a grave disadvantage. The mass media report politics; they are also, in every sense, political institutions of central importance to the functioning of Nigerian democracy.

The Federal Radio Corporation (FRCN), established after the dissolution of the old Nigerian Broadcasting Corporation, is a statutory corporation whose members are appointed by the Federal Government in Lagos. Since the return to civilian rule the corporation has claimed to adopt an attitude of impartiality towards the five parties. Leaders and officials of parties other than the NPN nevertheless complain that it does not give them fair treatment. Cases of actual bias against the four parties are difficult to find, except in the special case of one faction of the People's Redemption Party (PRP), which I shall come to shortly. What happens, I believe, is that a Federal institution like the FRCN tends to report Federal Government news more often and thus leans towards support for the NPN's view of things. This is not to suggest that Radio Nigeria, as the FRCN now describes itself, either ignores or is openly or blatantly unfair to the other parties. To take just one example, FRCN Kaduna's programmes like *Democracy in Action* and *Alkawari Kayane*, give coverage of political affairs from all states and from the point of view of all parties.

In its treatment of a split in 1980-81 within the People's Redemption Party (PRP), Radio Nigeria decided to recognize Aminu Kano's leadership rather than that of the rival faction. It did so after the Federal Electoral Commission (FEDECO) decision that the officially recognised PRP was that led by Aminu Kano. In FRCN's view, therefore, the two state governors who had been expelled from the PRP led by Aminu Kano in fact belonged to no party at all, and their claim to be in the official PRP had no validity. FRCN Kaduna took this argument a step further and in 1981 stopped reporting the activities of the two expelled governors or their supporters except when these were strictly official and non-political. Nigerian Television (NTV), also federally organized and centred, took the same view. An order to this effect came from the President's office.

However, this is not a simple case of total censorship or heavy government control. The Federal Government of Nigeria cannot stifle all news it does not like. The Nigerian constitution guarantees freedom of expression, 'including the freedom to hold opinions and to receive and impart ideas and information without interference'. It also defends the right for anyone 'to own, establish and operate any medium for the dissemination of information, ideas and opinions'. The only exception to this is that no one other than a state government or the Federal Government may operate a television or radio station without the approval of the President.[95] Some of the drafters of the constitution wanted specific guarantees of press freedom, but it was eventually decided that the press should enjoy the same freedom of any Nigerian citizen, there being no need for special treatment. Constitutionally, Nigeria's press is as free as any.

Nonetheless, constitutions may of course guarantee nothing if governments are determined to defy them and if there is no recourse to an independent judiciary able to act against unconstitutional practices. With Nigeria, after only just over two years of the new system, it is still too early to be sure, but in general governments at federal and state level appear to be respecting the guarantees of freedom of expression.

The freedom and diversity of the media in Nigeria taken as a whole has been guaranteed in a rather unexpected way. Newspapers, radio and television are mostly government owned, but there are no fewer than twenty governments! These governments are formed from different parties, each with different views on national and local issues, so that while each government operates a form of censorship over the media it controls, such censorship does not necessarily block the free flow of information. What one newspaper will not print another paper may be very happy to publish; what one state radio may silence may well be carried by another. A politician denied access to one television studio might find another welcoming him very readily. And the audience of a state radio station is not entirely limited to that state.

Each of the nineteen states has its own radio station. These stations are run by boards appointed by the state governments so that they tend to act as mouthpieces of the respective state governments. The extent to which they report the activities and reflect the views of other parties and political opponents varies. In certain states, broadcasters have been disciplined for reporting political opposition. But what is censored in this way in one state has often either found its way into the radio output of another or been reported by a newspaper. In addition to these nineteen separate state radio stations, there is the FRCN, with stations in Lagos, Kaduna, Ibadan, Enugu, Owerri and at the new federal capital now being built at Abuja.

The restructuring of broadcasting in Nigeria began at the end of 1978. The idea was to leave FRCN with the responsibility for national and international broadcasting: the Nigerian government would speak with one voice to its people and to the outside world. (Previously the independence of the Broadcasting Company of Northern Nigeria, BCNN, at Kaduna and its use of powerful short wave had meant that Nigeria had two voices in international broadcasting.) Henceforth the states would have responsibility for local or regional broadcasting and were to be autonomous. No state station was intended to operate short wave (SW), but in those states where existing radio stations already used it, they were allowed to continue doing so. Other states now plan, despite federal disapproval, to introduce SW transmission and so to broadcast longer distances. Meanwhile, the FRCN has found itself without an outlet in most state capitals. In many of these the state radio is hostile to the Federal Government; the latter has therefore decided to establish FRCN radio stations in every state capital.

After the return to civilian rule, the newly formed state radio corporations, which had been set up to be independent of Federal Government authority, were immediately subjected to local political control. Some general managers of state radio stations are former NBC men or women accustomed to thinking in a national as well as a local context. Their concerns now became far more parochial and ethnic, and party considerations undoubtedly began to play a greater part. The new system definitely means a reduction in employee mobility: appointments and promotions in state stations are frequently politically and ethnically motivated, and the chances of success for local people are greater than for those from other states. This was less often the case under the NBC. The state governments, of whatever party, attach great importance to the expansion of their own mass media facilities. A number of state stations have been opening second channels, some in stereo, yet many state governments are not content merely to expand radio. New television stations and newspapers are also being established: the NTV monopoly has already been broken. Lagos State, controlled by the Unity Party of Nigeria (UPN), now has its own television station on the air, but in early 1981 it was still not possible to watch this new state television service in central Lagos. Due to a dispute over wavelengths, Lagos State's television was effectively jammed by NTV. Anger against NTV is said to have been severe, with stories of NTV staff being attacked in public. In February 1981 the Federal Government decided that there was insufficient room on the VHF television band; the new state television services would therefore have to use the UHF band. At that time few television sets in Nigeria had the facility to receive UHF, and some state government spokesmen have accused the Federal authorities of deliberately making things difficult for any new state television station.

Until the commencement of the Lagos state television, NTV had a monopoly. Local radio stations in the state capitals were handed over to these states in 1978, but the same policy did not apply to television. The NTV, with its headquarters in Lagos, had television stations in all nineteen state capitals which link up at certain times – especially for the main evening news bulletin – and have federally appointed management. Governors of states whose ruling political parties are in opposition to the Federal Government have announced plans to start their own channels. In addition to Lagos at least ten other states have well-advanced plans for their own television stations. In Ondo, Kano and Plateau States new television establishments already exist, staff have been recruited, contracts with equipment suppliers have been signed and people have been sent abroad for training. Similar plans have been set in motion in Bendel, Gongola, Oyo and elsewhere.

In Jos, capital of Plateau State, the NTV station is still relatively new. The first General Manager there, Dr Girgis Salama from Egypt, has been asked by Governor Solomon Lar to set up Plateau State Television in direct competition with the television station Salama himself had launched. By early 1981 Dr Salama had already taken to the new station over half the NTV Jos staff, chiefly men and women he had originally recruited. The state allocated twelve million naira to the venture in the 1981 budget. The expenditure of public money on this, yet another television service, has been criticized in some quarters, but the Governor told me his decision was based on the fact, as he saw it, of NTV's pro-Federal bias. In his view the NTV paid insufficient attention to what the Plateau State Government was doing. When established, Plateau State Television will reach few people. Initially, the transmitters will serve only Jos, and others will later be built elsewhere; but most people do not have mains electricity. The use of UHF rather than VHF will further restrict the coverage possible. Television viewing will continue to be restricted throughout Nigeria by the high cost of sets, the difficulty of obtaining good, inexpensive maintenance, the underdevelopment of mains electricity supplies (power failures are frequent occurrences), and the insufficient number of transmitters.

What of the media that are federally owned, of which the most important are the FRCN and NTV? Politicians from those four parties not in the Federal Government claim that federal radio and television are ordered either to ignore or play down news favourable to them. At a meeting of some state governors from these parties in March 1981, an outspoken communiqué was issued:

> The governors considered what might have been the motive of the NPN Federal Government in wanting to monopolise the control of radio, television and newspapers. They recalled that in 1965, when elections were held into the then Western House of Assembly, the NNDP Government of the day announced false results and compelled all the mass media to carry false results... This led to a violent reaction by the people and to the collapse of the first republic. The governors noted that the authors of that incident are now in the leadership of the NPN. There is no doubt that if they gain control of all the mass media, they will repeat their trick of 1965 in 1983, by announcing false results, declaring themselves winners fraudulently and then proceeding to form the next government. The governors decided that the public must be alerted to the dangers inherent in the steps being taken by the Federal Government to monopolise the mass media so that public opinion may be mobilised to stop the NPN from plunging this great nation into another period of darkness.[96]

No evidence was produced to support this statement. The nine state governors of the Unity Party of Nigeria (UPN), the Great Nigeria People's Party (GNPP) and the People's Redemption Party (PRP) have nonetheless complained more vigorously about Federal policy towards the mass media than about almost anything else. They have complained, above all, that they are not adequately reported by the federally owned media during or after the monthly meetings which they have held regularly since coming to power in October 1979. There do seem to be some grounds for their complaint.

In February 1981, the nine governors were joined by three governors of states where the Nigeria People's Party (NPP) is in power. They issued a statement criticizing the Federal Government's proposals on the allocation of revenue to the various constituent parts of the federation, including the states. The statement, issued jointly by thirteen out of nineteen governors in the federation, was a newsworthy event by any standards, and yet it was either played down or ignored by the FRCN and NTV. The view of these two organizations, as far as I have been able to discover, runs something like this. The 'opposition' governors imagine themselves to be more important than they really are; they have state, not federal, responsibilities; their comments on federal matters should therefore not be regarded as of primary importance; and, if they were reported fully at all times, this would be giving them a greater prominence in national affairs than they deserve.

This argument is not without some validity. Nigeria's constitution is still very new, and no one yet knows how it really works. Politicians and others are trying to discover the limits of power. The news media can, by the way they report and by the significance they attach to personalities, events and the statements of individuals, colour the attitudes of the public and in turn influence the way in which the constitution is interpreted and the political system works. The problem for the media is that they find it very difficult to secure agreement across the political spectrum as to what would be accepted as impartially presented news.

Despite evidence of external controls, both the NTV and the FRCN are aware of the need to find a position of impartiality that can be perceived as such by political opponents. They are aware that to be labelled as the mouthpiece of the Federal Government alone, or worse still, as that of the ruling party, the NPN, would greatly damage their credibility. It would be simply untrue to charge either of them with strict censorship of controversy and opposition: they both regularly report controversy, including the most outspoken criticism of the Federal Government and its policies. The broadcasting of discussions and debates between politicians of widely different positions takes place regularly and, when interviewed, critics of the Federal Government appear to be given the same kind of deferential treatment as Federal spokesmen. For example, Dr Yusuf Bala Usman, political secretary to the then Governor of Kaduna State, was interviewed on NTV Kaduna in February 1981 and asked for his views on Libyan policies in Chad. Bala was outspokenly critical of Nigerian foreign policy which, he said, helped French 'imperialism' and French-supported 'puppet regimes' in West Africa. The tone of the interviewer was respectful, as if Bala Usman were an unquestioned authority on all matters concerning international relations.

Though neither NTV nor FRCN can be regarded as unqualified spokesmen for the Federal Government, the state radios are certainly partisan spokesmen for their respective state governments and are seen as such by their political opponents. Thus in July 1981 a violent demonstration took place in Kano against a particular policy of the Governor. A mob attacked Kano government offices and burnt down the state radio station. The radio was referred to by Governor Rimi's opponents as 'Radio Rimi'.

The attitudes of governors to the mass media vary, but most are reported to bring pressure to bear on the press, radio and television. In those states whose governments have refused to have anything to do with the presidential liaison officers appointed by the President to set up offices in the nineteen state capitals, radio station staff have been likewise forbidden to make contact. Censorship and control are nevertheless often made to look absurd. In the NPN-controlled Niger State in January 1981, a heated political controversy arose between the governor and the assembly. At first the state radio station did not include the matter in its regular news programmes; nonetheless, the story was being broadcast by the state radio. FRCN Kaduna's Hausa current affairs programme *Alkawari Kayane* had reports directly from its own correspondent in Minna which were carried in the FRCN programme being relayed there by Radio Niger. The station had two alternatives: either to drop a popular, well-produced current affairs programme that many could pick up direct from Kaduna anyway, or to report the story and reflect it in their own news bulletins. They chose the latter course of action.

Some state governments also spend large sums of money on the press. In 1981 Nigeria had fifteen daily newspapers, almost all of them highly partisan. A few were in the hands of private companies, but the majority were owned either by the Federal or state governments. State governments were planning to start new daily newspapers in Kano, Minna and Maiduguri. Yet there is insufficient advertising to support fifteen daily newspapers: more papers are chasing less advertising, in competition with both radio and television. State newspapers are therefore funded out of public money, and there have been attempts to follow the example of the *Daily Times*, funded from the profits made out of various commercial activities. In 1980 and 1981 Plateau State's *Nigerian Standard* was losing money heavily. Investments were made in a multi-storey office block in Jos in the hope that its rents would help pay for the newspaper, but the building was still largely empty six months after completion. Niger State hopes to fund its projected daily paper with revenue from the printing of exercise books and the like.

While it is difficult to give definitive answers to questions about control, the prevailing pattern does seem to be loose and informal: there seem to be few cases of actual censorship. Most media professionals appear to know what is expected of them in their various organisations, each of which has different political backers, and the media product tends to be created accordingly.

Nigeria has a pluralist mass media system. It is nevertheless a fractured kind of pluralism which reflects the political situation and in turn helps, to a large extent, to define and create the situation it reports. A great deal of attention is being paid to the media there. It is surely significant that when the government of newly independent Zimbabwe was seeking finance to buy out South African interests in the country's newspapers and establishing a new framework within which its press, television and radio could operate, it went to Nigeria both for finance and for advice. Nigeria's mass media are a vital part of the new democracy: everyone wants to be heard, each party wants a platform and each government wants a mouthpiece. At present the NPN and the Federal Government have access to, or a strong influence in, national radio and television networks and six daily newspapers. The seven NPN-ruled states each have their own radio station. The UPN has one state television station (a further four are planned), five state radios and three daily papers. The NPP is building television in its own states, while it has three state radios and three daily newspapers. The GNPP and PRP possess the state radios in the two states they each control, and the PRP government in Kano State has started newspapers there.

This is, of course, a crude over-simplification: in each case, there is a difference between the relationships. The *Nigerian Standard*, for example, can be described as the mouthpiece of the Plateau State Government and even of the Plateau State NPP, but not the NPP nationally. Kano State Radio is the mouthpiece of the government of Governor Abubakar Rimi, which is a very different thing from being a PRP radio station; indeed, the PRP, led by the late Aminu Kano, had the doubtful distinction of being without any mass media outlet at all during most of the period between the 1979 and 1983 elections.

In the two years following the return to civilian rule the activity of a considerable number of the news media became increasingly partisan. When President Shagari went on a state visit to Britain in March 1981, the large press corps accompanying him included no representative of any 'opposition' newspaper or broadcasting organisation. The only news medium represented which was neither federally run nor NPN-supporting was the Lagos newspaper the *Punch*. This paper, whose own political position is uncertain, is perhaps one of the freest spirits in Nigeria's mass media constellation.[97] On the day after President Shagari's arrival in Britain, one UPN state newspaper reported nothing of the visit, commenting instead in an editorial that he should not have left the country at a time when the doctors were on strike: it had been 'unpatriotic' for him to do so.[98] Most radio stations in non-NPN states had already stopped taking the national news from FRCN in Lagos, and so it is probable that they too ignored the event.

Concerned about its lack of a voice in local radio, the Federal Government has now decided to reverse the policy of the previous military regime which broke up the NBC in 1978. State governments will continue to have their own radio stations – that much is guaranteed by the constitution – but in 1981 the FRCN was authorized to draw up plans for the setting up of its own stations in every state. The reflection of political partisanship in the establishment of broadcasting stations could, if current trends continue, lead to a near-doubling of the present number of radio and television stations so that each state capital will have two of each: one which is part of the federal system and the other belonging to the state broadcasting service.

The mass media of Nigeria have political backers and are therefore given a political role which emphasizes the expression of opinion and places far less importance on the reporting of facts. In December 1980, there was a serious outbreak of rioting by religious fanatics in the northern city of Kano. The uprising was put down by the action of the police and the army, and an unknown number of people were killed, among them Muhammadu Marwa Maitatsine, leader of the fanatical sect which was at the centre of the trouble. At the tribunal of enquiry set up later, the police gave evidence that he had died of gunshot wounds and been found buried in a shallow grave. However, shortly afterwards, curio-sellers in Kano were seen to be selling photographs of the man, his wives and followers, and of some of the incidents that had taken place in December. One picture showed Maitatsine in police custody, apparently alive. This was later reported by the BBC and produced the following response in the *New Nigerian*, a Federal Government-owned newspaper published in Kaduna:

> Until recently, nobody doubted the official version of the circumstances leading to the death of Alhaji Muhammadu Marwa Maitatsine . . . He was said to have died of gunshot wounds at Watari village near Kano. Yet a BBC correspondent who claimed to have visited Kano during the fanatics' uprising . . . said that Maitatsine died while in police custody. This assertion would suit Governor Abubakar Rimi of Kano State very well. But my instinct tells me that this is but another way of discrediting the Nigeria Police Force. At best it is another attempt to set the country on another three billion naira wild goose chase. Enough is enough.[99]

Quite apart from the misreporting here, and the extraordinary exaggeration – the tribunal cost nowhere near three billion naira – the piece is notable for its complete lack of concern for the facts. Instead, what matters is to answer the question: 'In whose interests are "facts" reported or disputed?' There has been another, more recent, example of this. In March 1981 it was reported from Nigeria that troops from the neighbouring Republic of Benin had occupied villages in Sokoto State. A correspondent of the Federal Government's News Agency of Nigeria (NAN) reported that the Benin flag had been seen flying at places within Nigeria and beyond the recognised border. It was also reported that the Governor of Sokoto had decided to take up the issue with the federal authorities in Lagos. Then in April, President Kerekou of Benin visited Lagos. After his talks with President Shagari, the entire story was denied by both sides and attributed to 'enemies' of both countries. The *Nigerian Standard*, owned by the Plateau State Government, took up this theme in an editorial which described the reports as the 'handwork of some adventurers' and claimed that certain western nations were envious of the stability of African states and the cordial relations they enjoyed with one another. The paper urged its readers to be on their guard. It omitted to point out that the story had come entirely from Nigerian, and mainly official, sources.

There is a shortage of determined, energetic and independent-minded newsmen and women. Few journalists ever cover stories that require patience, time and money. Nigerian newspapers, radio and television stations compete for stories. As a result, stories pass them by – sometimes even those right under their noses. A spirit of enquiry is lacking: no one, save a few politicians, seems to ask questions. Journalists rarely investigate, tending to report only the words and actions of others. This is not entirely the result of political control, since the privately owned press shows no greater inclination towards investigative journalism. In Nigeria, freedom of the mass media seems to be valued mainly as the freedom to criticize rather than to discover something worth reporting. It may be that the task of thorough investigative reporting is really too costly and difficult. Facts and figures which are relatively easy to obtain in other (including many African) countries are extraordinarily hard to get hold of in Nigeria. The telephone service is still quite inadequate. Postal services between urban centres are slow and unreliable; reference works on that country, when obtainable, are full of inaccuracies. Generally, the only way to find something out is to go and see the individual concerned; however, appointments cannot be made when the phone refuses to work. One goes in person to see the relevant official who may be able to answer a question, only to find he is 'not on seat' – perhaps he, too, is trying to find someone! As a result journalists in Nigeria either depend on press releases, speeches, statements and hand-outs or go on hearsay, rumour and stories fed to them by politicians. Such material is generally impossible to check, and the only way to get a response may be to print or broadcast. The media regularly feed off each other's stories: a practice which may be defensible where the original story is an accurate one but which can otherwise lead to the dissemination of a falsehood.

In most liberal democratic countries there is some measure of agreement in the news media on political facts. News media which claim to be non-partisan attempt to discover the 'middle ground' and to maintain a balance between the different sides in political arguments. Such middle ground is as yet quite undefined in Nigeria, extremes being apparent on all sides. This fractured pluralism, as I have described it, contains few points of common agreement. Consequently, the man in the Kaduna street who watches an NTV report, hears the same story over the state radio and then reads about it in three or four daily papers receives several interpretations of the same event which are very different from one another – so much so that they may appear to be reports of separate events.

The interesting question for the future is: whose definition or interpretation of political reality is likely to win? On that hinges much of Nigeria's political future. The rival politicians know this, which is why they are paying so much attention to the news media.[100]

Notes

1   *Zambia Daily Mail*, 8th May 1972. Unless otherwise stated, I am referring to the mass media situation in Zambia during the period of my research, 1970 to 1973.
2   Graham Mytton, *Zambia Press Directory*, ZBS Research Project, Institute for African Studies (Lusaka, 1971).
3   Peter Fraenkel, *Wayaleshi* (London, 1959), p. 135.
4   Zambia Broadcasting Corporation, *Radio Listenership Survey of Zambia: Main Urban Areas* (Salisbury, 1965), tables 2 & 11.
5   Graham Mytton, *Listening, Looking and Learning*, Institute for African Studies (Lusaka, 1974), pp. 29-32. Expatriates were excluded from the survey.
6   *Ibid.*, pp. 34-37.
7   *Ibid.*, pp. 40-47.
8   For the most comprehensive analysis of the complex language situation in Zambia, see Mubanga Kashoki, 'The Language Situation in Zambia' in Sirarpi Ohannessian and Mubanga E. Kashoki, *Language in Zambia*, International African Institute (London, 1978).

⁹   For a fuller analysis and discussion of the broadcast language controversy, see Graham Mytton, 'Language and the Media' in *Language in Zambia* and *Listening, Looking and Learning*. During the national audience survey interviewers used only the seven 'official' languages in their interviews. Difficulty was encountered with only a tiny proportion of respondents. Listeners also admitted that they could understand the broadcasts in those languages intended for them. To give just one example, Chikunda speakers in Eastern Province had made demands to have their language recognized and broadcast. But none of them expressed any difficulty in understanding the broadcasts in Nyanja and all were able to answer questions put to them by us in that language.

¹⁰   *Times of Zambia*, 5th May 1972.

¹¹   SOFRECOM (Société Française d'Etudes et de Réalisations d'Equipements de Télécommunications), *Preliminary Study of a Plan for the Development of Radio Broadcasting in the Republic of Zambia* (Paris, 1967). The estimate for television assumed that at the same time a national network of FM stations would be built for the radio service to cover the entire country. Costs would therefore be shared between TV and radio. The radio share of the cost would have been between K16.8 million and K20.4 million. Without the simultaneous development envisaged, costs would be very much higher.

¹²   Zambia Parliamentary Debates, 8th January to 12th March 1971, col. 1288. It was not unusual for members of the government to speak out in Parliament against the policies of a department other than their own.

¹³   *Ibid.*, col. 1289.

¹⁴   *Times of Zambia*, February 17th, 1971.

¹⁵   *Zambia Parliamentary Debates*, 8th January to 12th March 1971, cols. 64-65.

¹⁶   *Ibid.*, col. 1314.

¹⁷   *Ibid.*, col. 1350.

¹⁸   I am indebted to Helene Freilem, Joseph Mwanza and Stephen Kapoyo for these interviews.

¹⁹   Some notes on radio programmes:
Nation and Humanism – political propaganda presentation, in all eight languages.
Pocheza M'madzulo – 'By the Fireside', a famous and immensely popular story-teller's weekly half-hour. Although in the Nyanja language, this programme was also popular among the speakers of other languages.
Kabusha Takolelwe Bowa – 'He who asks does not eat poisonous mushrooms.' Listeners' questions on various social issues are discussed and answered. This programme in Bemba was matched by similar programmes in other Zambian languages, including *Ndidzatani* in Nyanja.
Malikopo – one of the longest-running programmes on ZBS. It was a serial radio play with a kind of anti-hero, Malikopo, who was for ever getting into trouble of one sort or another. It usually had a moral point and it seemed to be very popular, not only among Tonga speakers.

²⁰   The letters were selected from those sent to *Kabusha Takolelwe Bowa* in April 1972.

²¹   Stephen Mpashi: *Chigeye*, Gallotone GB1847, quoted in Peter Fraenkel, 'Some African Songs of Northern Rhodesia'. I am indebted to Peter Fraenkel for permission to quote from his research into African music of the period. The translations are his.

²²   The Masuku Choir, *Tuli Mbombo*, Central African Broadcasting Service, Lusaka recording.

²³   *Shalapo Nomba Naya*, Gallotone GB1854. Alick Nkhata later became the Director of ZBS. After he retired, he became a farmer but was killed during a Rhodesian raid near his farm in 1979.

24   Thomas Mwewa, *Abanakashi ba Muno Kalale*, Central African Broadcasting Service, Lusaka recording.
25   ZBS English language news bulletin, May 2nd 1972, 0600 and 0800. Also seven Zambian language bulletins between 1245 and 1335.
26   ZBS English language news bulletin, May 1st 1972 at 1800.
27   Graham Mytton, *Listening, Looking and Learning*, pp. 53-63.
28   Ainslie, *Press in Africa*, p. 114.
29   *Five-Year Plan 1964-69*, pp. 62-65.
30   Tanganyika, *Parliamentary Debates*, 16th February 1961: 117.
31   *Ibid.*
32   *Ibid.*, 123.
33   *Ibid.*, 18th June 1962: 556-557
34   *Ibid.*, 19th June 1963: 623.
35   Although two Zanzibaris in succession were to hold this portfolio from 1964 to 1970, their responsibilities were confined to the mainland. The islands had a completely separate Ministry of Information.
36   *Parliamentary Debates*, 30th June 1964: 836.
37   William Tordoff, *Government and Politics in Tanzania* (Nairobi, 1967), pp. 163-164.
38   *Parliamentary Debates*, 30th June 1964: 841.
39   *Ibid.*
40   Tanganyika and Zanzibar, *Tanganyika Five Year Plan for Economic and Social Development 1st July 1964 - 30th June 1969*, 2 vols. (Dar es Salaam, 1964) vol. 2, pp. 62-63.
41   Tanzania, *Second Five Year Plan*, vol. 2, p. 2.
42   In the final year of the 1964-69 Plan, for example, Sh.2,067,200/- was spent on tourist projects in National Parks. No money was spent on information or broadcasting projects in 1969. Tanzania, *Appropriation Accounts 1963-1969*, p. 240.
43   *Five Year Plan 1964-1969*, vol. 1, p. 75.
44   Radio Tanzania, Dar es Salaam, Commercial Services, Advertising Rate Card (1967).
45   *Parliamentary Debates*, 8th September 1964: 14.
46   One Minister of Information who insisted on presidential news stories leading all the news bulletins on RTD said, when confronted with the objection that the President wanted the practice to end: 'That is just Mwalimu's modesty. He is, however, the President.'
47   *Ibid.*, 30th June 1964: 854-855. In December 1975 it was announced that no European music would be allowed on the National Programme. RTD, Swahili News Bulletin, 27th December 1975.
48   Tanzania, *Parliamentary Debates*, 16th March 1965: 40.
49   *Ibid.*
50   *Ibid.*, 21st June 1966: 563-564.
51   *Ibid.*
52   *Ibid.*, 15th June 1966: 249.
53   *Ibid.*, 24th June 1966: 887.
54   *Ibid.*
55   *Nationalist*, 16th January 1967.
56   The stark contrast in mass media policies between islands and mainland is illustrated by the fact that Zanzibar had the first colour television service in Africa in 1973, while even the importation of television sets was banned on the mainland.
57   *Nationalist*, 26th June 1965. There is some irony in this remark. Idris Wakil is a Zanzibari.

58 Interview with Ben Mkapa, Editor, *Nationalist* and *Uhuru*, 3rd November 1967.
59 Tanzania, *Gazette*, Bill Supplement, 1st March 1968, No. 2, pp. 15-16.
60 *Sunday News*, 31st December 1967.
61 *Nationalist*, 6th January 1968. The interesting point to note here is that the *Nationalist* made no reference to Kambona's activities in London until after the *Standard*. It is probable that the party paper would have ignored the story if it had not been reported in the *Standard*.
62 *Parliamentary Debates*, 3rd May 1968: 205-206. Given that three detentions took place on the same day that the paper was closed and that the Government had made a statement about subversive activities, this was a somewhat disingenuous reply. Otini Kambona was not in any position to put his side of the story.
63 *Parliamentary Debates*, 2nd May 1968: 96-97.
64 *Ibid.*, 97-98.
65 *Ibid.*, 98-99 and *Ngurumo*, 3rd May 1968.
66 *Parliamentary Debates*, 3rd May 1968: 188.
67 The Second Vice-President was referring to the section on the taking over of the major means of production, where the Declaration said that the way to build socialism 'is to ensure that the major means of production are under control and ownership of the Peasants and Workers themselves through their Government and their Co-operatives'. The major means of production are mineral resources, power, banks, etc. Communication was included, but in the context would appear to have referred to telephones, posts, telex and other means of communication of importance to commerce and industry. No one at the time appeared to think that 'communications' here referred to the mass media, and I had not seen this interpretation given anywhere else before this speech by Kawawa.
68 *Parliamentary Debates*, 3rd May 1968: 195.
69 It was often difficult to get the real meaning of a *Ngurumo* editorial. It seems however that the editorial writer was cleverly avoiding attacking the new Bill by saying that it would make no difference to *Ngurumo*. *Ngurumo*, 4th May 1968, and 7th May 1968.
70 *Ibid.*
71 Interview with Martin Kiama, Director of Broadcasting, 28th November 1967.
72 Justinian Rweyemamu, *Underdevelopment and Industrialisation* (Nairobi, 1973), pp. 126-127.
73 Julius Nyerere, *Freedom and Unity/Uhuru na Umoja* (Dar es Salaam, 1967), p. 186.
74 *Ibid.*, p. 187.
75 *Ibid.*
76 One of the most striking and popular examples of this was a song performed by the TANU Youth League Choir, *Azimio in Arusha* ('Arusha Declaration'), which used traditional melody forms with western-style harmony. This and other similar songs could accurately be described as national (rather than tribal) music.
77 Wilfred Whiteley, *Swahili: The Rise of a National Language* (London, 1968), p. 65.
78 Whiteley, 'Language and Politics in East Africa', *Tanganyika Notes and Records*, June-September 1957, pp. 159-160.
79 Mohammed H. Abdulaziz, 'Tanzania's National Language Policy and the Rise of Swahili Political Culture' in *Language Use and Social Change*, ed. W.H. Whiteley (London, 1971), pp. 160-161.
80 Whiteley, *Swahili*, p. 3.
81 *Ibid.*, p. 107.
82 *Ibid.*, p. 52.
83 *Ibid.*, pp. 60-61.

84 Marcia Wright, 'Swahili Language Policy 1890 - 1941', *Swahili*, 35, March 1968.
85 Whiteley, *Swahili*, p. 12.
86 *Nationalist*, 1st August 1966.
87 *Ibid.*, 27th June 1966.
88 W.H. Whiteley, 'Ideal and Reality in National Language Policy: A Case Study from Tanzania', mimeo, University College, Dar es Salaam (no date).
89 Tanganyika Broadcasting Corporation, *Audience Survey Report 1960*, pp. 1-7.
90 TBC, *Annual Report, 1960*, p. 9.
91 Tanganyika, *Parliamentary Debates*, 19th June 1962: 621-623.
92 *Ibid.*, 15th February 1961: 115.
93 TBC, *Annual Report 1962-63*, p. 7.
94 William Hatchten, *Muffled Drums* (Ames, Iowa, 1971), p. 144.
95 *Constitution of the Federal Republic of Nigeria* (Lagos, 1979), pp. 18-26.
96 *West Africa*, April 6th 1981.
97 It is significant that the *Punch*, which is privately owned, is not distributed widely. It concentrates on sales in Lagos and some other more easily accessible centres, presumably to maximize advertising revenue and reduce overheads. The political press spends much more money on distribution with the obvious intention of increasing political influence.
98 *Nigerian Tribune*, 18th March 1981.
99 *New Nigerian*, 18th March 1981.
100 Moreover, the government's concern about the political impact of the mass media was reflected in the new Electoral Act passed in August 1982. The Act, which will govern the elections to be held in 1983 and all subsequent elections contains a significant section on the mass media. It requires that all newspapers, radio and television owned by either the federal or state governments should, for a period of three months before the election and one month after, come under the supervision of advisory councils made up of members of all parties. The intention is to ensure that no party in control of any government anywhere in Nigeria can control the news or other content of publicly owned media during the election. The provision does not apply to the privately owned news media. Critics of the Act have pointed out that committees, however well-intentioned, can hardly be expected to work with the speed required by a competitive news medium. They also point out that if a newspaper or radio or television station disobeys the instruction of these advisory councils, there is nothing that can be done. The freedom of the press to report is protected by the constitution. When signing the Bill on August 6th, President Shagari said he did not like this section and hoped the National Assembly would think again. *FRCN*, Lagos, 6th August 1982.

6
Roles and Controls

The relationship between communications and social and political structures is a close one. Indeed, as I hope I have shown, the discovery of the lines of communication in society can tell us a great deal about the nature and structure of society. In that sense, as in many others, this book has been more than a little inadequate: I have concentrated on modern forms of mass communication and have largely ignored other types. I have been struck particularly by the fact that in very recent history an enormous number of people in Africa have become members of that modern collectivity, the mass media audience.

It has been noted that the post-war increase in the number of states on the world map coincided with the arrival of radio in the less developed areas of the world, especially in Africa. However, the members of the nationalist movements in most of the new countries came initially from within a fairly small political élite. In certain countries they were able to use the fledgling mass media to build up a nationalist movement, whilst elsewhere the sentiment of nationalism proved difficult to establish and maintain beyond a relatively limited, select group. Some new countries have been established on weak foundations and had little popular support. The creation of popular commitment to new political structures was often viewed by the new rulers as a task of high priority: a vital component had to be the establishment of networks of communication without which no kind of human organisation could exist.

Radio can play a major part in developing such networks. The fastest and most cost-effective of the modern mass media, it can overcome the barriers of distance and illiteracy; and, though providing a somewhat restricted kind of national communications network wherein the authority and voice of central political power can be greatly enhanced, it can also be effective in supplying limited but vital information to constituent parts of the new societies.

What we see in Tanzania, Zambia, Nigeria and elsewhere is an uneven development of communications. Radio sometimes reaches remote places before roads have been built. In Nigeria, colour television and a wide choice of daily newspapers have arrived before the provision of adequate telephone and postal services. The mass media cannot replace other forms of communication and are limited in what they can do. In Africa, these inevitable limits are frequently made even more restrictive by the way the media are run. In most cases the media are centralized; consequently, the information they carry tends to come from the political centre. Because of this they generally provide few links between the separate constituent parts of the wider political or national system. Radio in particular provides a greatly improved means of downward communication, superior to any other, but it receives little feedback: a fact which may have serious consequences for the political system – and for society as a whole – as the mass media audience grows. Radio stations, television stations and newspapers in the less developed countries do little to improve communications from the constituent parts of a society to its political centre. They rarely possess the facilities which would enable them to take this kind of activity very far.

The content of mass communications in many new African countries has tended to be heavily dominated by exhortation and command. The communicators – who are, not unfrequently, employees or even members of the government – are less receptive to information coming back from the people they address. Thus the mass media may actually increase the widening gap between rural and urban life and culture. It is in the towns that most journalists work and most photographs are taken; it is also there that news copy is written, programmes are produced and, finally, that papers are printed. This represents a major departure from the communications patterns that preceded the mass media. We see the arrival of specialized, skilled, professional communicators who generally operate within a particular section of the society they are communicating with. While it is true, as we saw in each of the three case studies, that the media usually make efforts to reflect the broader society, the attention given to urban affairs, problems and culture is nevertheless greatly disproportionate.

My intention in this final chapter is to attempt to see if there is any sense in which we can talk of a mass media role. Do they have a distinctive and identifiable role? There will probably be a distinction between the role designed for the media by those who own and control them and the part they actually play in day-to-day social life. One might also expect there to be a difference between the media's own self-image and what can be demonstrated by looking at the media from the perspective of sociology or political science. What follows is in no way comprehensive, but I hope it will lead those studying their own national media to look more closely at what the media really do and what the audience actually use them for.

The media in Africa and in many other less developed areas of the world are frequently established, supported, subsidized and staffed by the State. They are sometimes part of the very apparatus of government, requiring inputs of cash and other resources in order to survive. They are usually judged by those in power as being of considerable importance for the exercise of that power. In situations where State and government become identified as one, the news media become the public voice of the State and no alternative voice may be permitted.

This is not, of course, the case everywhere. There are privately owned newspapers and, in Nigeria, there are even alternative voices in television and radio. In such a situation the news media may provide platforms or publicity for alternative groups. It was partly this factor which led the Tanzanian Government to take further control of the press in 1968. News media capable of reaching an audience independently of the government or the State are perceived as a threat to the existing power structure. In the new states, where the institutions of government are fragile, and economic and development problems are acute (and, in many cases, getting worse rather than better), a free press permitted to question policies designed to deal with these problems is unlikely either to last or to remain free for very long.

The modern mass media do not merely replace traditional means of communication by providing them with new means of achieving the same result: radio, television and the press actually introduce social relationships that are entirely new. In Tanzania, certain individuals who held positions of political power feared this aspect of mass communications. The mass media have the power to speak directly to a large, scattered and undifferentiated audience; through them, information can now be transmitted independently of socially structured lines of authority and status in society. However, in practice, access to the media is not public, equal or free, and control of it generally passes to those who already have political power. At the audience end, too, the direct impact of radio, for example, can be mitigated by powerful social factors. The first people to have radio (or television) tend to be those occupying positions of authority or prestige in the existing social order. Thus Wilbur Schramm noted the arrival of a radio set in a previously isolated Arab village:

> I watched a radio receiver, the first any of the villagers had seen, put into operation in the head man's house. The receiver promptly demonstrated that knowledge is power. It became a source of status to its owner; he was the first to know the news and controlled the access of others to it.[1]

I also noted in Tanzania that people with status and position in society were significantly more likely to be radio listeners and newspaper readers. Their position did not arise initially from their access to the mass media – in many cases, they had held posts of authority or high social status before the arrival of radio – but their possession of a radio set or ability to read a newspaper served to enhance their authority.

However, this situation was unlikely to last. Already in Tanzania radio reaches the homes of many hundreds of thousands who are illiterate and hold no position of social or political importance. Here and elsewhere radio has brought new relationships into being. Schramm expressed this point well in another observation made in the same village:

> The most impressive demonstration of the impact of that radio was the scene when a group of villagers – who had previously known higher government chiefly through the tax collector or a soldier – heard for the first time a spokesman of their leaders invite them to take part in governing their country. The surprise, the incredulity, the rather puzzled hope in their faces made an unforgettable picture.[2]

Looked at from the perspective of the 1980s this may now seem unrealistic, yet twenty years ago it was genuinely and widely hoped that radio would provide the means of involving large numbers of illiterates in the democratic process. It was hoped that the radio networks of these new states could provide the kind of information necessary, but the results have been disappointing. Radio has nonetheless produced some change in this direction: it has challenged the old hierarchical order by its ability to reach directly into people's homes. Yet it is this same achievement which has rendered it most liable to political control. Though the social and political consequences of any innovation may be unknown, they can be imagined or speculated about by those in power, and if the media are seen to be promoting opinions and attitudes likely to bring about social change, it is probable that attempts will be made to control what they say. This is probably true of all societies. I saw recently, on a wall in London, a slogan (painted by some witty anarchist when no policeman was looking) which read: 'If voting changed anything, they would ban it'. The anarchists of Western Europe argue that democracy is a sham: political power continues to be exercised by the same class, whichever party wins. This argument is, I believe, a spurious one, but not entirely without substance. When something really does challenge the existing way of doing things, moves are often made to control or curb whatever is producing that challenge. Societies can cope with gradual change, but most have a vast array of built-in safeguards against major upheaval.

Direct access to the minds and lives of the audiences is available to anyone with access to the media; this is, of course, a facility highly valued by advertisers. Advertising is an integral part of modern industrialized capitalist society, where goods are manufactured to meet demands which are in turn promoted by direct appeals through the mass media. Advertising is in fact a human activity unique to societies with means of mass communication: the former could not exist without the latter. Access is also very important to politicians. As we saw in the case of Nigeria, in a political system with an element of public competition, politicians need access to mass media in order to publicize themselves and their parties. Control of the media enables this access to be controlled. Like many other countries, Nigeria has a constitution which guarantees freedom of speech and of the press, but this does not guarantee equal and free access to the mass media for all who seek it. Because the media are vital to the exercise of political power they tend to come under political control, whether direct or indirect; alternatively, they are used in the furtherance of certain political interests. Such promotion of political interests is not distributed evenly between the various possible and actual contenders for power in that country. In Britain, the printed mass media are heavily biased in favour of the Conservative Party. The electronic mass media try to maintain a balance between the rival parties, but they do so on the basis of parliamentary representation, political groups offering alternative strategies and policies being accorded far less access, if any at all.

In one-party states, access and control converge. The ruling party and government usually have direct or indirect control over the entire mass media. Yet in this situation the mass media should not necessarily be regarded as speaking with one voice or having no role in political competition. Even in such tightly controlled and centralized systems as obtained in Tanzania and Zambia, they could be used by rival groups eager to promote their own causes.

However, the media are concerned with more complex transactions than these. The individual members of the audience are, to a large extent, autonomous: there is no guarantee of what they will listen to or read and no way of ensuring how they will interpret what they receive. Hence there arises the important question of what the audience goes to the media for. It was obvious from my own studies in Zambia and Tanzania that, while the usefulness of radio in public information and enlightenment may be considerable, this was not the reason why people bought a radio set in the first place. They saw it chiefly as a source of entertainment and diversion. In western industrial societies, the mass media are the single most important source of entertainment. It is, for example, very difficult nowadays for entertainers in these societies to make a full-time living from music, drama or dance unless they are patronized by the media. As a result of this the mass media have become the major arbiters of taste and purveyors of popular culture. This is less true of the developing countries, but even there the media have made singers, dancers, comedians and story-tellers into nationally known figures. And of course entertainment, whether musical, dramatic or anything else, carries with it cultural and ideological messages which are no less powerful than the more patently ideological content of news and current affairs programmes.

The media can give their audience a sense of identity and a group membership. There is no doubt that in both Zambia and Tanzania the radio made citizens conscious of their identity as Tanzanians or Zambians by its portrayal of events and its use of cultural material which was mostly of national origin. At the same time, as I noted, the media as a whole tended to portray urban rather than rural life and to cater more for urban demands than rural ones.

It is self-evident that any society, regardless of its size, requires an effective system of communication: information has to be passed to those who require it. The size of the modern nation-state makes mass communication essential but, as we have seen in the case of Africa, the media do not perform this function of informing society with uniform success. Indeed, almost everywhere one can discern a failure to inform. Nigeria's newspapers and radio stations have neglected to investigate the failure of the country's electricity authority to provide a reliable service; Ghanaians have been offered little in the way of helpful analysis concerning their country's severe economic difficulties. Western news media have not always provided adequate information on matters of importance. Though, for example, their coverage of events in Iran between 1978 and 1981 appeared to be comprehensive and detailed, they omitted to report something essential. There was little understanding of the reasons for the Shah's overthrow and even less understanding of the popularity of the Ayatollah Khomeini, with the result that bewilderment still exists as to the causes of the extreme outbursts of anti-western sentiment expressed by many Iranians in the name of Islam. Press coverage has produced stereotypes but not much knowledge. It is possible that the complexities of the modern world defy ready explanation and analysis, and yet the attempt has to be made if the media are to fulfil their function. Failures like the ones outlined here have led some to argue that the role of the modern mass media is now not so much to inform as to divert: to provide an entertaining and relaxing escape from unpleasant realities.

It is often said in the West that the media have a vital role as the watchdogs and guardians of liberty. The Watergate scandal in the United States is cited as an example of a time when a free press functioned at its best, exposing high level corruption and the abuse of power. It is said that without a free press the whole affair would never have come to light.[3] The press has similarly been able to expose the lies and deceits of the Kennedy, Johnson and Nixon administrations during the long war in Vietnam, when government officials tried to cover up or conceal US policy. This investigative role is not one very often seen in the less developed countries, and it is easy to see why: the problems of political instability are too great and the institutions of government too fragile. Freedom of the press, it is argued, can so easily be used to promote the claims of those hungry for power. The mass media are given a different task, that of development – of facing up to and attempting to overcome the massive problems of poverty, ignorance and disease.

Nevertheless, there is an unsolved and possibly insoluble dilemma here. The government seeks to use its power over the media to exhort its citizens to greater effort and at the same time to prevent the media either from questioning policy or being significantly critical of political authority. Yet such power is unlikely to be used for very long, if at all, in a disinterested and public-spirited way; it is more likely to be used for the furtherance of political ends than in the service of public enlightenment. This is true even when it might be of advantage to the State to encourage the kind of media independence that could lead to greater public understanding of problems. One can take as an example the case of Mali in the years 1978 to 1980. A series of demonstrations and riots among secondary and tertiary level students led to a complete shutdown of the educational system lasting many months. The chief cause of the trouble was the students' demand that they be promised jobs in the government service as a right. Malian students had grown up seeing their predecessors from the same educational establishments going on to well-paid jobs in the state system, and they now expected similar treatment. Yet there was a limit to the number of people the State could take on, and this limit had been reached. The same story has been repeated in a number of other African countries. It was clear from the beginning that it would happen: after the initial post-independence Africanization and the rapid promotion of recently qualified local personnel, a reduction in recruitment was inevitable. Yet it was hardly ever mentioned in public or in the media. A feature of the news media everywhere, whether controlled or not, is a tendency to avoid uncomfortable truths; and yet, if they are to fulfil the social role of providing appropriate and useful information, they have to be able, free and willing to report and investigate the often unpalatable truth.

This raises the matter of the so-called 'revolution of rising expectations'. Early writers on the mass media in the new states foresaw the danger that the new media would engender a desire for the products of industrial society without showing the legitimate means of obtaining them. To put it crudely, the media were seen to be good at stimulating demand but poor at encouraging hard work. That this has happened there can be no doubt. The mass media are themselves part of a new kind of life which has, for many, a great deal of attraction and glamour attached to it. The products are enticing, whether actually displayed in commercial advertising or merely in other media content. The media may show that more comfortable, more prosperous and more healthy lives are possible. The reaction of the audience to this may be one of resignation, even fatalism, but this is not always so: there are many cases of people making demands based on what they have learned through the media about conditions elsewhere. No matter how far they are controlled, those who are poor, diseased and without any apparent hope are still able to see, however unclearly, that a different kind of life is possible. At the other extreme, it might be argued that the media are even more likely to encourage demands among the privileged for more of what they already have. It would be absurd to blame the arrival of the mass media for the growth of materialism in the modern world and increasing demands for expensive and luxury consumer goods. Yet it must be admitted that by and large the modern media are part of the process of advanced western capitalism, which encourages the consumption of more and more goods and links personal success with the acquisition of certain brands of cigarette, cosmetics, alcohol, motor cars or clothes.

The new media of Africa are torn between two alternatives, neither of which is very attractive. The kind of freedom allowed for the press under the Nigerian constitution leads to numerous problems, some of which have just been outlined. At the time of writing, Nigeria's mass media are moving in the direction of limited commercialism on the one hand and intense political competition on the other. What will the effect of this be on a society of such enormous differences in wealth and poverty, health and disease, privilege and disadvantage? It is still too early to say how Nigeria will fare.

Other governments have taken an entirely different approach. They see a necessity to control their news media, restrict commercialization, limit political competition, and suppress or discourage the expression of political opinions at variance with those of the ruling group or party. Here we encounter the notion of journalism for development, clearly illustrated in our study of the Tanzanian situation. In Tanzania, as in many other less developed countries, there has emerged a theory for the media which encourages an engineered, controlled press committed to government objectives and priorities:

> All national resources – including the resource of information – must be directed toward development. If information is allowed to cause dissent or loss of international prestige, it detracts from the greater goal. By this reasoning, the control of news is not only a legitimate right, but also a national necessity.[4]

The problem here is that the State is called upon to do something which it may not be fitted to do in the general interest. As I noted earlier, the exercise of political power has rarely been characterized by motives as altruistic as that of the service of the public good, whatever rhetoric may emerge from governments and ruling parties to this effect. The fact that a government holds the power to protect the public from harm is no guarantee that the same power will be used in that interest. Development journalism requires that governments or their agencies supervise, decide, judge and act in a field in which they are subject as well as object. Reporting on governments and their activities is a legitimate part of the media's function: therefore governments are not reliable and independent arbiters of what the media ought to be doing. Because their own activities form a major component of the news, governments have a very obvious and immediate interest in how they are reported. Yet despite the widely held view that they should not be directly involved in the business of reporting, the trend in the world is quite the opposite. The notion of development journalism is now the majority view both among the less developed countries and – of great importance internationally – within UNESCO. Even in Nigeria, where the media are constitutionally free, the majority of mass media institutions are under the control and direction of the government, whether at federal or state level.

A number of arguments can be used to support government intervention and control of the media in the less developed countries. It can be said that, for all their competitiveness and conflict, the western mass media give overall support to the existing economic social and political system, the status quo. If radical in their political or social stance, they are reformist rather than revolutionary. It is, for example, very clear from Woodward and Bernstein's book on the Watergate scandal (which eventually brought down the Nixon administration) that the authors were not questioning the American system of government. They and others would doubtless argue that their ability to investigate and their right to call into question the integrity of the man occupying the highest office in the land were a vindication of the democratic, constitutional process of which a free, uncontrolled press is a vital and strategic part. Throughout that period one can remember feeling that whatever came of the legal, journalistic and political investigations, the American system of government would survive with its institutions intact. There might be some change in the rules, some adjustment in the basic institutions, even some alteration to the structure of power but – and I think I can say this in all fairness – the American system of government was never either in question or seriously threatened. Nixon resigned, but his place was immediately taken by Ford in accordance with the constitutional rules, and the American government continued – shaken but not fundamentally altered.

In an important sociological study of Canada, Porter wrote that the mass media were a vital institution in that enormous country in that they promoted a system of values which encouraged cohesion and unity and conferred a sense of validity on the existing social order. He rightly described this as an ideological function of the mass media. It provided the reason for the economic, judicial and political systems, all of which were depicted as flowing naturally from Canada's traditions and culture. Porter went on to show that in their recruitment policies the Canadian media maintained this ideological function by ensuring that personnel fitted the tradition.[5] Changes do, of course, occur over time, but these tend to be gradual: the essential element is continuity.

There is no such established pattern for the mass media in the majority of less developed countries. A press of some kind has long existed in many African countries, but only relatively recently has it reached an audience large enough to enable one to refer to Africa's press as a *mass* medium. Radio and television are very recent phenomena and, significantly, the rapid growth of the radio audience in recent years has largely come about since the gaining of independence. The most important mass medium in all African countries, radio has come into its own at a time when the new institutions of government have been at their most fragile.

Although the mass media of the less developed countries made attempts to draw on traditions from outside, especially those of the former metropolitan powers, these have often been at variance with local conditions and problems. It may be argued that, either because they chose to adopt an unsuitable tradition or because they really had no idea what their role ought to be, a role was imposed upon them. It is hardly surprising that in countries such as Botswana, Mali, Niger, Upper Volta, Somalia and even Tanzania, where governments have judged it necessary to put funds into media development – without which there would probably be few, if any, media outlets at all – the State should seek to outline a fairly strict code of behaviour for the new media. Rarely was this policy worked out very carefully or coherently: very often it was done in a rather unpraiseworthy attempt to hold on to power come what may. Yet it is difficult to argue in a coherent or sensible way for any alternative. In a poor country with impoverished resources and little hope of any significant improvement in living conditions for the mass of people, how can the media expect to be funded by the State and at the same time adopt a role that might threaten the existing fragile order? This may look very like an apology for dictatorship and the suppression of freedom, which it is not intended to be. Nevertheless, it is hoped that the student of the mass media in Africa will not ignore the need to understand why the media are as tightly controlled as they are. It could be that, lacking the type of role that has evolved historically in certain developed, industrialized democracies, the media have had a role imposed on them. Hence we have the notion of 'development journalism' in which the mass media are seen as a nation-building tool, from which it follows that if they pose any threat to the existing order they will be controlled and curbed.

In any event, the major constraints on the media in Africa are neither political nor social but economic. Africa's press is now stagnating and even, in places, going into decline. The cost of newsprint, machinery and ink, all of which have to be imported, has forced certain papers to cut their circulation. Some newspapers are heavily subsidized; if they charged their readers the real cost of production and distribution, they would further reduce their sales. In 1981 one major Nigerian daily which was attracting insufficient advertising cost one naira (about US $1.50) per copy to produce, of which a mere tenth was being met by sales: the subsidy was provided entirely by the state government that owned it. Nigeria has the funds to do this, but few other countries can afford the considerable expense.

Since I made my study of Tanzania, export income has shrunk in real terms while an ever-growing proportion of meagre foreign exchange is having to be used to service debt and pay for oil imports. The purchase of newsprint, ink and printing machinery from abroad may not be possible for very much longer. The *Daily News* in Tanzania has cut its print run from 60,000 to 45,000 copies.

Radio also suffers from this trend in the economic life of the continent. Its development both at the transmission and receiving end has slowed down in most countries. The greatly increased cost of batteries for portable sets has cut listenership in some countries, while in Zambia, for example, transmitters have been off the air for months at a time when foreign exchange for spare parts has not been made available. The only countries in sub-Saharan Africa whose mass media appear to have suffered little from the world-wide recession of the 1970s and 1980s are Nigeria and South Africa.

This lack of resources impoverishes Africa's media, weakening their potential and restricting their achievements. Two stark alternatives are possible here. The first is that the less developed countries do the best they can with what little they have, which might mean that newspapers appear less frequently than every day, that a smaller number of copies is printed, that the number of pages is reduced or that printing standards are lowered. It might also mean an end to the publication of papers for small language groups, the dropping of plans for the improvement of radio reception (such as the building of new transmitters) or the abandoning of television altogether. The other alternative is that they become increasingly reliant on outside assistance, which presents a major obstacle. The relationship between the less developed countries and the rest of the world is an unequal one in which the rich, mainly western, nations dominate the media both in terms of technology and content. Few African countries have the resources or expertise necessary to design, establish or maintain communications systems which would present a true and appropriate reflection of their own culture. Poverty makes cheap foreign merchandise all but irresistible; thus, often through so-called foreign aid programmes, the less developed world is led to rely not only on the technology of the West but also on its films, television programmes, gramophone records, syndicated newspaper material and the international news agencies. All of these, issuing from the established western and communist sources are cheaper than any comparable material which may be produced at home.

One writer sees it all as a deliberate system of exploitation and control: the western economic and political levers of power keep the less developed countries in the position they occupy by perpetuating demand for the products, tastes and values that keeps the West on top.

> The marketing system developed to sell industry's outpouring of (largely inauthentic) consumer goods is now applied as well to selling globally ideas, tastes, preferences, and beliefs. In fact in advanced capitalism's present stage,

the production and dissemination of what it likes to term 'information' become major and indispensible activities, by any measure, in the overall system. Made-in-America messages, imagery, lifestyles and information techniques are being internationally circulated and – equally important – globally imitated . . . Today, multinational corporations are the global organizers of the world economy; and information and communications are vital components in the system of administration and control.[6]

This is perhaps an extreme view. Personally, I find the idea that western multinational companies and governments could conspire together in this way faintly ludicrous – such a global conspiracy would surely never work. The dominance of the western media is probably all the more effective for not being planned.

One does not have to look far to see those effects. Let us take television as an example. Those African countries that have decided to invest in television have discovered they now have no choice of whether to go into colour or use simpler, black-and-white technology: the latter is no longer available, because the main users of television technology in the West no longer require it. If you want to operate a television station you now have to buy colour equipment. Similarly with radio, much of the new studio equipment involves the use of labour-saving devices for the playing of tapes and discs, whose prices reflect the high labour costs in the places where they are made. In the newspaper industry, new techniques in page-setting involve the use of word-processing computers, which will mean journalists' writing their copy straight on to the printing machines without the intervention of typesetting. These and other new techniques have been designed in the West to avoid and reduce the use of personnel. No such need exists in the less developed countries, most of which have a surplus of labour. However, the mass media of the Third World have little choice: though the technology is inappropriate, it is often all that is available. This will become increasingly true as the development gap widens, and with inappropriate technology come inappropriate attitudes of mind, values and ideology. Technology is not ideologically innocent.

One of the best and most readable studies of the whole subject is a recent work by a Canadian scholar which looks critically at the dominance of the West and assesses the response to it by the less developed countries through UNESCO. While not in favour of the kinds of control of the international media now being envisaged by some countries, the author argues that there is a case to be made against what the West has done and continues to do in this field. He is particularly critical of western scholarship:

Given its predilection with audience research, American mass communication study has not concentrated upon research investigating the ties which bind media institutions to other sources and structures of power, whether domestic or international. In essence, development communication experts have taken for granted that more Western-type technology and communication hardware was beneficial to more Western-type economic growth which was equated with development. In fact, the policies they supported did not advance development and the quality of life, but in fact tended to foster a colonial-type dependence on the West, to aggravate an unbalanced distribution of benefits by concentrating new communication power in the hands of ruling elites, and to create tensions and frustration in less developed countries by promoting inappropriate and inaccessible Western ideals and further expand the economic gap between the West and the less developed countries.[7]

One hopes that African and other Third World students of the mass media will avoid these mistakes and be more critical. There can surely be no doubt now that to make sense of the media the researcher needs to take a broader view than has been the practice in the past.

The same strictures apply to western attitudes towards the present vexed but important question of the so-called 'new world information order' which has been aired in UNESCO. This calls for a restructuring of the way news flows around the world; in particular, it seeks to redress the imbalance between rich and poor or between North and South, parallel to the attempt being made to establish a new world economic order. It is argued that just as the media in one country tend to support the existing economic and social order so also the international news media, dominated as they are by the West, support the international social and economic order. The world is therefore seen through relatively prosperous western eyes.

The response of the West to this argument is to admit that some inequity has existed but stress that to tamper in any way with the international flow of news would be to threaten freedom. The debate is complex and one that has by no means been resolved. My intention here is not to examine it in detail but merely to show how very important is the entire issue of freedom and control of the mass media. It is a reminder of the vital truth that no country can be isolated from the international news media, and that no study of any country's mass media is complete without consideration of that country's place *vis-à-vis* international communication. At present, international communication is subject to innumerable controls. Western countries and western news agencies point to the restrictions on access imposed by some countries, saying – correctly – that these are hampering the process of free and accurate reporting. By contrast, some of the less developed countries complain that a far more significant factor and a far stronger evidence of unfreedom is the fact that international reporting is dominated by a few agencies based in rich countries possessing the funds and technology to allow them to dominate and to decide how the world should be portrayed to itself.[8]

The idea behind the promotion of a new world information order is that there should be a more equitable flow of world news and a better balance in it. Furthermore, it seeks to stop countries from becoming the information 'colonies' of others and to encourage the development of mass communications policies which take proper account of each country's conditions and aspirations. But, say the critics, take a closer look at the present policies of less developed countries: true, their mass media may possess a certain degree of autonomy, but their governments are still empowered to suppress criticism and the truth. This argument deserves serious consideration.

The Kenyan journalist Hilary Ng'weno has made this entire issue his speciality. His remarks at an international press meeting in 1968 were noted earlier. More recently, he has been highly critical of the way the debate is being conducted and of the kinds of sentiment now being expressed through UNESCO. When UNESCO was about to meet in Nairobi, the independent news magazine *Weekly Review* published an article by the Kenyan Minister of Information stating that attempts to secure a more balanced flow of news around the world were being attacked by the United States and 'some un-African black allies'. The Minister explained the United States' emphasis on press freedom as being due to that nation's history and its rebellion against Britain: it still needed 'rebel mass media'. But Africa, he said, did not need this: 'What we need are totally committed African mass media . . . and not a replica of either the East or the West'.

Not everywhere in Africa would a minister expect his views to be challenged, but in the same issue of the magazine Ng'weno published his own reply to the argument that because freedom of speech led to serious problems there ought to be strict government-imposed controls. The title of his article summed up his view: 'All Freedom is at Stake'. Ng'weno wrote that the UNESCO debate had concentrated on the international flow of news, which was not nearly so important as the problems of news flow within each country. Taking as his example Ghana, a country of limited resources, he asserted that a Ghanaian journalist's right to report freely from China was not as fundamental or urgent as his right to report freely within Ghana itself. That aside, there was a great deal wrong with the way international news was collected. Ng'weno criticised the ignorance of some western journalists who saw the Third World in terms of the cold war and the split between East and West, when often these were completely irrelevant. He agreed that the freedom of the international press could pose very serious problems for the stability of those countries whose 'fragile political structures . . . cannot withstand endless scrutiny of the shortcomings of those in power or of the failures of economic and social development programmes'.

These and other serious complaints by the less developed countries, plus a sense of frustration at their own impotence in the face of the cultural dominance of the West in all relationships, had led many such countries to support policies at UNESCO which Ng'weno regarded as extremely dangerous – dangerous, because they saw government control as the answer. The UNESCO proposals would lead to the curtailment of the flow of information in the world: they would not provide a solution to the problem. Supporters of the demands for control wished to replace one kind of distortion, that of western dominance and bias, with another based on political bureaucracies. Ng'weno concluded that it was not possible to find a halfway house between the two positions of freedom and control. Though he was clearly on the side of freedom, it should not be inferred from this that he was in favour of the present western dominance and bias. This situation could be changed by journalists' putting their own house in order: it was not a matter for the State. Control of the press was inherent in totalitarianism and, while it might be theoretically possible for a government-controlled press to place the interests of people before that of the State or the regime, 'in practice this has not been the case anywhere'.[9] He established connections between the workings of the mass media and the nature of the State, thus endorsing the view, expressed earlier that the mass media of any country are an integral part of the political and social system which they both reflect and support. The media do not exist independently and must always be seen as parts of a wider picture.

Freedom of the press, as enjoyed in the West, is of course subject to social and economic controls. Nonetheless it remains true that journalists in western democracies rarely go to gaol for reporting things the governments do not like. Newspapers and radio stations are seldom taken over or closed on the whim of the party in power. Freedom of the press and of public comment is regarded as an essential part of progress. The scientific and technological advances of the past two to three hundred years are considered to be direct results of the successful challenge to both ecclesiastical and aristocratic dominance over communication and scholarship. Is there then a link between the lack of freedom and underdevelopment? Does the one produce the other? Though this might sound simplistic, it seems fair to say that an atmosphere of oppression and fear is unlikely to liberate the human mind for its greatest achievements. Only through the application of reason and knowledge to problems can they be solved, and that may well prove impossible if the free flow of necessary information is hampered. The State is not the body best qualified to decide what is necessary. To this argument Marxists retort that, in the capitalist State, necessary information is withheld not so much by any action of the State as by an institutional process whereby the structure of the entire system ensures that whatever does not fit is filtered out.

If we recall the remarks quoted earlier of Hilary Ng'weno and Babatunde Jose we can agree that total freedom of the press does create difficulties. Let us look at a practical example. In 1968, when working in Tanzania, I attended a party at the Ministry of Information. Three Tanzanian journalists present disagreed on how to deal with a story which was beginning to come through. A village settlement scheme had failed very badly, involving the loss of large sums of money, and villagers who had been brought to live at the settlement had left. It was argued that inadequate preparations had been made and that problems which should have been foreseen had been overlooked. The three journalists were now discussing what they were to do with the story: should they investigate it fully, or should they leave well alone? Were there any other alternatives? Three views emerged from their discussion.

The first journalist argued that they should all ignore the story. The government and TANU had only recently launched the policy of *ujamaa* (socialist) villages, which was difficult to put across and of which many peasants were suspicious, even afraid. To report the failure of an earlier attempt at village settlement would not help in persuading peasants that moving to new village settlements was a good idea. Indeed it would reinforce the doubts and prejudices they already held. He argued that the duty of journalists to report important events should always be tempered with concern for the effects likely to be produced by certain kinds of information. Writing about such failures would only spread confusion and disaffection at a time when the government was launching a political education campaign through the party and the mass media to encourage positive attitudes towards living in the new villages. Any investigation of what went wrong on this settlement should be left to the government and to TANU. The argument was a familiar one, very similar to that used in wartime Europe to justify the censorship of negative news about the progress of the war.

The second Tanzanian journalist poured scorn on this point of view, saying it was not the business of the press to protect the government from the effects of its own policies, nor to abuse the people's trust in the press. They expected it to report fully and accurately what was going on. The government and the press each had a different task to accomplish: if the government had a duty to serve the people in whatever way it thought best, then the press also had a duty to go out and investigate impartially exactly how the government was performing its role. The only thing that could or should hinder any press reporter from following up the story was whether he had the resources and the time to do it justice. The story in question was a newsworthy one. Taxpayers' money had been spent, apparently wastefully. Someone was to blame, and it was the duty of the press to investigate, so preventing the government from 'sweeping the whole affair under the rug'. So far as the government's good intentions and policies were concerned, he said, appropriate policies should be based on accurate information and knowledge of all the facts. If newspapers were not free to report facts, including uncomfortable ones, then how could policy makers be expected to make good decisions? Policies would fail solely if they suffered from a lack of information and were inappropriate. The only way to ensure effective and sound government was to have a free press able to report stories like this; if the press worked hand in hand with government so that embarrassing stories were hushed up, then that press would cease to be trusted by its readers. His argument was one familiar to western democracies: that the press should act as a 'fourth estate' in the nation, remaining separate and distinct from political and social institutions.

The third journalist took a view that differed from either of these extremes. He agreed that the press had to say something about the failure – it had, after all, reported the initiation of the scheme with a loud fanfare – because it would lose credibility if it ignored stories when things went wrong. If journalists wanted to be trusted, then they should not ignore things just when they went sour. If bad news were not reported, it would encourage misinformation and rumour, which were far worse. Moreover, the press had a duty to report the facts so that lessons would be learned from mistakes. Thus far he agreed with the second journalist, but, he said, the first one had a point too. Tanzanian journalists were operating in a context not unlike that of war, everything had to be written with the utmost care. The journalist had to be conscious of the possible effects of what he wrote, taking pains to present things in such a way as would not discourage others but instead show them how to succeed by avoiding mistakes. Journalists had no business campaigning against elected governments: it was legitimate for the government and ruling party in Tanzania to expect co-operation from the press. Village-building policies had been drawn up in good faith, and no one could disagree with the basic aim of improving life for the very poor and disadvantaged. The press could help by making sure that people understood what was involved in the government's decisions and what was expected of them as Tanzanians.

These three positions will be familiar enough to anyone who has worked in the mass media in a less developed country. They display three views of the role of the media, and the reader will, I hope, have noticed how all of them have been seen operating in the three case studies outlined earlier.In Tanzania, official policy on the part of government and media aligned itself with the third view, but very often it was the first view that prevailed in practice. In Zambia, the situation was very similar, although at times and on certain stories the press did investigate quite freely. In Nigeria, under the new democratic system of government, the second view prevails officially at present; however, in those media owned by state governments, it was the first view which prevailed when it came to reporting the activities of the government concerned. I have introduced this story here not to draw any conclusions but to illustrate the three roles that can be assigned to the news media. These roles are not necessarily mutually exclusive, although they obviously conflict in many ways. In my opinion, all three views are currently being expressed and all three roles attempted by Africa's media. The remarks made in the Tanzanian parliament in support of the 1968 measure which increased government power over the press were made in terms of the danger of people being 'confused' by press reports – an opinion not dissimilar to that of the journalist who recommended that the village settlement failure should be ignored. At the time of writing, Nigerian newspapers and radio stations owned or controlled by parties not in the federal government regard any move by the federal authorities to curb either immoderate language or unsubstantiated allegations as a fundamental attack on the constitutional freedom of the media. They are using the argument of the second journalist, who spoke in favour of complete freedom to publish the facts.

I hope that the issues raised here will assist students to look closely at their own media, discovering how these approach similar stories and what reasons they give for the way they report. I hope also that arguments for restraint will be regarded as not motivated solely by a desire on the part of the ruling power to conceal the truth in its own interests: new political systems may require an atmosphere of constraint and moderation for their good health and survival. Nigerian readers might consider whether the present highly charged atmosphere conveyed by their mass media – with daily newspapers making frequent strongly worded attacks on political opponents – will not eventually threaten public confidence in democratic civilian rule, which, for success, requires at least some measure of reason and tolerance.

It is difficult to assess fully what power the media have in these new states: so much depends on resources, control and on content, which are somewhat variable. Moreover, very little research has been done. Some things can nevertheless be said with a fair degree of certainty. The media are very often responsible for presenting the public image of the new system, and thus they can either bestow legitimacy or withhold it: for example, the way in which a person or event is described may define attitudes from the outset. While this does not mean that we will all think alike on the subject, it usually means that the possible range of interpretations of news available to us is limited and defined. Think about or examine the way the media in your country described the latest African *coup d'état* and ask yourself how your view of that coup was coloured by the manner of reporting. Then ask or try to find out whether the story was written from local sources, from sources in the country concerned or by the international news agencies. It is highly probable that the way in which coups are described by these or other sources in the initial stages affects international attitudes to them. The words used in news stories are far from neutral. Consider them: 'rebels', 'revolutionaries', 'liberators', 'usurpers', 'militants', 'Muslim fundamentalists', 'extremists', 'right-wingers', and so on. These and other labels commonly employed by the media pass into the language we use in our own discussion of events, but are rarely much help when it comes to understanding the events themselves, except in a highly superficial way. News has to be simplified but, in the process, ideological interpretations tend to be unavoidable. This dilemma has been outlined simply by Golding and Elliott:

> News attempts to be a comprehensive account of significant events in the world. Yet also, being finite, it has to be selective . . . Much therefore is omitted, and selection necessitates partiality and the intrusion of personal judgement. The . . . second dilemma derives from the commitment of news to convey objective, factual accounts of events, and at the same time make them meaningful and comprehensible to audiences.[10]

This process of selection and of making sense of events involves interpretation, which in turn involves attitude and ideology. The student of the media needs to equip himself with the skills of interpretation necessary to discern these processes at work.

It is partly concern about this which has led to the contemporary debate within UNESCO already referred to. We have seen examples of similar fears being expressed elsewhere in this book. President Kaunda noted how the international media could legitimize a regime or, equally, do the opposite. Tanzania's Vice-President noted, somewhat ruefully, how by using clever presentation and the 'tricks' of the media professional, a newspaper could either build up or put down an individual.

Certain governments have been attempting through UNESCO to control the international news media which are seen to be dominated by the western news agencies and the big battalions in the television, film and photo agency fields. Just as the media in one country, despite their differences, tend to support the existing economic and political institutions, the status quo, so also the international news media are conservative. The world they portray is one seen through rich western eyes.[11] Ng'weno's argument against imposing controls on the international news media is that the cure would be far worse than the disease. He feels that it may be better to have distortions, which the intelligent and informed can pick through and decide on, than no facts at all. It might be more appropriate to set up alternative news agencies, like the Non-Aligned News Pool and the Pan-African News Agency; yet these are new and untried.

In analysing attempts to control the media, it should be remembered that control is not an easy matter. Quite aside from the legal obstacles in force in those countries where constitutional protection exists and is supported by the legal system, any form of censorship or control requires a bureaucracy. Bureaucracy costs money, as trained staff are required. Most often there is no direct censorship: governments ensure that editors and journalists know what is allowed and what is not, having learnt by experience what they are expected to do.

Yet even this form of control presents problems. There are nearly always alternative sources, sometimes within the same country. We saw in the case of Nigeria how a listener denied a story by censorship of one source can obtain it from another. Moreover, radio broadcasting is international, and it is known that during periods of tension and increased censorship of the press, radio listeners tune in more often to international networks such as the BBC.

Then there is the evidence of one's own eyes. The government-controlled media may say that there are no shortages of food in the shops or omit to mention strike action by, for instance, bus drivers, but in these and similar cases the audience is able to see for itself. Thus the credibility of the local media is undermined. This can produce serious consequences for the government, which may later wish to use the media to announce something truthfully and in good faith, only to find that the audience no longer trusts the source.

Another consequence of the suppression of news may be even more serious for society as a whole. Any large society organized on the scale of the modern nation-state increasingly needs mass media to act as its eyes and ears. Effectively organised and staffed, the mass media can supply vital information to a wide range of people and institutions, thus enabling appropriate and timely decisions to be made in response to difficulties, opportunities and changes in conditions. If instead the media are starved of the necessary resources and required to publicize only the activities of a few prominent leaders while suppressing or ignoring the kind of stories which really affect people's lives and futures, then they have little social value and will not promote the growth and development of society. Any tendency to block criticism or ban reports of adverse news or conditions in the country, regardless of whether or not these reflect badly on the government, may prevent vital information from reaching not only the public which reads newspapers and listens to the radio, but also from political authority, in particular those sections of the administration which may need that information most.

The problem with the mass media is that we are still not quite used to them! Bad news gets reported and – in consequence – the news media can often give the impression that conditions around us and elsewhere in the world are very much worse than they really are. Reports of disorder in relatively few places within a country can easily give the impression that the social order in general is breaking down. Numerous examples of this come to mind. Late in 1968, in Britain, a series of prison escapes took place which were reported widely because the prisoners involved were notorious criminals: escape from prison became an 'issue' for the media. For weeks any escape by any prisoner was given priority treatment. An enquiry was set up by the government of the day to look into prison security. In fact, prison escapes during those few months did not take place at a higher rate than normal – the media merely gave the impression that this was the case. Similarly, in a less developed country where the audience is even less accustomed to the phenomenon of mass communication, reports of a seriously infectious disease such as cholera or of violent unrest in scattered places may suggest serious dangers to the public in general, disconnected events becoming connected in the public mind. One can be opposed in principle to government control but still understand why controls are introduced in such a situation.

A more appropriate response than mere government control may be to increase greatly the amount of money spent on the training of journalists and the improvement of media facilities. It is argued by some that only in this way will the media become more responsible and more aware of the problems that they might unwittingly create. This may or may not be the answer. Unhappily, in a world of increasing disparity in wealth and growing economic problems – especially in the less developed countries – it is hard to feel confident that significant funds will be made available for facilities and training in the field of mass communications.

Notes

1   Wilbur Schramm, *Mass Media and National Development*, p. 20.
2   *Ibid.*
3   See Carl Bernstein and Bob Woodward, *All the President's Men* (London, 1974).
4   M. Rosenblum, *Coups and Earthquakes: Reporting the World for America* (New York, 1979), p. 206.
5   J. Porter, *The Vertical Mosaic* (Toronto, 1965), pp. 460-486.
6   H. Schiller, *Communication and Cultural Domination* (New York, 1976), p. 3.
7   Thomas L. McPhail, *Electronic Colonialism* (Beverly Hills, 1981), p. 79.
8   Students may wish to study the debate in more detail. Well worth reading are Rosemary Righter, *Whose News?* (London, 1978); Jeremy Tunstall, *The Media are American* (London, 1977); Oliver Boyd-Barrett, *The International News Agencies* (London, 1980); and Thomas McPhail, *Electronic Colonialism* (Beverly Hills, 1981). Those interested in the UNESCO Commission's report on the subject should consult *Many Voices, One World* (Paris, 1980).
9   *Weekly Review*, November 8th, 1976.
10   Peter Golding and Philip Elliott, *Making the News* (London, 1978), p. 17.
11   Examples of this are only too easy to provide. One of the most striking was an agency story in 1974 about a conference held in Europe to consider the 'problem' of rapidly rising commodity prices. The story was written as if the then temporarily high price of some of the primary products from less developed countries was a world problem, and went out to all customers around the world in these terms; however, for most producer countries, the 'problem' had been very good news indeed! For the record, the good news did not, of course, last long. From the West's point of view, the 'problem' soon disappeared: most primary products quickly slumped again in price.

Select bibliography

The African Book World and Press: A Directory, 2nd edition. Oxford, 1980.
A useful directory of the whole field of printed publishing in Africa
including details not only of publishers and printers but also of major
bookshops. Each country's newspapers are listed – not accurately in every
case.

Ainslie, Rosalynde, *The Press in Africa*, London, 1966.
Invaluable historical study of Africa's press, containing much material not
published elsewhere.

Berelson, Bernard, and Janowitz, Morris *Reader in Public Opinion and
Communication*, New York, 1966.
Useful collection of American writings on the subject, including many on
mass communications research.

Boyd-Barrett, Oliver *The International News Agencies*, London, 1980.
The organizations of international reporting, the owners, their customers
and how they pay their way. A thorough piece of media research.

Curran, James, Gurevitch, Michael, and Wollacott, Janet *Mass Communication
and Society*, London, 1977.
Designed as the basic reader for an Open University course, this valuable
collection of articles, many of them specially commissioned, represents a
good cross-section of the current field of mass communications research in
Britain.

Deutsch, Karl *The Nerves of Government*, New York, 1966.
Hypothesis about the connection between networks of communication and
the exercise of political power.

Fraenkel, Peter *Wayaleshi*, London, 1959.
Long out of print and now difficult to find, but well worth the effort. A
fascinating account, by a participant, of the early days of broadcasting from
Lusaka.

Golding, Peter, and Elliott, Philip *Making the News*, London, 1979.
A study in Ireland, Sweden and Nigeria of how news is reported by
television. Valuable for its profound insights into how television professionals look upon news in differing social, economic and political circumstances.
Some surprising contrasts and similarities.

Hatchen, William *Muffled Drums*, Ames, Iowa, 1971.
The author has been able to study African newspapers and radio stations at first hand. This book makes a special study of the mass media in Nigeria, Ghana, Zambia, Kenya, South Africa, Ivory Coast and Senegal. Some useful description but few insights.

Head, Sydney *Broadcasting in Africa*, Philadelphia, 1974.
Mainly descriptive account of broadcasting systems in all African territories, with useful sections on technology, training and related matters. Out of date now, but a useful history.

Katz, E., and Wedell, G. *Broadcasting in the Third World: Promise and Performance*, London, 1978.
An attempt to assess the achievements of mass media in some Third World countries. Based partly on field research in, among other countries, Senegal and Nigeria.

Klapper, Joseph *The Effects of Mass Communications*, New York, 1960.
Classic academic work on the state at the time of mass communications research. Best known for its attempt to say something unconfusing and unambiguous about the effects of mass communication, following a period of conflicting and inconclusive research in the United States.

Kurian, George Thomas *World Press Encyclopedia*, 2 vols, London, 1982.
A valuable reference work with histories, contemporary data, bibliographies and details of laws affecting the press in each country. Includes data on both printed and electronic media.

Lawrence, Robert de T. *Rural Mimeo Newspapers*, Paris, 1965.
How newspapers can be produced successfully using simple technology which saves importing expensive high technology and requires less skilled manpower to run.

McPhail, Thomas *Electronic Colonialism*, Beverly Hills, 1981.
Scholarly, critical and balanced account of the debate over the imbalance in world communication.

McQuail, Denis *Towards a Sociology of Mass Communication*, London, 1969.
Readable and thoughtful work which tries to set mass communications in a sociological perspective. A very useful bibliography.

Mytton, Graham *Listening, Looking and Learning: A Report on a National Mass Media Audience Survey*, Institute for African Studies, Lusaka, 1974.
An account of a three-year study of the mass media audience, its preferences, comprehension of languages and geographical spread.

Mytton, Graham 'Language and the Media' in *Language in Zambia*, Mubanga Kashoki and Shirarpi Obannessian (eds.), International African Institute, London, 1978.
An account of languages in the press and radio and of how comprehension of languages is not sufficient for many members of the audience for whom

language is a badge of cultural identity. The extent and significance of multi-lingualism in Zambia.

Schramm, Wilbur *Mass Media and National Development*, Paris, 1964.
Classic and influential work of optimism about the media and what they might achieve.

Tunstall, Jeremy *The Media are American*, London, 1977.
The dominance of US media exports, especially in the English-speaking world, is the subject of this very useful and readable study. It shows how the United States media industry owes its success to a combination of production methods and economy of scale.

UNESCO *An African Experiment in Radio Forums for Development: Ghana 1964/1965*, Reports and Papers on Mass Communication, no. 51, Paris, 1968.
One of many such accounts of the use of radio in campaigns for agriculture, health, etc. through organized listening groups.

UNESCO *Many Voices, One World*, Paris, 1980.
The report by the international commission set up by UNESCO to study how to bring about a 'new, more just and more efficient world information and communication order'. Written by a committee, but contains some valuable international analyses.

UNESCO *Statistical Yearbook*, Paris (annual).
Data on mass media of every country.

Whiteley, Wilfred *Swahili: The Rise of a National Language*, London, 1968.
The history of the language, with some valuable insights into how it helped the growth of mass media in East Africa based on a local language – one of the few areas in Africa where the mass media have been able to spread using mainly one local language.

Wilcox, Dennis *Mass Media in Black Africa*, New York, 1975.
Suffers from an American bias, but is nonetheless useful and mostly accurate.

Williams, Raymond *Communications*, Harmondsworth, Middlesex, 1968.
A critical look from a radical perspective at mass communication in western capitalist society.

World Radio-TV Handbook, Hvidovre, Denmark (annual).
The guide to all radio and TV stations in the world. Comprehensive and informative.

List of addresses of centres in Africa for the study of mass communication

Algeria
Institut des Sciences Politiques et de l'Information
B.P. Alger 493
37, rue Larbi Ben M'Hidi
Algiers

Cameroon
Ecole Supérieure Internationale de Journalisme de Yaoundé (ESIJY)
B.P. 1328
Yaoundé

Egypt
Department of Mass Communication
American University in Cairo
P.O.B. 21511
Cairo
Faculty of Mass Communication
University of Cairo
Orman
Ghiza
Cairo

Ghana
School of Journalism and Communication
University of Legon
P.O. Box 53
Legon
Ghana Institute of Journalism
32, Second Avenue
P.O. Box 667
Accra
National Film and Television Institute
P.M.B. G.P.O.
Accra

Kenya
School of Journalism
University of Nairobi
P.O. Box 30197
Nairobi

Kenya Institute of Mass Communications
P.O. Box 42422
Nairobi
Communications Training Centre
All-African Conference of Churches
Nairobi

Nigeria
Department of Mass Communication
University of Nigeria
Nsukka
Institute of Mass Communication
University of Lagos
Lagos
Department of Mass Communications
Bayero University
P.M.B. 3011
Kano
Department of Journalism
Ogun State Polytechnic
Abeokuta
Nigerian Institute of Journalism
Breadfruit Street
Lagos

Senegal
Centre d'Etudes des Sciences et Techniques de l'Information
Université de Dakar
Dakar

South Africa
Institute for Communications Media Research
University of Durban-Westville
Private Bag X 54001
Durban 4000
Institute of Communication Research
Potchefstroom University
Transvaal

Tanzania
Tanzanian School of Journalism
Ministry of Information and Broadcasting
Dar es Salaam
Nyegezi Social Training Centre
P.O. Box 307
Mwanza

Tunisia
Institut de Press et des Sciences de l'Information
Université de Tunis
Montfleury
Tunis

Zaire
Institut des Sciences et Techniques de l'Information (ISTI)
Université Nationale du Zaire
B.P. 14.998
Kinshasa 1

Zambia
Department of Mass Communication
University of Zambia
P.O. Box 32379
Lusaka
Journalism Training Department
Evelyn Hone College
P.O. Box 29
Lusaka
African Literature Centre
P.O. Box 1319
Kitwe

Uganda
School of Journalism
Institute of Public Administration
P.O. Box 21005
Lugogo
Kampala

Index